'While numerous works on Buddhist meditation are av
is still a need for an accessible and understandable ha
you are holding is precisely such an exhaustive work. E
of the basic methods, it offers us a detailed map with
about the path leading to tranquillity and insight. This book is the fruit of
the author's many years' experience of meditation and teaching, with a
wealth of advice – for those who are taking their first steps on the path, as
well as more experienced practitioners.'

Žarko Andričević, founder of Dhammaloka, Zagreb, Croatia.

'This enhanced new edition guides readers more clearly into the meditations
and draws out their significance more fully, now explicitly oriented around
the "system of meditation". This system provides a fine framework both
for understanding where various practices fit in and for reflecting on the
nature of our own spiritual experiences. Kamalashila has also woven in an
appreciation of a view of the nature of mind that in the Western tradition
is known as the imagination, helping make an accessible link to our own
philosophical and cultural traditions.'

Lama Surya Das, author of *Awakening the Buddha Within*, founder of
Dzogchen Center and Dzogchen Meditation Retreats, USA.

'A wonderfully practical and accessible introduction to the important forms
of Buddhist meditation. From his years of meditation practice, Kamalashila
has written a book useful for both beginners and longtime practitioners.'

Gil Fronsdal, author of *A Monastery Within*, founder of the Insight
Meditation Center, California, USA.

'His approach is a clear, thorough, honest, and, above all, open-ended
exploration of the practical problems for those new and even quite
experienced in meditation.'

Lama Shenpen Hookham, author of *There Is More to Dying Than Death*,
founder of the Awakened Heart Sangha, UK.

Buddhist Meditation

Tranquillity, Imagination and Insight

Kamalashila

indhorse Publications

Published by
Windhorse Publications
169 Mill Road
Cambridge
CB1 3AN
UK

info@windhorsepublications.com
www.windhorsepublications.com

Typeset and designed by Ben Cracknell Studios
Photographs © Alokavira/Timm Sonnenschein
Cover design by Dhammarati
Cover image: photograph of cat. 27c 'Head of a Buddha', Northern Qi dynasty (550–
557), from Qingzhou Municipal Museum, China, from p. 61 of *Return of the Buddha*,
Royal Academy of Arts, London, 2002.
Despite numerous communications with The State Administration of Cultural
Heritage, The People's Republic of China, the copyright holder of this image could
not be located.

Printed by Bell & Bain Ltd, Glasgow

British Library Cataloguing in Publication Data:
A catalogue record for this book is available from the British Library.

ISBN: 9781 907314 09 4

Contents

List of tables

List of figures

Preface to the third edition

This is a completely rewritten edition of the original *Meditation: The Buddhist Way of Tranquillity and Insight*, published in 1992.

When I started the project in the mid-1980s, meditation and Buddhism were hardly known about in the general population, and certainly not widely practised as they are today. A comprehensive manual of Buddhist meditation practice from a Western teacher was virtually unique. My basic material, a seminar on Zhiyi's (Chi-I's) *Dhyāna for Beginners* given by Sangharakshita in 1975, contained plenty of practical, traditional teachings about the way to develop both the dhyānas and insight in Buddhist meditation. This was a good, reliable source, to which I added my fledgling teaching experience, but for comparative Dharma texts I could choose only from the few available in those days, such as The Songs of Milarepa and Suzuki Rōshi's *Zen Mind, Beginner's Mind*. As for other meditation manuals, I found virtually nothing: I used a scholarly survey of the *Visuddhimagga* by Vajirañāṇa Mahāthera and a somewhat impenetrable work by Yogi Chen, who had been one of my own teacher's teachers. Both texts were entitled 'Buddhist Meditation'.

The book was well received, and has sold steadily and modestly since its publication. But so much has changed since 1992. Everyone knows about meditation, Buddhism is a standard subject in schools, at least in the UK, and mindfulness has become an important form of therapy. Meditation is well taught by many Western teachers in numerous traditions, and there is an abundance of good written advice on meditation if you know where to look. So the challenge, when Windhorse Publications broached the possibility of a rewrite, was whether this well-aged book could add to or enhance any of that.

The original material on the principles of meditation practice and much of the practical advice about supporting a deeper application of meditation still seem relevant and valuable. But I have long felt I could produce a better book by improving the writing and drawing on developments in my own practice over the past twenty years – an idea initially planted in my mind by Jonathan Shaw in 2000. I hope the new edition guides readers more clearly into the meditations and draws out their significance more fully.

The main change is that the whole book is now explicitly orientated towards the system of meditation devised by Sangharakshita in the 1970s. This brings out how the practices I have described fit together as part of an integrated path to Awakening. I have also woven in an appreciation of a view of the nature of mind that in Western tradition is known as the imagination, as it makes an accessible link to our own philosophical and cultural traditions. Imagination is not just another way of viewing our mental and emotional reality, it is also helpful as a connection with meditation because we are familiar with it from our own arts and literature; it speaks in a more poetic voice than the technical language of the Pali texts.

The other major change is a greater emphasis on the Buddha, who taught most of these meditation methods in the first place. In the earlier editions, I cited many other teachers, but the practices that they have taught all derive from the Buddha himself and aim at the state of Awakening he discovered. I have tried here, within the limits of the original text, to establish the Buddha as the principal reference point and inspiration for the whole tradition of Buddhist meditation. I have made more references to the historical Buddha and also have updated the material on *sādhana* meditation practice to include less formal, more experimental ways to connect with the living reality of the awakened mind. Finally, I have wanted to emphasize the balance required in an effective meditation practice between active and receptive approaches. So the Buddha's teaching of mindfulness has a larger place in this new edition, along with the practice of Just Sitting.

In the original edition, I quoted Ryōkan:

> *Not much to offer you – just a lotus flower floating*
> *In a small jar of water.*[1]

In reoffering my lotus along with some fresh water, I feel the same tentative and ironic pleasure. I'm somewhat more aware, twenty years on, of this book's failings as a container, yet I know the lotus flower of the Dharma floating in it is the real thing. I hope I have made meditation practice understandable so that you can accept, use and enjoy it.

As always, many other hands, eyes and hearts have helped, so numerous that individual thanks are impossible. I can, however, mention how important an influence on me over the years has been the community of experienced teachers growing among our Triratna community: they continually challenge and encourage me to come up with material that works. May our amazing diversity continue to unite us in our understanding of the Buddha's teaching, and long may our connection endure! In that community I include Sangharakshita, my teacher for over forty years, whom I thank from my heart for refreshing my outlook with frequent gusts of fresh air.

This has been an extensive rewrite, taking place over a couple of years. Throughout that period, my partner Yashobodhi has been an unfailing source of encouragement and comfort during a difficult transition from a simple life in a remote Spanish wilderness to the bustle of London, where I now work. Moving back to the UK was eased by the EcoDharma community in Catalunya, which I thank for their help and patience over that time, and the West London Triratna Centre, which offered reassuring support when we really needed it. I also thank Devapriya, who offered accommodation in London when we had nowhere to go, and Hugh Roper, our generous landlord, who accepted us on the basis of a phone call, Buddhist names and all, and gave his study and super-solid desk for the writing.

Kamalashila
West Hampstead, London
8 July 2011

Introduction

··

The great transformation

> The different headings employed in this book, such as …
> transcendental powers and wisdom, tranquillisation and reflection …
> are all derived from the same source… . If you trace out this source
> and terminus, or should trace out the practices and attainments of
> the Buddhas, they would all alike be found in this practice of dhyāna
> [meditation].
>
> Briefly speaking, the dhyāna which our Master [Zhiyi] had practised,
> and the samādhi which he had experienced, and the lectures which he
> had delivered with such eloquence, were nothing but the manifestation
> of this [tranquillity and insight].
>
> Or, in other words, what the Master had been teaching us was simply
> the narrative of the operation of our own minds; and the profound
> teaching of the T'ien-tai School, and the voluminous literature to be
> studied, are no more than an elaboration of this single subject.
>
> Bhikṣu Yuen-tso, of his teacher Zhiyi in Tranquillity and Insight
for Beginners,[2] a classic meditation manual (sixth century CE)

Meditation is based on 'the operation of our own minds', on the
everyday and mysterious experience we refer to as 'me', my mind or
my heart. Buddhism calls it *citta* or the heart-mind. Master Zhiyi and
his disciples spent their time on T'ien-tai Mountain delving into this
through meditation, study, reflection and the practice of community.
Their generation, in a similar way to ours, was starting to see the
relevance of the 'foreign' Buddhist methods. Zhiyi was re-formulating
Buddhism for his time and culture.[3] His example inspires this book,
as does that of the Buddha, the Indian wanderer Gautama who had
originated the tradition of Awakening a thousand years before and

who actually taught most of the practices described in this book. By practising what the Buddha taught we can emulate his achievement and make contact with the living energy of his Awakening.

And it is the mind – the very same mind that's trying to make sense of these words – that can do this. Its state from moment to moment, whether happy or unhappy, wise or ignorant, compassionate or cruel, is the most important influence on personal development. According to one of the earliest recorded sayings of the Buddha, our whole life is the creation of our mind. If we act with a pure mind, the result will be joy; if we act with an impure mind, the result will be suffering.

> *Experiences are preceded by mind, led by mind, and produced by mind. If one speaks or acts with an impure mind, suffering follows even as the cart-wheel follows the hoof of the ox (drawing the cart).*
>
> *Experiences are preceded by mind, led by mind, and produced by mind. If one speaks or acts with a pure mind, happiness follows like a shadow that never departs.*

Opening verses of the Dhammapada, transcribed
from oral tradition in the first century BCE[4]

But what *is* mind? We find the phenomenon of mind impossible to describe or to define fully. Despite humanity's achievements in the philosophical, religious, scientific and psychological fields, no one, not even of the greatest Buddhist teachers, has been able to say definitively what the mind actually is. We can of course describe it, say a great deal about how it functions and map connections with the brain and the nervous system. We can detail at length the workings of memory, feelings, knowledge, perceptions and thoughts and also explore the unconscious mind. But though we acquire more and more information about how these phenomena work, we still cannot get access to what is really happening. Why do 'we' – or why does mind – exist in the first place? What is it and what are we?

Our problem is that we cannot get beyond the framework of the mind to take an objective viewpoint on our world, for any observation is coloured by the subjective assumptions of the observer. Nor with this kind of mind can we understand what the outside world essentially is, because again the world is always our own perception of it, our particular experience of it. With this kind of mind, we can never get to the thing itself beyond our own subjective view of it. This problem has been well attested in philosophy, and science has now started to acknowledge its effect on experimental methods. But from the point of view of spiritual development, the revelation that we are ignorant of the very nature of our existence is profoundly exciting – even if it is profoundly unsettling too.

The mind is, in a way, our all and everything, and it's natural that most of the time we simply regard it as 'me'. Yet the me-sense is a relatively small part of our experience. It is the tip of an iceberg compared to what happens below the conscious surface. What a contrast there is, for example, between waking and dreaming life. Sometimes as we settle into bed at night we can observe the imagination coming to life as we sink into a half-sleep. It seems the dream world is always there, its striking images expressing themselves in a rolling drama under the surface of conscious awareness. By watching what happens as we fall asleep and cross the borderline of consciousness, we can sometimes even glimpse our entry into the dream state. It shows that being conscious is not just a question of being awake or asleep (as though we could be switched either on or off) but something that continues unbroken into other realms of experience.

The imagination

There is clearly more to the mind than our subjective selves, and Buddhism offers ways to explore it further. Suzuki Rōshi suggested that, in reality, the mind is far 'bigger' than we suppose.

> Usually we think of our mind as receiving impressions and experiences from outside, but that is not a true understanding of our mind. The true understanding is that the mind includes everything; when you think something comes from outside it means only that something appears in your mind.
>
> Suzuki Rōshi[5]

What is particularly interesting from a Buddhist perspective is the mind's capacity to extend beyond me-based limits and see through the layers of habit and ignorance to what actually is there. This can trigger a transformation in the inner structure of the mind so that it becomes not only a faculty we use but also something far bigger than us that is teaching profound truths.

Our own pagan, nontheistic traditions of mental development – they began with the ancient Greeks, were revived in the European Renaissance and later in the Romantic Revolution and continue in contemporary poetry, philosophy and art – contain many connections with this sense of 'big mind'. The notion of the imagination is especially helpful in making these connections. Imagination is both our creative capacity and the nature of consciousness itself. What most characterizes it is, of course, the mind's faculty for making images. To read or talk with someone on the phone or to take in the atmosphere of a novel or a poem involves us in a constant image-making process. It is extraordinarily rich and everyone does it differently. The images that unfold inside us are often not visual pictures at all but some kind of felt sense. Have a look yourself, or listen, sniff or poke around, at what you are doing inside when you read this. Is there not some kind of physical sensation in the body, a feeling of some kind and then deeper, in the heart of it, some kind of image or perhaps a mass of them?

We also have some kind of image of our own development, of what it is we are striving towards or would like to be. It is awakened when something inspires us, when we are affected by another, external, image. This comes in very different ways for different people. As a child my imagination was sparked by Norse and Greek mythology: the stories communicated a sublime sense of 'other', a perspective on existence from the outside that I hadn't realized was possible. After that introduction, I found as I got older that many other things could arouse it too: music, books, particular films, drugs and, later on, some aspects of Buddhism. In every case, an external image sparked off an internal image – an image of some kind of awakening, speaking to an image of my own life. Certain images do seem to have a special ability to communicate something inspired and awakened. One of the clearest for me is the image of the Buddha. It's all there somehow – the enlightened individual who has a personal history and connections just as we do, yet who possesses timeless wisdom and compassion. There is the teaching and understanding flowing from those qualities, and the realization that we can discover them for ourselves now by following his example. All of that, for me, is encapsulated in his image. But the Buddha's image can also affect me in ways over which I have no control and cannot imagine on my own; it is bigger than my imagination of it. Images have tremendous power to transform us when we are able to trust and open up to them.

In terms of Buddhist practice, the development of the imagination can also be seen in a progression from simple, unreflecting consciousness through reflexive consciousness (self-awareness) to a mode of consciousness that is in some way beyond self and other.

Reflexive consciousness is the awareness that we are aware and the knowledge that we know this. It's what brings colour, depth and pain into our lives. Sometimes we can feel that it's all just too much; we avoid self-awareness and retreat inside a shell or deliberately distract ourselves. When we close down into this unreflecting, one-dimensional state, life loses its richness and seems painted in unrelievedly grey shades. But when we take courage and fully acknowledge our existence, we soon start living in full glorious colour – perhaps harsh and garish at times but also often beautiful.

I have often heard it said that in contrast to animals, reflection is the distinctively human factor from which we get our supposedly unique sense of humour and our ability to think creatively and to empathize. Contemporary observations have discredited such assumptions with regard to quite a few animals. Moreover, human beings aren't self-aware all the time: we're often absorbed rather blindly in our thoughts and sense experiences in the very state of 'simple' consciousness that we ascribe to animals. The real advantage of being human is not so much the ability for self-awareness itself but the increased opportunity we have for developing it. Self-awareness is not difficult to develop; it just needs appreciating when it's there and to be encouraged to grow.

A good strategy for reconnecting with ourselves when that certain something seems to be missing from experience (no spark and it's all grey) is reconnecting with the physical body. Body awareness, and the lack of it, affects us deeply. It may be very difficult to connect physically at such a time; but seeing the need and then persisting with the attempt creates a foothold in reality, and from there it is easier to pick up on the feelings and thoughts of the moment. That little shift from simple consciousness to self-consciousness, especially through body awareness, is a skill that, as we'll see, is strengthened by mindfulness training.

Occasionally we get a glimpse of a dimension further on from this: transcendental consciousness, sometimes also called universal or nondual awareness. What is transcended is the view that 'I' am a completely separate fixed entity in relation to other similarly fixed entities. That is a very tenaciously held view; it strongly affects the way we all perceive the world and act within it. But as a result of an insightful reflection or a spontaneous moment of illumination, experience can also open out so that we see 'me' and 'the world' in a more universal way – and suddenly those words no longer fit what we are experiencing. Thich Nhat Hanh evokes such an illumination:

> *Forest.*
>
> *Thousands of tree bodies and mine*
> *Leaves are waving*
> *Ears hear the stream's call*
> *Eyes see into the sky of mind,*
> *A half smile unfolds on every leaf.*
> *There is a forest here*
> *Because I am here.*
> *But mind has followed the forest*
> *And clothed itself in green.*[6]

A potential transformation, an enlargement of the way we experience our lives, thus extends from simple consciousness through self-consciousness to consciousness beyond self and other. Like a softly glowing lamp, spiritual practice brings to light marvellous qualities previously obscured by confused emotions and attitudes. Gradually the obstacles to our freedom show themselves and start to dissolve: confusion is displaced by clarity, ignorance by wisdom and negative emotion by positive emotion. In this way, meditation and mindfulness gradually transform our whole life in the great transformation mapped out over the course of this book.

A systematic overview of meditation principles

Before beginning Chapter 1, I would like to offer an overview of meditation principles that we can refer to as we go on. This system of meditation was developed originally by my teacher Sangharakshita. We shall find it a good framework both for understanding where various practices or approaches fit in and for reflecting on the nature of our own spiritual experiences.

Buddhism has a rich tradition of meditation methods. The Buddha himself was credited by the fifth-century CE commentator Buddhaghosa with teaching forty of them, most of which, in some form, appear somewhere in this book. Thousands more have been added since his time as the Buddhist tradition entered many Asian cultures. The variety of methods may come as a surprise, as mainstream Buddhist communities these days generally focus on just one meditation technique.

It is certainly normal in Buddhist tradition to introduce newcomers to a single method: this is usually a variant of mindfulness of breathing (*ānāpānasati*) and possibly also the development of loving-kindness (Mettā Bhāvanā). A few traditions start with some kind of Just Sitting or mindfulness practice or with chanting. The Buddha himself taught these three crucial areas of Buddhist practice, and individuals have pursued them in various Buddhist traditions. Almost every newcomer to Buddhism starts with these, and probably with the first, because when starting off, everyone needs to become 1) more integrated and concentrated, 2) more friendly and loving and 3) more deeply aware.

In my own tradition, the Triratna Order,[7] we call these key areas 'integration', 'positive emotion' and 'mindfulness'. The first two are similar in that they involve directed effort: we cultivate concentration and develop our ability to love. But in its basic form the third, mindfulness, is not about cultivating anything; it's simply being aware of what is happening. Thus 1 and 2 are active meditations but 3 is receptive. The full, extended practice of mindfulness, as outlined in the *Satipaṭṭhāna Sutta*, does have an active developmental aspect. However, the basic mindfulness practice is receptivity and openness to the actuality of all experience, and that is equivalent to the Just Sitting meditation (see Chapter 3).

Here emerge the main principles in our system of meditation. First comes the difference between those practices that actively cultivate particular qualities and those that receptively 'take in' current experiences. Then there is an ordering, a sequence of regular steps: concentration, positive emotion and mindfulness are basics everyone needs to have established before attempting in any depth the more advanced stages of meditation, which are concerned with insight or wisdom. It may certainly happen sometimes that we do experience levels of awareness or insight that seem very much beyond our current stage of realization, but these experiences are usually temporary. Soon we have to drop back and continue putting down roots in the here and now.

To begin with, you help your mind to become concentrated and unified; you develop **integration**. This makes it easier then to develop love, confidence and kindness, in other words **positive emotion**.

Table 1: Integration and positive emotion

Active	Integration	Positive emotion
	1) Concentration: ānāpānasati	2) Loving-kindness: Mettā Bhāvanā
Receptive	Mindfulness and Just Sitting	

The next chapters are concerned with the details of these processes. Chapters 1 and 2 in particular, and most of those up to and including Chapter 6, focus on the stages of integration and positive emotion. Mindfulness is covered in Chapters 3 and 4. Chapters 7, 8, 9 and 10 introduce the stages of meditation that are concerned with insight into the real nature of existence and the compassion that is inseparable from that insight.

Insight meditation is the other main factor in our system. It is something very different from integration or positive emotion but can be sustained only once our work in those stages has established a positive, integrated state of mind known as dhyāna. Dhyāna is fresh, open, clear and concentrated at a level that makes it possible to explore in depth the nature of our existence and to see through our over-literal assumptions and views. Without at least the beginnings of dhyāna, our insight meditations are likely to be unclear and unfocused; they will not result in any actual insight.

The realm of practice aimed at cultivating dhyāna, equivalent to the stages of integration and positive emotion, is generally known as *śamatha* or 'calming' meditation. The realm of insight meditation is known as *vipaśyanā*, which means 'seeing'.[8]

Practised within a state of well-established śamatha, vipaśyanā methods eventually produce results: we really do see through our views and assumptions. A moment of true seeing is radical and something of a shock; it can set off a process that culminates in the collapse of everything we have previously taken for granted. It is the most crucial transition in anyone's spiritual life. We therefore call it the stage of **spiritual death**, which is not putting it too strongly: like death, real insight is always unexpected, always resisted, always life-changing. 'Death' also suggests the possibility of a renaissance, a rebirth into a new kind of existence. Until our old ways finally die off, nothing new can come about.

Seeing into the truth makes it easy to abandon delusion, to let it go and to let go into the positive state of insight. Here we enter the area of insight meditation. It is concerned not so much with breakthroughs and realizations but with the process of becoming fully awakened, in which the practitioner starts to be transformed in a permanent way. This phase of the system of meditation is termed **spiritual rebirth**.

Table 2: The system of meditation

Active approach	Realm of śamatha		Realm of vipaśyanā	
	1. Integration Mindfulness of breathing; concentration-orientated practices; active mindfulness	2. Positive emotion Mettā, brahma vihāras, bodhicitta	3. Spiritual death Reflection/direct seeing vipashyana, e.g. six-element practice	4. Spiritual rebirth Sādhana or *Buddhānussati*, connecting with the Buddha
Receptive approach	5. Mindfulness and Just Sitting Some aspects of sādhana meditation; Just Sitting meditation; receptive mindfulness			

The system of meditation

Each of the four cumulative stages is associated with methods that typically cultivate it, but with experience comes the ability to cultivate any phase with any practice. Most methods can be approached from either a śamatha or a vipaśyanā angle or both. All the practices will be explored in some depth as the book progresses.

1) **Integration** is associated with concentration meditation, such as mindfulness of breathing.
2) **Positive emotion** comes about through loving-kindness (Mettā Bhāvanā) meditation and the family of practices that Mettā Bhāvanā comes from, i.e. the four brahma vihāras.
3) **Spiritual death** is arrived at through vipaśyanā meditations such as the contemplation of conditionality or the six-element practice.
4) **Spiritual rebirth** is especially associated with sādhana (visualization) meditation. As will be seen in Chapter 9, sādhana is often a complex of practices within practices, an aspect of which is an active cultivation of the Buddha's qualities. Thus this phase of the system of meditation can, like the previous three, be associated with the active approach. However, since sādhana especially involves receptivity to the living qualities of the Buddha, it also links very naturally to the receptive approach.
5) **Mindfulness** has the unique place in our system of making sure that the meditator does not lose his or her grounding in tangible, felt experience by overemphasizing the active approach. Mindfulness refers to many different kinds of practice, but in terms of meditation it is especially associated with Just Sitting. More will be said in Chapter 3, but the essence of this approach is to stop doing things and come into relationship with immediate experience. The effect on the practice is refreshment and renewal at every level.

Chapter one

....

Integration

You probably know how it feels when you are trying to get through to someone whose mind is on something else. They just seem unable to give you their attention, and it's a frustrating experience. Yet some of that exists in your experience all the time: you rarely give your *undivided* attention to anything! You have so many things on your mind that your attention is constantly dissipated; distraction is a normal part of your life. T. S. Eliot commented in 'Burnt Norton' that we are 'distracted from distraction by distraction ... filled with fancies and empty of meaning'.[9] So side-tracked are we from our original purposes that we lose sight of what is most important and precious to us. Like one of those dreams in which everything conspires to prevent us from doing something, there is a frustrating sense that there was *something* we really wanted to do but we cannot remember what it is.

You can gain much by going against that trend and strengthening your ability to concentrate. Bring the threads of attention together and your direction clarifies; you uncover something deeper and truer in your nature. This is what mindfulness of breathing achieves. It teaches you how to relax the mind and to focus, without conflict, on a single object.

How can you remove the conflict of attention that prevents concentration? Aside from giving the mind an initial direction, you can't simply force it to concentrate – it won't stay there for long. If you try too forcefully to fix your attention, there will be an emotional reaction that will either destabilize or dull the mind. Full concentration requires the emotional faculties to be in harmony with the reasoning mind, which is giving directions. But most people can easily think about something without knowing what they feel about it or get emotional without any clarity of thought. This mental imbalance obstructs their ability fully to engage and to concentrate.

It's easy to see this disconnection in others. When you say things such as 'Be careful what you tell Ellie this morning; she's really not herself' or 'I'm sure you'll like old Joe – he's so much himself', you are assessing their inner balance of reason and emotion. In fact, 'being oneself', in the fullest sense, is the primary aim of concentration meditation. That's what 'integration' means. In psychological terms, integration means bringing together the different elements of your personality into a dynamic and harmonious whole. Indeed, you can aim for a certain inner harmony straight away in meditation. Initially your work will be in strengthening your ability to engage your attention, so that you can become fully absorbed in what you are focusing on.

Many factors are involved in giving attention. Some people have a greater natural ability; others' attention is more scattered. It is also easier to concentrate in particular situations and at different times of day: external circumstances and emotional pressures all make a difference. A normally cool and collected person may lose that calm aura in a crisis; an enthusiastic person may become anxious when there is nothing for them to do. But we all possess the faculty of concentration to some degree, and can learn to strengthen it, making it less dependent upon circumstances.

> When a meditator is first counting his breaths he should count late, like a grain measurer does (after each measure).
>
> Then he should count the breaths early, just as a cowherd counts his cattle.
>
> A skilled cowherd takes pebbles in his pocket and goes to the cow pen in the morning – sitting on the bar of the gate, and prodding the cows in the back, he counts each one as it reaches the gate and counts 'one, two', dropping a pebble for each.
>
> The cows have spent an uncomfortable night in the cramped pen, so they come out quickly in parties, jostling each other as they escape. So he counts early, saying 'three … four … five' – and so on up to ten …
>
> With the help of that counting, the mind becomes unified, just as a boat in a swift current is steadied with the help of a rudder.
>
> Ancient instruction manual (Buddhaghosa, fifth century CE)[10]

The essential method of this practice is very simple: give continuous attention to the touch sensation as the breath comes in and out of the body. Each time the attention strays, gently and firmly return to the breath sensation.

As the practice continues, mental wandering tends to lessen as the attention in the body becomes deeper and more constant. Scattered energies gather together, rounded up like the cattle Buddhaghosa mentions, as you keep returning attention to the breath. Experiencing the mind coming together in this way is deeply satisfying, and you feel increasingly peaceful, relaxed and clear-minded. Once you can rest the attention continuously in the breath, there is a sense of complete absorption – a tangible sense of integration, of being totally 'yourself'.

In principle, you can use any object as a focus; breathing is just one of thousands of possible meditation objects. You could concentrate upon any small visual object such as a matchbox, an orange or a black dot, but the trouble with something so humdrum is that you're likely to become bored or hypnotically fixated. Some objects simply work better as images for carrying the aspiration for Awakening. What is especially evocative about the breath is that it is as alive as you are, and as mysterious and vulnerable. Breathing is inherently interesting too, with its rhythmic, sensuous quality, and the subtlety of its sensations engages your interest while allowing a relaxed flexibility. The latter is important: if attention is allowed to become stiff and wooden, the energy and inspiration will be lost.

Perhaps because it is so basic to your existence, the quality of breathing at any time mirrors your physical and mental state. It quickens as you get emotionally stirred and quietens as the body relaxes. And as the breathing stills, the mind becomes correspondingly composed.

But even though breathing can engage the attention in so many ways, an effort will still be needed in order to stay engaged with it for a whole meditation session. Now and again you will find yourself becoming distracted, perhaps completely losing track of what you are doing. This is why the method in the initial stages of the mindfulness of breathing meditation is to count each breath from one to ten. It helps to maintain the attention.

You can try the meditation right away if you wish. Just make sure you are sitting in a position that will be comfortable for 15–20 minutes and understand the following overview.

Mindfulness of breathing meditation

Brief instructions

Begin by sitting quietly for a minute or so, just to relax, settle down and gather your energies.

1. Feel the touch of the breathing as it flows in and out of the body. Just *after* each breath leaves the body, note it mentally with a count. Count ten breaths in that way, from one to ten, and then start again at one. Keep doing that for a predetermined time (start with five minutes for each stage, glancing at a timepiece placed in front of you).
2. Now note each breath *before* it enters, counting in the same way as before.
3. Now stop counting and simply experience the touch of the breathing as it constantly changes.
4. Now direct your attention to the point where you most feel the touch of incoming air – probably around the nostrils or the upper lip; the exact location does not matter. Simply choose any point that seems suitable. Rest your attention continuously on the subtle sensations of the air stimulating that point.

After the meditation, take a minute or so to sit quietly absorbing the experience.

Table 3: Stages of the mindfulness of breathing meditation

Preparation	Make sure you are comfortably seated. Sit quietly for a minute or two; relax, settle down. Experience the sensation of your breathing.
Stage 1	Count just after each out-breath.
Stage 2	Count just before each in-breath.
Stage 3	Stop counting; experience the general flow of the breathing.
Stage 4	Maintain your attention at the point where you most feel the touch of the flow of air.

Detailed instructions

Stage 1. Counting after each out-breath

Find a good sitting position cross-legged, kneeling or on a chair. Arrange whatever cushions and blankets you need in order to be comfortable. Have your hands resting together in your lap or on your knees. It is best to close the eyes; but if you feel drowsy, have them half open and rest your gaze at a point a metre or so away on the floor.

First, take a minute or so to relax and settle down. Then start to take your attention onto the breathing. As much as you can, let each breath come as it will without altering the natural flow. Don't try to breathe 'normally'. Just allow the breaths to come short or long and to feel as awkward, rough or self-consciously controlled as they like. The breathing may be sighing or gusty at times; at others, it will become smooth, subtle and hardly perceptible. Be confident that in experiencing each breath just as it is, you are practising correctly. The point is not to breathe well but to use the breath as an object of concentration (though, in fact, your growing concentration will probably make the breath gentler and calmer). The aim is to experience it *exactly as it is*, and any sense that you are over-controlling the breath will subside in the natural course of practice. The basic instruction is to stay with the present-moment experience of the touch of the breath in the body.

Now, to make your attention more continuous, tag each breath with a count. As the out-breath finishes, silently count: one. Feel another breath coming in and going out: two. Feel another in-breath, another out-breath: three. Keep noting each out-breath like that; and once you get to ten, return to one and repeat the sequence.

Keep the counting sequence going throughout the first stage and stay with the breath's sensations. Whenever you notice that your attention is wandering, bring it back immediately to the touch of the breath and continue counting. Get into the habit of returning straight away to the breath sensation; don't waste precious momentum wondering why or how you became distracted. Have confidence that it's fine to think no more about it. It may sometimes be useful later on to explore what happened, but for now keep returning patiently to the breath sensation again and again. And that essentially *is* the practice, for now at least. As you become more familiar with this, it will become easier to stay fully absorbed in the breathing.

Stage 2. Counting before each inward breath

Now count before each breath comes in. Count one, and experience the flow of a breath coming in and going out again. Then count two, and again feel the inward and outward breath. Count three, feeling once again the in- and out-breath, and continue counting each in-breath in that way until you get to ten. Then return to one and repeat the sequence.

It's a very slight change, but it makes a difference. You'll probably find your attention sharpening up a bit, and now you have to take a slightly more active stance. This stage helps to establish concentration more firmly. Maintain the counting sequence as before, patiently bringing your attention back to the breath sensation again and again when it wanders.

Over these two stages you will probably have built up a degree of absorption. It may not be especially noticeable, as distractions may still be present. So don't analyse too much. Just have confidence; and when the time comes, move on to stage 3.

Stage 3. Experiencing the flow of the breath

Now let go of the counting method and feel the natural flow of breathing coursing through all the body. Pay special attention to the turning points, where the tide of breathing turns from out to in and from in to out. This stage generates awareness of the whole volume of the breath, helping to maintain your concentration from breath to breath to breath.

Allow the breathing to quieten naturally, and let both your mind and your body quieten with it. Your attention and your physical posture are likely to become calmer and more refined now. As you tune in more to the body, feel its energy and include that in the meditation. When you do that, it can feel as though the concentration is coming from the body as much as the mind. As you become more experienced, it becomes possible to include a subtle sense of body posture throughout the meditation. That deepens and grounds the sense of integration.

Stage 4. Experiencing the subtle sensation of the breath

Next, focus on the sensation at the point where you feel the air entering and leaving your body. Choose any point that seems right and remain focused there. The sensation will be clearest around your nostrils or upper lip, or perhaps further in or down towards the throat.

As your breath passes this point, you may feel it as a soft, brushing sensation that is cool as it enters and warm as it leaves. Remain with that single point of sensation as uninterruptedly as you can. Be receptive to the slight changes at each phase of the in-breath and the out-breath and at the turning points between them. Focus so closely that you almost listen to the sensation.

Because the sensation is subtle, its quality changing at each moment, following it will require some agility. Eventually the sensation may become so subtle that it is almost imperceptible. It may indeed seem to disappear completely. In this case, the breathing has not actually disappeared but it has become so subtle that the practice demands you to seek it afresh. You need to soften and quieten your concentration in a new way. The mind needs to become extremely gentle and fine in order to re-establish connection with this more subtle object.

Have confidence that this will come in time. As the breathing relaxes at this new level of quietness and subtlety, the mind is able to achieve a new depth of calmness. This joyful calm marks the beginning of dhyāna, full concentration or higher consciousness, to be explained in Chapter 6.

Ending the meditation

When you bring the practice to an end, be gentle. Open your eyes slowly, take in what has happened and sit quietly for a while before getting up. Resist any impulse to get up abruptly and do something vigorous. Rushing into the next thing will jar your mood and may leave you feeling oversensitive or irritated.

The transition between meditation and the rest of the day is very important for when you come to sit again. It affects the way you feel about both of them. To rush out of meditation straight into a busy schedule can squash the good effects of the practice and prevent them from being absorbed into your life. On the other hand, leaping into meditation without much preparation usually just brings a disturbed mind to the meditation. Such habits undermine the resolve to meditate by reducing its benefits and turning the experience into a struggle. Really, you need to make suitable preparations for meditation and also to notice all the transitions you make between activities in your day, so that you feel less rushed and more fully present in what you do.

On days when you have more time, it is helpful to allow plenty of open space around meditation. Don't rush into it, and for a while afterwards just do something quiet; let your mind absorb what has happened. Gaze out of the window, take a short stroll and let your thoughts unwind a little. This all helps the process of integration.

The essential conditions for meditation are a comfortable sitting **posture** and a suitable **place**. These conditions will enable you to sit still with no interruption for some time and without minor discomforts building up and nagging you.

A stable and comfortable **posture** with an upright back is essential. The way you achieve it does not particularly matter: you can sit on a kitchen chair, kneel on a high pile of cushions or sit cross-legged in the traditional style. There are longer-term benefits to the cross-legged and kneeling styles, so if they come reasonably easily, sit in either of those ways. Appendix 2 explores the different ways of sitting for meditation, and some of the illustrations will give ideas for experimentation. If, like most people, your hips are stiff and you can't sit cross-legged for very long, then the best posture is probably to kneel on a thick blanket or to sit on a stool or several cushions. The blanket under the legs helps to prevent them from getting numb, and the high pile of cushions is important for most normal people in helping to prevent the back from slumping. These points apply to cross-legged positions too – have plenty of cushions. And have a folded blanket under the legs if possible. Certainly use a straight-backed chair if it seems better, but it's not good to lean the weight against the backrest unless you actually have back trouble. That gives rise to the tendency to slump, which causes mental dullness.

You also need a quiet **place** for meditation, and it's best if you can be certain that there won't be any disturbances. For example, it's a good idea to turn off your phone or mobile. Guaranteed quiet will make a big difference to your ability to relax and let go into meditation, so it's worth going to some lengths to get it. The effort of concentration makes you extra sensitive to distractions, so music or a conversation in a nearby room is likely to become a source of irritation. Avoid such things as much as possible, but don't get too fussy about it because there will always be external distractions of some kind. Even when you are alone in the depths of the countryside, there are all kinds of sound for your mind to attach itself to. So once you have eliminated all the distractions you can, be patient, relax and let go of the desire for perfect quiet. Allow the sounds to come and go as they wish in the background while you focus on the breathing.

If you intend to take up meditation as a regular practice, you will soon need more personal guidance than this book can provide. You can find out about Buddhist meditation classes in your area and also contact fellow practitioners who follow the methods outlined in this book.[11]

It is important to read the basic instructions and make sure you understand clearly what you are supposed to be doing in each stage, so that you won't have to stop in the middle of them and check. Timing the stages on your own might seem tricky but timer devices or applications are available. Some people find them helpful, and I often use one myself. But it is not necessary to have exactly equal stages, and it's easy enough to use some kind of timepiece. If it is distracting to open the eyes and check the time, then it's fine simply to move on to the next stage of the meditation when ready. Once concentration feels sufficiently established in one stage or enough time seems to have passed, just go on to the next stage. If a stage has finished but your concentration isn't as good as expected, it is usually better to move on to the next stage. The various stages are ways to work on concentration from different angles, so it's useful to gain experience in all four stages. You will often find that, despite a difficult start, a later stage has a surprisingly concentrating effect. In meditation as in the rest of life, you can never assume that you know what's going to happen.

Chapter two

....

Goodwill

> May all beings live happily and safe
> And may their hearts rejoice within themselves.
>
> From the Buddha's Discourse on Loving Kindness
> (*Karaṇīya Mettā Sutta*)[12]

The Buddha is frequently referred to in the Pali scriptures as 'the Happy One', and his friendliness immediately struck those who encountered him. In that spirit he taught a wide range of spiritual practices to a great variety of individuals, instructing them according to temperament and spiritual need. Two practices he frequently recommended were mindfulness of breathing, which was introduced in Chapter 1 and Mettā Bhāvanā, literally 'the meditation that cultivates a quality of goodwill'. This quality focuses strongly on relationship. It is the desire to help, to be a friend and to be open and interested in people. The opposite to the anxiety to get things, it's a desire to give – the very spirit of generosity. It's also an ethical, responsible quality: one cannot bear to harm or to exploit others.

Mettā is a positive emotion. Its essence is the wish for someone to be truly happy. This wish is also at the heart of Mettā Bhāvanā meditation, in which you wish happiness – and, importantly, its causes – for four kinds of people with a special place in your life: you (and that's vital), good friends, neutral people and those you find difficult.

But what is happiness and what are its causes? I find myself using the terms 'true happiness' or 'real happiness' because the common idea of 'happiness' often corresponds to what people think they would experience if only they had a better partner, house, car, computer or mobile. A genuinely happy person will surely enjoy pleasant living, but their life couldn't consist of uninterrupted pleasure. Happiness also encompasses what Buddhism calls skilful pleasures, for many pleasures don't entail happiness at all, heroin, revenge or gluttony for example. Our human tendency is to chase happiness and to end up craving more while enjoying less.

Happiness is when you enjoy more and crave less, when you feel satisfied, fulfilled, independent and strong. It is closely connected with your ethical state; it relates to whether or not you feel good about yourself, whether you feel you have acted appropriately or have done what needed doing. When you know you have lied or exploited someone or somehow betrayed yourself, you don't really feel happy (though you may pretend you do). Acting ethically provides you with a pleasure and enjoyment that has subtle, gentle strength. The Buddha distinguished it from the more self-centred sources of pleasure and encouraged its cultivation as the way to liberate the heart.

Mettā, the friendly wish for someone's true happiness, underpins all this. Here is how its quality can be made to grow in everyone's life.

Mettā Bhāvanā meditation

Brief instructions

This brief description gives an idea of the stages of Mettā Bhāvanā practice. Then follows a more detailed explanation. After that, we'll discuss some related issues.

Prepare for meditation. Sit quietly, settle down, connect with your body and with whatever you are feeling and thinking.

Cultivate mettā for yourself. Consider your life and experience how it feels to be you. Feel the truth of your experience, perhaps joyous, perhaps sad. Acknowledging whatever feelings are present, wish yourself happiness. Maybe say to yourself, 'May I be well and happy.' Then just keep setting your attention back on to that wish (five-plus minutes).

continues overleaf

Cultivate mettā for a friend. Switch to the impression in your mind, whatever form that takes, of a friend – maybe this will be an actual visual image, but a simple feeling is fine. They should be roughly your age and not someone you particularly have sexual feelings for (keep it simple!). Experience your true response and wish them happiness as you did earlier for yourself (five-plus minutes).

Cultivate mettā for a 'neutral' person. Think of someone for whom you don't have a particular liking or dislike. What you feel when you bring them to mind may not be very clear but stay with what's there and encourage a friendly response, wishing them happiness. It's good training to maintain this in relation to someone you don't naturally find interesting, so keep it up (five-plus minutes)!

Cultivate mettā for a difficult person. Turn your attention to someone you're not getting on with. Experience truthfully how you feel now without being misled by how they 'always' make you feel. Cultivate a fresh response, wishing them real happiness, even though that might go against the grain. Real happiness makes everyone more likeable and has little connection with superficial pleasure or advantage. So let go of any animosity or resentment you're harbouring (five-plus minutes).

Cultivate mettā equally for each person. Now concentrate on all four people – you, your friend, the neutral person and the difficult person – and develop mettā as equally as you can towards each. From there, **cultivate mettā for all beings everywhere.** Let your mettā expand like the warmth of the sun towards all beings everywhere in the world. Here is one way. Start with those nearest you, in the same room or the same building. Then include everyone in the street, town, city or area you are in. Let your imagination take your good wishes out in ever-widening circles. Include everyone in the country, the continent, the other continents, the entire Earth, the whole universe. Recall how all those beings, non-human as well as human, are undergoing every kind of experience even as you are meditating. Think of them all with equally strong love and kindness.

Detailed instructions

Start by sitting in a comfortable position. If you sit as still as possible, it will help to keep you focused on how you are feeling. Mindfulness, especially mindfulness of feeling and emotion, is an important key to Mettā Bhāvanā. But body awareness is also needed in order to experience feeling: emotional energy comes from opening up to what is here physically. Fully experience the pleasantness, the unpleasantness or just the absence of feeling that is present. If there are painful feelings, don't pretend that they don't exist. Realize that there's no need to be angry or despondent because of them. Simply experience them mindfully. It's the same with pleasant feelings – recognizing and enjoying pleasure without getting overinvolved. And if there seems to be no feeling at all, which is common enough, turn and face that space of (apparent) nothingness. Actively experience it. It could be that you need to re-establish contact with your core experience, with the body and the senses, because you've lost touch. But it is just as likely that, quite naturally, your experience is somewhat neutral at the moment. Whatever the case, to help with the meditation sit very still and simply 'listen' receptively to the experience, even though it may feel as though there is nothing there. Rest attention within the body, on the breathing, the muscular relaxation or tension and the general flow of physical energy.

Don't worry if feelings are weak or hardly noticeable; if they are subtle or uncertain, this only indicates that they need to be given space for their meaning to become clear. Thus feeling doesn't have to be powerful and strong before you can do something with it. If you stay with the experience as it is, you can build mettā effectively, even when the feeling is subtle and barely perceptible.

As often as not, you have to acknowledge pain. Human experience is a bittersweet mixture; it is never 100 per cent pleasure. When feelings are pleasant, it is easy to be kind and friendly. But when they are painful, you need to be patient and avoid reacting with emotions such as denial, ill will, frustration or self-pity, which easily become habitual. It is helpful, if you can, to continue experiencing them, patiently understanding that all feelings, pleasant, painful or neutral, are temporary and that your reactions to pain actually end up making it even more painful. So allow space for something new to enter. At first, the response of loving-kindness may not be very strong; but once it gets started, you can build on it.

1) In the first stage, **cultivating mettā for ourselves**, you can explore and use any method you find helpful. It may help to say to yourself the traditional phrase 'May I be happy, may I be well, may I be free from suffering.' But avoid repeating it automatically. Consider the real meaning of happiness – clarifying this is essential in meditation – and allow time for a response of some kind to emerge. Mettā Bhāvanā works on the principle that wishes and intentions get stronger, clearer and more effective when you concentrate on them. So once you have contacted the need for happiness, and the more genuine benevolence that comes from perceiving that, put your heartfelt energy into it.

If you look, you'll discover an image in your mind of what you are trying to do. This is not easily describable but it is a quite tangible sense or feeling that you can trust as being your true wish for happiness. It is something very simple. If you can rest fully in it, the feeling of mettā will deepen and become more established. Then, as the practice progresses, instead of getting lost in thoughts about what you're doing, you can stay with that simple core and keep returning to it. This is where the practice can go deeper.

By the end of the first stage, you're likely to feel a little better towards yourself, or at least a bit more settled into the practice. But don't be put off if nothing much seems to have happened. That's often how it is. Once the time is up, it's best to move to the second stage without lingering in the hope of a more tangible result. The feeling that 'not much is happening' is common in the first stage of any kind of meditation because we're still warming up. In meditation practice generally, the best approach is to tackle each stage as it comes without wasting energy judging one's performance. In Mettā Bhāvanā you are learning to tune in to your experience and to treat yourself with kindness and appreciation. It is a long-term project and you can relax into it.

2) Next, remaining in touch with the feeling you already have, **generate mettā towards a good friend** – anyone towards whom you already have natural friendly feelings. Just choose them fairly quickly, without dithering, and rest the attention on their image. The impression may be visual, a felt sense, a set of thoughts or something else again; but in whatever way you imagine them, stay as steady as you can with that image, trust it and return to it every time you notice that the mind has wandered. Using the methods already described, wish them true happiness. If it helps, you can apply to them the traditional phrase mentioned above or use any method that evokes, deepens and refines your wish. In this you need to be emotionally truthful and experience the actual response that is aroused. Your responses change all the time – so maybe this time, despite the friendship, your friend's image does not actually evoke strong friendliness at all (our best friends are the people we usually take most for granted). Recognize that situation as your working ground. In Mettā Bhāvanā the art is always to create something new out of how you actually feel right now. You can learn something every time about yourself and your relations to others.

3) Then, without losing touch with the changing feelings, transfer the mettā towards your internal image of **a neutral person**. This is somebody for whom you have no particular feelings at the moment: you neither like nor dislike them. They may be someone you hardly know, perhaps someone you often see but never speak to yet have an impression of. It could be the postman or a neighbour or someone you know well and don't dislike but find uninteresting. Just as before, develop mettā in response to the way you actually feel about them right at this moment. There will be an image of some kind. Most likely, you'll feel very little, in a way similar to when (seemingly) you feel nothing in the first stage. But if you trust the process of giving attention, over time you will eventually find more feeling; and that will start to reveal subtler feelings of pleasure or pain, to which you'll feel more able to respond with mettā.

4) That extension of our emotional capacity takes a step towards the biggest challenge as, in the fourth stage, you **direct mettā towards someone you dislike** or who seems to dislike you. You can choose someone you're not getting on with at the moment, with whom there is either some temporary misunderstanding or long-term, habitual noncommunication. You could indeed choose an out-and-out enemy, someone you really hate. However, it is best not to make the practice impossibly difficult. And remember that the whole point of the exercise is to generate loving-kindness for all beings. If your negative feelings are very powerful, you'll probably end up strengthening them.

As in the previous stages, remain aware of the actual feeling that arises. Whenever you get distracted, return to your core experience (body, sensation and feeling) together with the actual impression, the image you are holding of this person. Have the view that even though you currently find them difficult to get along with, things can and do change. Reflect that their experience will differ from your perception and that, like you, they often experience frustration and real suffering. If you can see this, you can relax your perceptions (and perhaps a little pride) and genuinely wish for their happiness and well-being. If they were truly happy, you would surely perceive them differently. Indeed, you would almost certainly find them more likeable.

5) The final stage begins by **imagining each of the four people in the practice** – you, your good friend, the neutral person and the difficult person – all together. Remaining with the core experience and the feeling of mettā you've been building up, work to **equalize the mettā between all four persons**. Direct mettā equally strongly towards the friend and the neutral person, yourself and the difficult person and the difficult person and your friend. Work with images as described. It needs plenty of practice and concentration to do this well and to get fully engaged. The method is an effective way to sharpen awareness of all the feelings you have about all the people you know. If time is limited or you're just starting the practice, a more basic approach is to let mettā flow equally towards each person without analysis or comparison. Simply imagine that the mettā is equal towards all.

Then **extend the practice to include all beings.** Equalizing the mettā starts a process of opening it up and universalizing it. Open out to include the entire world, far beyond you and your three companions.

In doing this, use your imagination freely. For example, you could try, first, to develop loving-kindness towards yourself and anyone else in the room you are in. Then start opening out to include everyone in the house, building or wherever you happen to be. Once that's established, include the area round about, then the whole town or city. Next, imagine the county or state and the country and expand the friendliness to include the whole continent. Include the other continents too, until the wish is for everyone in the world without exception to be happy, well and free from suffering. Whatever beings there are, human or non-human, connect with their lives and wish them happiness. The Buddhist tradition is that there are life forms throughout the universe, so don't stop with Earth – wish every being well. Finally, develop mettā not only towards all present life but also towards whatever living beings there might be in the future. As you meditate, try to get a sense of totality, of completeness, of *all* beings. Let go completely and expand the attitude, emotion and feeling beyond all conceivable limits.

Table 4: Stages of the Mettā Bhāvanā meditation

Preparation	Sit comfortably and still.
	Tune into your experience.
Stage 1	Develop friendliness towards yourself.
Stage 2	Develop friendliness towards a good friend.
Stage 3	Develop friendliness towards a neutral person.
Stage 4	Develop friendliness towards a difficult person.
Stage 5	Develop friendliness towards each person equally.
	Extend friendliness to all beings everywhere.

Going deeper into Mettā

The Buddha radiated goodwill. He once said that 'spiritual friendship is the whole Buddhist life'. And just before his death, it was the impending loss of his kindness that struck the most grief in the heart of his long-term assistant and companion Ānanda.

Friendship is a capacity that can be developed. From the point of view of most people's spiritual development, it is at least as important as concentration, and often a more effective way to make personal changes. Someone dominated by hatred can never become wise. You know that when you're grumpy and irritable, your understanding is at its most limited and that when you're happy, it's much easier to feel friendly towards others. The method of Mettā Bhāvanā shows this in the first stage: it seems to indicate that if you really want to befriend another person, the friendship will be flawed unless you at least try to befriend yourself.

That is a wise principle, but it can be difficult to put into practice. People I know genuinely feel very appreciative of others' merits, but have an amazingly strong reluctance to accept that there's anything at all good about themselves. This sometimes arises out of modesty, whether real or false, but more fundamentally it seems to stem from a lack of self-confidence. So Mettā Bhāvanā practised over time will strengthen our self-esteem and deepen our faith in our potential.

I sometimes hear concern that mettā will make people arrogant or self-centred if they direct it towards themselves: it seems too ego-affirming. This is a fundamental misunderstanding of the nature of mettā. To wish ourselves true happiness encourages us to be kind to ourselves and to allow our good qualities space to emerge. The reality that we so often treat ourselves harshly is hardly ego-affirming – it's a challenge! Looked at in another way, the first stage of Mettā Bhāvanā *is* ego-affirming, in the positive sense we all need. You benefit from encouraging yourself to do what you need to do. There is always some ability to make positive changes.

It also helps to look more broadly and appreciate our existence in itself. When you really look, you can see what a precious, mysterious quality you have in being alive and human. You may have many problems, but there's also much to rejoice in.

> [Human existence] is called precious, because it is similar to the Wish-Fulfilling Gem, as difficult to obtain, and very useful. This human body has the power to reject evil and to accomplish good, to cross the ocean of conditioned existence, to follow the path towards Enlightenment, and to obtain the perfect Buddhahood. Therefore it is superior to other forms of life such as gods and serpent demons, and it is even better than the Wish-Fulfilling Gem.
>
> It is called 'precious' because of the difficulty of obtaining this human body and because of its great usefulness. Yet, though difficult to obtain and very useful, it easily breaks down, because there are many causes of death and without waiting it passes on to the future.
>
> Therefore, because of the difficulty of its attainment, of the easiness of its breaking down, and of its great usefulness, you should think of the body as a boat and by its means escape from the ocean of conditioned existence.
>
> Gampopa, 1079–1153 CE) [13]

Gampopa is talking here about escape from the states of mind that condition a repetitive, destructive and, possibly for us, self-blaming lifestyle. He is also pointing to the amazing potential of the human condition to develop affirmative, creative states of mind. You would probably have no difficulty in liking yourself if you had this in focus. You would also have a truer sense of the value of others' lives, and then friendliness towards them would probably be more heartfelt. Confidence in this comes through reflection – through stepping back from the distractions and emotional pressures of your workaday lives and, in a space that's free and relaxed, considering the important things of life. The ability to create that kind of space comes especially from the inner calm of regular meditation practice.

> If ... you practise realising the good qualities of other people, there will come a feeling of great compassion for all sentient life. In this connection you will have vision and recollection of your parents, your close kinsmen, your intimate friends, and your hearts will be filled with inexpressible joy and gratitude.
>
> Then there will develop similar visions of compassion for your common acquaintances, even for your enemies, and for all sentient beings in the five realms of existence.
>
> When you rise from the practice of meditation after these experiences, your hearts will be full of joy and happiness and you will greet whoever you meet with kind and peaceful faces.
>
> Zhiyi [14]

It is only natural that your inner attitude spontaneously expresses itself in actions. And your actions directly affect other people, including the global environment of living beings and their habitats. The extent to which you actually feel mettā shows itself in your appreciation that others have needs and points of view. Your capacity to empathize with the lives around you is the basis of ethics, because understanding them makes you more sensitive and kind towards them. This is why friendship is an essential practice. Indeed, it is an ideal practice for the real world: by irritating, flattering, ignoring, disparaging and frightening you, don't others provide endless opportunities for seeing your negative emotions and developing positive ones?

Some people conceive of spiritual life in terms of getting rid of faults, and they have a point: ethics, meditation and wisdom do indeed purify whatever obstructs your path. However, your path to Awakening is better understood in terms of encouraging your positive qualities. When you develop such qualities, harsh and unhelpful emotions tend to dissolve naturally. To think always in terms of 'getting out of negative patterns' may subtly reinforce them.

In the cut and thrust of daily interaction, it's not always easy to see opportunities for changing your attitudes towards other people. Mettā Bhāvanā offers a unique solution, a space where you can experience all the detail of your responses without the complexity entailed by others' actual presence. Real interactions often give you no time to reflect on your feelings, so you may tend to react blindly, in a slight panic, often without fully knowing what you feel. Meditation allows you time to understand that you can transform these habits, and the habit of inner reorientation also transforms your behaviour spontaneously, without you having to think about it.

Still, meditation on its own, in a bubble, is not enough. The world needs people to go out and befriend others; there is just not enough kindness and friendship around. And the obvious way to train in Mettā Bhāvanā is in our existing relationships, especially our friendships. With a friend you are freer to be aware of the emotions you are experiencing and expressing. Real friendship allows you to disagree and to bring emotional difficulties out into the open. At the same time as friends enjoy the connection, it is vital to any friendship that each expresses what they truly think and feel. These are important ways for you to learn about yourself.

Look at those you know and consider the extent to which they, like you, are governed by moods. The reasoned explanations people give for their actions are just part of the truth. Everybody is influenced by powerful, complex emotions that are often unconscious and over which they have little control. Many feelings are triggered in one way or another by other people. You have grown up in a family of some kind, you live with and around other people, you work with them, read about them, know about them – people are continually in your thoughts and your dreams. You may sometimes be reluctant to admit the strength of the emotions you have about others, but the fact that a particular person or creature makes you feel inspired, relaxed, jealous, irritated or scared matters deeply to you. Responses like these are largely habit: they are pre-existing emotional tendencies ready to be set off by specific people and behaviour.

Day and night, the currents of emotion build up into moods and then disperse as changeably as the weather. These moods affect the content of your thoughts, your level of energy and your creative ability. You would do well to become more aware of your typical emotional weather patterns, yet they can be so painful and confusing that you may relapse into indifference from fear of acknowledging the really difficult emotions.

Simultaneously you may also have a sense of alienation, of separation from emotions. The raw feeling may have gone underground. The urbanized life most of us lead allows little contact with the natural world. Precious resources such as food, water and transport are taken for granted. Animal life is virtually absent on city streets apart from a few pet dogs on leads, and any insect is an inconvenience to be eliminated. People are oblivious to the energy of the waxing and waning moon. In winter even the presence of daylight seems irrelevant, all heat and light being provided by technology. Entertainment and information technology feed our imagination; they are a constant stream of data that excites, disturbs and numbs us.

Being in a state of continual overstimulation while also being cut off from elemental nature can cause many of us to lose touch with basic feelings about things. You even may not think that you have much feeling, because you don't experience it very consciously. But despite being imprisoned, it remains powerfully alive. So an essential preparation for Mettā Bhāvanā meditation is to reconnect with your core experience – the immediate message of your body and senses.

The way in to a deeper engagement with the emotions begins when you acknowledge pleasure and pain, the most basic of all feelings. These strong, simple signals are often ignored or hastily covered up. However, as they are the point where emotions emerge, you need to acknowledge what's happening. Make it a constant practice to ask yourself whether or not you like this experience and whether you feel anything or not. If you do feel something, is it pleasant or painful? If you are truthful with yourself about what you feel, you will become clear-minded and self-confident, not pretending that you're enjoying something when you aren't or convincing yourself that some experience will be unpleasant when you know very well that you will enjoy it.

Being honest with yourself in this way brings emotional awareness, and that gives you leverage over conditioned responses. No one gets angry, jealous, possessive, secretive, grumpy or insecure without a cause. These emotions arise in response to particular situations. As feelings about a situation rise, an emotional response starts forming. You become relieved, elated, anxious, irritated or envious, for example. At that point, there is a degree of choice. It may be almost imperceptible, and you may well choose to ignore it; yet you do have an opportunity at least to temper the anger, resist the anxiety or climb down from the elation. In this endeavour every little bits counts, and you can count any successful circumvention of these powerful patterns as a real victory.

Such emotions are ready-made responses (probably formed long ago) that you are now in the habit of releasing if certain triggers are pressed. Of all triggers, pleasure and pain are the most basic, and naturally you want pleasure and don't want pain. When you don't see the emotional process behind your responses, the danger is that you may do almost anything to anyone in order to get pleasure or to avoid pain. Exploitation has emotional unawareness at its root; it is caused by the loss of empathy that is alienation from experience. On the other hand, it is very easy, if you want, to be connected with your experience and to respond positively. Someone with a friendly heart will never knowingly exploit another, whether that other is a human being, an animal, a plant or a landscape. Mettā is not only the positive emotion of goodwill but also an ethical sensibility that arises from goodwill and manifests as a non-exploitive, generous attitude.

As we have seen throughout this chapter, mettā arises from the realization that all beings want simply to be happy and that their wish to be happy is operating in all they do, however unethical or foolish their activities. Happiness really comes from ethics – from helpfulness, generosity, contentment, truthfulness and awareness – and mettā is the desire for all beings to find that kind of happiness.[15]

Chapter three

....

Mindfulness and Just Sitting

This chapter introduces mindfulness, another core principle of meditation practice. The other principles considered so far are integration and positive emotion, whose primary methods are mindfulness of breathing meditation and Mettā Bhāvanā meditation respectively. There are two more principles to be explained. And eventually, in the full system, Mindfulness becomes the fifth stage, as its essential position is outside the four active developmental stages (see Table 2, towards the end of the Introduction).

Mindfulness as a principle is receptive, open, non-interfering and non-developmental, and its primary method is Just Sitting. Receptive, open-minded awareness is the basis for the system of training in mindfulness taught by the Buddha via the four *satipaṭṭhānas* – domains or fields of mindfulness – in the *Satipaṭṭhāna Sutta*, Majjhima Nikāya 10.[16]

Note, however, that mindfulness *as a system of training* takes on as well an active, developmental aspect. This contributes to the development of Integration, for example. Thus in the fourth satipaṭṭhāna and elsewhere, the open awareness of mindfulness is combined with active reflection and comparison, with receptive looking and active transformation working together. The principle of mindfulness works in this way within each of the other developmental stages.

Four fields of experience

The immediate concern of mindfulness is the question 'What is happening, right now, in my experience?' This enquiry demands continual curiosity, receptivity and openness, and it gives birth to the Just Sitting meditation practice and to walking meditation.

....

The Buddha identified four basic aspects of human experience: our body, our current feelings, our general mental state and the particular objects in our mind at present. He called them the 'domains of mindfulness', four fields of experience that unfold out of one another.

Try taking a little of your attention away from reading this and settle it in your body. Take your awareness through the different parts of your body and experience whatever sensations you find. There may be a little resistance at first, but relax and continue and you'll get into it. (A tip: don't skip to the next instruction until you are directly experiencing what the present one is referring to.)

Feel the skin on your face and the variety of different physical sensations there. You will find tensions, tingles and a whole variety of sensations. Experience these for a while and relax into the realm of body sensation. Then allow your attention to shift from the sensations in the eyes to those at the lips, then to the forehead and scalp. As you do this, you may feel other parts of your body relaxing in sympathy. Next move down to your shoulders, upper arms, forearms, wrists, palms, fingers and thumbs. Then take the attention minutely down through the rest of your body – first the chest and abdomen, next round to the back and down the spine, then the hips, buttocks, thighs, knees, calves, ankles, feet and toes – experiencing the sensations right down to the tingles on the soles of your feet.

A body scan is a good way to prepare for any meditation because body awareness provides a way in to awareness of the subtler aspects of experience – feelings, emotions, thoughts – that you work with in meditation. Mindfulness works from the ground up. The fact that you are in touch with your body, the first field of mindfulness, allows you to tune into feeling. The fact that you are in touch with feeling (pleasant, painful or neutral), the second field of mindfulness, allows you to tune into your emotions and their accompanying thoughts. For example, when you are angry, you have angry thoughts; when greedy, you have greedy thoughts; and when hungry, you tend to think about food. Angry mind, greedy mind and hungry mind are examples of moods or general mental states, the third field of mindfulness. When you're in the habit of noticing moods, the mind has a new spaciousness in which you more readily notice the specific objects of your attention. Here begins the more complex and active fourth field of mindfulness, (objects of) attention. It enables you to check the effects of your moment-by-moment activity against your aspirations (and particular teachings of the Buddha) and to make choices about the ways in which you respond.

1. Body

Awareness of the body is essential. Consider the great joy of being physically aware. If you let your awareness flow along with what you are doing physically, even the simplest sensations – your feet on the ground, the air on your skin – can become rich and absorbing. It brings richness and significance into day-to-day life.

The crucial thing that body mindfulness does is to bring you into the present. It brings you down to earth, out of the clouds of proliferating thoughts. At first, you may resist letting those go, but with a little persistence you'll appreciate the reality of the here and now. When you bring awareness to the body, your activities begin to assume a certain harmony. You feel more in touch, more on the ball. And this is a pleasure, so you relax. Your whole approach to life slows down yet you don't get less done. In fact, by tuning in to a more effective way of living, you achieve more.

Body awareness can teach you a good deal about how your posture and movement mirrors how you feel. You can easily see in others that the body holds habitual attitudes and emotions. You can also feel it in your own physical sensations, postures and movements. Facial expressions give out the most obvious messages, but body language instantly communicates interest, uncertainty and aggression too. On seeing a joyful spring in someone's step, you know instinctively that they are happy. Or you sense immediately that something is wrong when a friend even slightly bows his head and rounds his shoulders.

2. Feeling

One of the first changes that happens once you get in touch with the body is that you more readily experience what you feel across a spectrum from pleasure to pain. So ask, on the basis of that body scan you just did, is the physical sensation as you sit here (or maybe you're standing or lying down) pleasant or is it not? No doubt it seems more complex than that, but focusing on the pleasure/pain axis opens a door into seeing more deeply. Feelings can also be mental: your ideas, memories and perceptions *feel* pleasant, painful etc. These feelings might seem quite obscure but, even so, making the enquiry has a powerful effect.

Then it's easier to connect with the more complex emotions running around in the mind. If your body experience is a bit unpleasant, are you perhaps also responding with irritation, embarrassment, aversion or fear? If it's pleasurable, there will be a different range of emotions; but the point is that from the perspective of meditation, it's very useful to notice more clearly what goes on inside. For example, let's say that you are sitting here reading, aware of a particular set of sensations in your body that you normally associate with hunger. The sensations are slight yet you can acknowledge that they're slightly unpleasant. With that acknowledgement you can see that (as usual) you're already responding with an emotion – at this stage one of equanimity. OK, you're a little peckish but it's no big thing. You are more interested in continuing to read. Later on, you would start getting uneasy, even having strong cravings and thoughts about food. Alternatively, if you hadn't noticed the basic discomfort at all, you might have become confused without knowing why and then become distracted.

'Feeling' here means pleasure or pain, strong or weak. These feelings are automatic, and people have little control over them: chocolate automatically gives most of us pleasure; toothache automatically gives us pain. Feeling is usually so overlaid by emotion (and streams of emotionally loaded thinking) that you don't see it as a separate layer. Yet its nature is different. Chocolate may produce an automatic feeling of pleasure, but that pleasure need not be followed by craving for more or by planning about how to get it. That craving and planning would be a further, emotional overlay in which you might expend enormous energy. Toothache (painful feeling) may have a potential to draw you down into a depression (negative emotion), but you do have some degree of control over that. Even when apparently very slight, it is the space where the pattern can be changed.

Mindfulness of feeling is an essential transformational art, because people are so accustomed to living in a secondary reality of complex emotions and thoughts that they are cut off from raw experience. The essence of Buddhist practice is staying, as far as possible, with the central core of sensation and feeling, before the habitual emotional reactions kick in. From that core it is possible to change the knee-jerk responses. Emotions are always responses to some feeling somewhere. By carefully watching your inner reactions, you will see the continual pattern of feeling/response, feeling/response, feeling/response. You will see the basic attraction to whatever gives you pleasure and the basic repulsion to anything that gives you pain, attraction and repulsion being the most basic emotions: you want to move either towards or away from feelings.

When we feel inadequate to deal with an emotion, one tendency is to cut off. It is easy to feel uncomfortable with strong emotions such as anger or sexual desire; this leads many people to deny them and become distanced from their experience. It's also just as common to become gripped by such an emotion and to start acting out of it more or less blindly, often at someone else's expense. In bringing you more deeply in touch with feeling and emotion, the purpose of mindfulness is to cultivate skilful, helpful responses. You can't change your feelings, for pleasure and pain will arise whatever you do. What you can do is to learn to change the way you respond to those feelings – you can learn to develop patience, love and compassion, and to let go of impulses towards craving or hatred.

This also involves awareness of thinking, as thought and emotion are more or less inseparable, each providing a key to the other. Once you notice a thought, the underlying emotion becomes readable. Connect with an emotion and you can see the thought process that's going on simultaneously. Such techniques are essential to the training. Often you have no idea what your thoughts are, even though you spend long hours pursuing them. How elusive they can seem, billowing forth like clouds or darting like minnows through obscure waters. Mindfulness practice develops the ability to spot thoughts and to know the direction they are taking. In particular, you learn to see when a train of thought comes out of an emotion – whether, for example, an opinion is actually a rationalization of your preference or the result of objective consideration, or whether the way you are describing things to yourself is useful or an unhelpful distortion based on fear or prejudice.

Looking more closely allows you to clean up your thinking by 'testing statements on the touchstone of conscience',[17] as D. H. Lawrence puts it. Clarifying the relationship between your thoughts and emotions will allow you to rediscover what you actually think and feel. Most of your thoughts are a mish-mash of other people's ideas, and that's normal: everyone takes in ideas from parents, friends, books, media and the Internet. But fully facing the power of these influences is an important step towards thinking more clearly and independently. It increases your ability to reflect upon or to direct your thoughts. This is an essential quality, as we'll see later when we consider the cultivating of insight.

3. Mood

> And how, monks, does he in regard to the mind abide contemplating the mind?
>
> Here he knows a lustful mind to be 'lustful', and a mind without lust to be 'without lust'; he knows an angry mind to be 'angry', and a mind without anger to be 'without anger'; he knows a deluded mind to be 'deluded', and a mind without delusion to be 'without delusion'; he knows a contracted mind to be 'contracted', and a distracted mind to be 'distracted'; he knows a great mind to be 'great', and a narrow mind to be 'narrow'; he knows a surpassable mind to be 'surpassable' and unsurpassable mind to be 'unsurpassable'; he knows a concentrated mind to be 'concentrated', and an unconcentrated mind to be 'unconcentrated'; he knows a liberated mind to be 'liberated', and an unliberated mind to be 'unliberated'.
>
> From the section on 'Mood' from the *Satipaṭṭhāna Sutta*,
> the Buddha's main teaching on mindfulness[18]

The third field of experience as mapped out by the Buddha is a comparatively simple one. It's your current mental state, what you can call your mood. According to Robert E. Thayer, a mood is a relatively long-lasting state that is volitional. It contains various connected thoughts and emotions, though it differs from those thoughts and emotions 'in that (the mood is) less specific, less intense, and less likely to be triggered by a particular stimulus or event'.[19]

Hello! How are you today? Needy, irritated, obsessive? Tunnel-visioned, self-absorbed? Confused, distracted, can't focus? Or crystal clear, concentrated, never been brighter? Like glancing at the sky and observing the weather, it's easy enough to roughly gauge your current mood. However, I suspect that you don't do it very often, even though it's mostly just a question of deciding to take a look and even though you would benefit, as would your friends, if you looked more often. To know quite consciously, for example, that your mind is 'contracted' – perhaps owing to lack of sleep – is helpful because if you know, you'll be less inclined to overstretch and harm yourself or to lash out at others. It is also helpful because when you understand your mental state, you tend to stay connected with your experience. And this is perhaps the most important thing of all: you need to be sensitive to your experience. Many problems arise when you don't even notice that you are in a particular mental state – irritated, for example – and go off unawares in a mental bubble, disconnected from the reality of your impressions, feelings and emotions. Alienation makes you difficult to live and work with, quite apart from the fact that it dissipates your energies and makes you, in the long term, less happy.

4. Objects of attention

The fourth and in some ways the subtlest field of experience is your moment-by-moment attention to the objects in your current awareness. There are the objects of your physical senses, the familiar sights, sounds, smells, tastes and touches, along with the current thought constructions, perceptions, recognitions, memories – every kind of image within what Buddhism calls 'the mind sense'. All these phenomena come and go in your attention so fast that you miss most of the detail. As meditation becomes more concentrated and your mindfulness becomes more thorough, you'll notice more of them. It is quite astonishing sometimes to see how much actually passes through the mind.

Of course, these objects of attention are equally the concern of the other areas of mindfulness, but here the purpose is a little different. In the *Satipaṭṭhāna Sutta*, the Buddha recommends that you contemplate the experiences in every field in a way that is 'diligent, clearly knowing, and mindful, free from desires and discontent in regard to the world'.[20] He suggests that you explore each of these internally and externally and that you be aware of their arising, passing away and both. You should be mindful of each to the extent that is necessary for knowledge and continuous mindfulness and should maintain a spirit of independence, 'not clinging to anything in the world'.

The Buddha now also asks you to measure your present experience against a number of his principal teachings, including the five hindrances to concentration, which are explained in Chapter 4.[21] In this way the practice of mindfulness becomes a complete training in Enlightenment: the first three fields train you in getting a clearer experience of your life and the fourth maps the moment-by-moment detail of your experience against various teachings that can be used to transform it.

Just Sitting

Done properly, mindfulness of breathing and Mettā Bhāvanā cultivate mindful awareness of your current experience in the ways we have just been exploring. However, they then do something *with* that awareness: they use it as a basis for concentrating the mind and generating kindness and love. This active cultivation was described just now in the fourth field of mindfulness. It's excellent to act on the basis of awareness; this is the path in a nutshell. However, there is also much to learn through cultivating mindfulness without such an agenda. Sometimes it's helpful just to notice what's there in your experience before you leap in to change it. Moreover, you need to allow extra space for the things you habitually avoid, misinterpret or find uninteresting to come to the surface. This is where the Just Sitting practice is important.

The practice

Just sitting means exactly that: the practice involves just sitting there. There is no cultivation of anything. But you don't sit passively like a sack of potatoes. There is a method, which is to maintain attention in the present moment as constantly as possible, fully facing every aspect of experience as it arises and opening to it. Have a strong commitment to being open, trusting that in each moment there is more to feel and to perceive than you currently realize. Each time you sense that you've lost that openness, stop and return attention to your present experience – especially to the body – as its sensations are tangible and definite. This stopping and starting again is in the spirit of Just Sitting. Yet apart from the continual adjustment to maintain basic openness, the practice should be fluid and relaxed, with no other effort to make things happen.

This attitude is embodied in the posture too. The eyes are open and the gaze is soft, relaxed and still, settled upon the floor a few feet away. This expresses a naturalness and receptivity to the activity of the senses. Similarly, in the seated posture you should have the arms open and the hands resting on the knees rather than the palms of the hands held together in the lap as is more usual. In terms of body language, this indicates confidence and an open heart.

It is a good idea to set a time for a session: anything from fifteen to thirty minutes is fine as a start. That may seem short; but Just Sitting can be quite an intense practice, and shorter sessions are easier to sustain at first. Later, sessions can be as long as one wishes.

You just sit there, naturally aware and receptive, not trying to do anything special and not trying to suppress anything, allowing thoughts, feelings and emotions to come and go as freely as they like. Take the attitude that you are ready to welcome anything that may arise in your experience with an equally open, detached mindfulness and to let it change and pass on without obstruction. Open eyes are a way to participate very actively. Closed eyes, by contrast, are normally associated either with sleepy, dreamy states or with deliberate concentration and withdrawal from the senses. It may be necessary to remind yourself that you are not meditating in the usual way, by withdrawing attention from sensory input. This method is helpful for concentrating attention.

But Just Sitting is not a meditation practice in that sense: it is a direct application of mindfulness. Since you are not trying to avoid *or* to change experience but to look directly and non-analytically into its nature, the mood is one of openness to experience and not withdrawal. Everything is viewed as interesting and significant, including the experiences you dread or find painful or tedious. At bottom, you can't insist on Just Sitting being purely a receptive process, even if that is its defining quality. Being open becomes something very active – you are confidently opening into a positive sense of reality.

Sooner or later, Just Sitting becomes a doorway to insight. As the mind settles into the mood of this practice, it becomes possible to observe in a very direct way the impermanence of each perception and each momentary transformation of 'you', the perceiver. Seeing the impermanence of both starts to dissolve the distinction conventionally made between the subject and the object of experience. Generally, by relaxing into an experience of things before labelling them, you start to see their real nature. In this way Just Sitting can combine a very simple, direct mindfulness with the long-term aim of perceiving reality in accordance with the teaching of Perfect Wisdom, *Prajñāpāramitā*.

Besides being a practice in its own right, Just Sitting works well as a preparation for meditation. Just sitting quietly for five or ten minutes, tuning in and becoming more relaxed and sensitive helps you to disengage from the mood of the previous activity and to take proper stock of your present mental state. A short period of Just Sitting can also be a good way to end a meditation and absorb its impact. Simply sit on, without trying to concentrate any more, and just remain mindful of the body and the feeling tone of the meditation. This allows its effects to be properly incorporated. It is a gentler disengagement from meditation and a smoother transition to ordinary activities.

Walking meditation

When the sitting practice you are doing, whether Just Sitting, Mettā Bhāvanā or mindfulness of breathing, comes to an end, it is a good idea to get up from the cushion and take that experience for a walk. Generally, it is important that you find ways to take the awareness of body, feeling, mood and attention generated in meditation into the main, active part of your life. Walking meditation is a way to experiment with that transition and is also an effective practice in its own right.

The Buddha spent the greater part of his life in the open air, and mindful walking was a significant aspect of his personal practice.

Walking meditation – it can also be done indoors too – is a very useful complement to sitting practice. It is an excellent support as well for all other practices (not only Just Sitting) and is especially useful for breaks between sessions of meditation or at times when you can't do sitting meditation. Because it supports reflection very well, it is also a way to clarify your ideas and to find perspective on the spiritual path.

The recommended way of practising is to find a straight path on a flat piece of ground (ideally outdoors) and to walk mindfully up and down. The attention is absorbed in a general practice of mindfulness, in a way similar to the Just Sitting meditation. That is, your attention should rest in the body and its movements while you are in the present experience and acknowledging whatever feeling, emotion, thought or other perception comes up as you walk. The pace you choose must allow you to maintain mindfulness. Because walking will dissipate the attention, it helps a bit to retain some awareness of the breathing – not focusing exclusively on the breath but noticing its touch as a continuous, relatively stable aspect of the overall experience. I find it helpful to absorb myself in the relation between the breathing and the walking by noticing the way the breaths rise and fall with each step. I normally find that there are three breaths to each step, which can extend to four as the body-mind starts stilling and relaxing. Those numbers aren't important at all, and my lung capacity is less than average, but I find this a good way to rest attention more thoroughly in the experience.

I favour the up-and-down method because the regular pause and turn at the end of the path creates a natural moment for refocusing and recollecting oneself. However, you can also walk in a continuous circle, as is often done in group meditation sessions, or in any other walking pattern you find suitable (the up-and-down route can be adapted to a curved path, for example).

Because it is body-based, walking up and down is a good way of relaxing and clarifying your thoughts. Any excess of energy in the head is brought down into the body. This can be a way of absorbing an experience, such as reading or a session of meditation, or it can be preparation for meditation or another activity. It is ideal at times when sitting meditation would be difficult, for instance if you are tired or emotionally unsettled. You should not expect walking meditation to support a very focused concentration, though more focus will come with practice. The quality of concentration tends to be more general owing to the body's constant movement and the need to stay aware of the setting. Concentration also requires time to build up: you may need to allow even fifteen or twenty minutes for it to be established in any kind of continuity. Some people will find this initial period too boring or distracting for their patience, but perseverance pays off. With continued body awareness, concentrated mindfulness will emerge over time, along with the inspiration normally associated with meditation.

The walking speed should be chosen to match the current state of mind. If you are dull, you can walk more briskly, or move slowly if restless. On the whole, the pace should be fairly slow and measured, though it usually works to walk a little faster at first and gradually slow the pace as the mind harmonizes with the body and becomes concentrated. The effect, as more vivid mindfulness arises, is to expand the experience of walking so that you perceive far more of the detail of tiny body movements, such as the foot lifting. In these circumstances it may feel natural to slow right down to a pace whose movements might be hardly perceptible to an observer. But the right pace is the one that feels most comfortable to you as you deepen into mindfulness. Walking very slowly and deliberately can induce deeper concentration in itself, though that won't come automatically: if you try to force it, the concentration will be narrow and unfeeling. The key is to maintain a breadth of mindfulness. Movement can be as slow as you like as long as you are physically relaxed and able to walk, if at a snail's pace, in a free, natural manner. If you feel tense, it may help to walk faster for a while and let the tension dispel itself. (There is no virtue in slow walking in itself other than as a means to cultivating awareness.)

Walking meditation is also a good use of time when you feel like meditating but don't have a quiet room available. At work, for example, if you have some time spare during a lunch break, try using it for walking up and down in a quiet street or a park. The best practice to choose would probably be a run through the four fields of mindfulness. If you are agitated, with much on your mind, perhaps include a gentle Mettā Bhāvanā or simply 'just walk' up and down.

Once it has become fairly familiar, you'll find that walking meditation is a very useful method to have available. It is excellent when you don't feel like meditating but know you need to, for example when you are very agitated or very restless. It can also break up and invigorate dull mental states. Walking meditation generally has a smoothing, integrating effect on whatever you bring to it.

The open enquiry that is mindfulness – whether it is applied to walking meditation, to Just Sitting or in the general training in mindfulness – is central to cultivating the path of your development.

Chapter four

. . . .

Sustain the practice

Oh now, when the bardo of life upon me is dawning!
Abandoning idleness – there being no idleness in (a practitioner's) life –
Entering into the reality undistractedly, listening, reflecting and
  meditating,
Carrying on to the path knowledge of the true nature of appearances
  and of mind,
May the Trikāya be realised,
Once that the human form has been attained,
May there be no time or opportunity in which to idle it away.

The Tibetan Book of the Dead[22]

As this ancient text is vividly telling you, you are alive! And your human life, though temporary and fragile, holds tremendous potential. You should take this precious opportunity now and use it for your spiritual benefit and the welfare of the world. This means not only meditating and gaining insight into reality but also making ordinary life significant in a way that can sustain the depth of your potential realization. This chapter is about appreciating and providing for your need for that sustenance.

Zhiyi says that as you meditate with increased conviction, your respect for the practice naturally increases.

> If you are practising right dhyāna, there will come into development
> all kinds of meritorious qualities … the body will become bright and
> transparent, fresh and pure; your minds will become happy and
> joyous, tranquil and serene; hindrances to your practice will disappear
> and good thoughts will spring up to help us. Your respect for the
> practice will increase and your faith in it will deepen; your powers of
> understanding and wisdom will become clear and trustworthy; both

your body and mind will become sensitive and flexible; your thought
will be less superficial and more profound.

Zhiyi[23]

These improvements are the direct result of meditation, but you must
do it.

Regular practice

To experience lasting results, you need to meditate regularly. It is
best to practise every day and to build up a routine. The practice will
then develop a momentum of its own, its positive benefits will stand
out more clearly and you will feel more like doing it. There is an art
to keeping motivation fresh. To maintain interest, it's important to
see that your meditation practice is working for you generally, even
if some days seem better than others. The art of sustained meditation
requires self-discipline, but that doesn't mean forcing yourself. It
means finding ways to make regular practice enjoyable and satisfying.

One idea is to make a habit of meditating at the same time every
day. Any part of the day or night will do as a start; just create a
meditation slot that's regular. For many people the early morning,
when their mind usually feels more peaceful, is the best. I know people
who always get up before the rest of the household, being careful not
to wake anyone. Practising at a quiet hour gives them a fresh start to
the day, whereas there are problems with meditating later. Maybe in
the evening they tend to be tired or it's a time for visitors, talk and TV.
Other people's mornings lack peace. Maybe they have children to look
after. And all they can think about is what needs doing on the day.
Everyone else around is in a rush. But in the evening their day is over;
they relax easily and forget about work. For them the evening can be
an excellent time to meditate. In the city it can be pleasant to meditate
late at night, as street life quietens and traffic noises die down.

Meditating with others

To be sustained, regular meditation needs the support, encouragement
and inspiration of other practitioners. This book gives you some

information and maybe some confidence about meditation, but it won't be enough to support your practice. Live contact is more meaningful – you'll more easily get a point when you see how a teacher is delivering it. If you go to a meditation class, you also get opportunities to ask questions and join in discussion. All this can reassure you that you are on the right track. It matters, because if the practice is done exclusively alone, your assessment of it will lack perspective.

Contact with more experienced meditators shows more clearly what is happening. Everyone has periods when their meditation seems to be getting nowhere, and at such times simply having contact with more experienced meditators is very helpful. It isn't necessarily that you have to go to them with your problems; you may not know what your problems are. But your vision of things often becomes clearer just by being around them and seeing how they approach things. You usually learn something important even if you don't have particular questions to ask. It also helps to make friends with other new meditators, your peers, because you see how meditation is changing them and that they often experience similar difficulties. If you like the approach of this book, you could seek out a Buddhist centre that teaches in this tradition.[24] If you live a long way away, it is worthwhile making contact by email or phone. Simply making a connection could make all the difference to your engagement with meditation. And you may discover that a teacher is visiting your area or that a meditation weekend or a longer retreat is available.

Going on retreat

Once you have been meditating for a few months, go on retreat. A retreat involves going somewhere quiet, getting away from the bustle of day-to-day life and spending more time meditating. Attending an event like this will give you a deeper experience of what meditation can do and help you to establish the practice on a firmer footing. Many retreats are organized by Buddhist centres and may be of any length, from a day or a weekend to a fortnight or more. A weekend is enough at this stage. Different kinds of retreat cater for different levels of experience, but the essential point of all retreats is to take a complete break and concentrate upon meditation practice. The improved conditions will allow you to connect more deeply with meditation. The event will be held in the country, or at least somewhere reasonably quiet, and the opportunity to meditate without disturbance can make a great difference. On retreat you can experience your mind at its best, so it's worth making the effort to go to one as soon as you feel ready. There will be more to say about how to make good use of retreat conditions in Chapter 5.

Preparation

Sometimes you seem to be in the mood for meditation; at other times you don't. But you don't have to be completely controlled by your moods. There are ways to actively encourage a more meditative frame of mind. This is an important skill to acquire as you learn the art of creating a sustainable practice. The first thing is preparation. Preparing well can make all the difference to the ability to concentrate. If you leap enthusiastically upon your cushion immediately after an involved conversation or directly after work or if you find yourself there the last thing at night when you are tired and overstimulated, it will probably be difficult to meditate. Nor if you try to meditate with a full stomach or straight after a physical workout will you be properly ready. The result is again likely to be a distracted meditation. To meditate properly, you need to be able to forget the rest of your life and concentrate just on the present moment. It's a matter of wholeheartedness.

You need to be able to let go of unfinished tasks, matters you want to discuss with others and preoccupations of every kind. Unless you can let them go, they will linger in your mind and interrupt you when you are trying to concentrate. So every time you sit, you need as much space as possible from your preoccupations and the ordinary activities of your life. This can be achieved by taking a break with a cup of tea, going for a brief walk or anything that calms you down and brings you back to yourself. During this time, you should try to become as aware as possible of your body, your feelings, your mood and your thoughts, so that when you start to meditate you are fully present and in harmony with yourself. If you always deliberately make some space like this, you'll find that when you sit to meditate, your energy will be much more available.

Finishing

It matters that you finish a session of meditation properly. Just as the way you say goodbye to a friend can affect the future of your relationship with them, the way you leave a meditation session can have a strong effect on your overall practice. It is important, for example, to conserve any calm and clarity that you gain in a session by leaving gently and quietly. After a meditation session, it is helpful to spend a few minutes quietly, uninvolved, before entering into the hustle and bustle of the day – and certainly to avoid getting up abruptly and immediately involving yourself in a stimulating activity that will scatter the concentration you have developed. Leaving meditation in that way can have a jarring effect that creates a feeling of resistance to further meditation. So you should take care to leave with a positive feeling towards the practice; it encourages you to return for later sessions.

When you have a busy schedule, it can seem impossible to avoid quick transitions, but in fact it is nearly always possible to avoid haste. You could say that it is a matter of time management – planning so that you always have time to spare before the next activity – but what is more essential is to nurture a continual concern for maintaining positive mental states and all the conditions that support them: all the good habits that help to sustain meditation through the ups and downs of regular practice. Ongoing meditation is a living process needing care and protection.

An attitude of kind concern, in which you are mindful of the importance of meditation for your life, helps to avoid a build-up of resistance to practice. In individual sessions it is fairly normal to experience a little resistance, especially at the beginning. This isn't usually a problem, because it disperses in the course of the practice. But when resistance gets strong and even dampens your enthusiasm for practising meditation, there is some other cause. Maybe you have been rushing things, meditating at irregular times or have lost touch with why you are meditating in the first place. Perhaps it's time for that retreat and some extra space for reflection.

Environment

Resistance to meditation could also have something to do with the environment you meditate in. External conditions have a big impact on everyone's ability to concentrate, so make sure you give yourself the best conditions you can. If it is very noisy and difficult to concentrate, try to do something about it if possible. But the appearance and atmosphere of the practice environment can make even more of a difference by inspiring you to meditate. If you can, set up your sitting cushions permanently. Then decorate this spot in a way that evokes a peaceful atmosphere. I have a shrine with an image of the Buddha, candles and often some flowers, but there are as many approaches as there are people. Some I know tend to be 'minimalists', and like a very simple, clean and almost Zen-like space for daily practice. Others veer towards the other extreme, with a profusion of decorations, Buddha images, framed pictures, coloured hangings and even (horror of horrors) soft toys. It is all a matter of personal taste. The important thing is that it should inspire you. When you actually sit down to meditate, fresh air and the fragrance of smouldering incense or essential oils can calm the mind. Don't dismiss the value of such things. Creating an environment in this way can genuinely make a difference in preparing the mind for concentration.

Ritual

Another practice that can make a big difference is any ritual that clears the atmosphere and sets the scene for deeper practice, say offering incense or flowers, chanting or bowing in respect to a shrine. Such observances leave some people cold, but they can also give appropriate expression to the relationship that is building up with the practice and the place where you do it. Each person needs to find their particular approach to ritual and to experiment.

It's like gardening: if you give the practice the conditions it deserves, internally and externally, it will flourish. Here is a short dedication ritual that can create a rich atmosphere in a meditation room before a session. It can be followed by mantra chanting. For example, the mantra of Śākyamuni Buddha, Oṃ Muni Muni ... Mahā Muni ...

Śākya Muni … Svāhā, can be sung over and over – there are traditional tunes you can learn, but one-note recitation is fine too – in order to evoke the spirit of the Buddha's application to meditation practice.

Dedication Ritual[25]

I /We dedicate this place to the Three Jewels,
To the Buddha, the ideal of Enlightenment to which I aspire,
To the Dharma, the path of the teachings that I follow,
To the Sangha, the spiritual fellowship with others that I enjoy.

To the observance of the five precepts
I dedicate this place,
To the practice of meditation
I dedicate this place,
To the development of wisdom
I dedicate this place,
To the attainment of Enlightenment
I dedicate this place.

For the happiness of all beings,
For the benefit of all beings,
With body, speech and mind,
I dedicate this place.

Oṃ Muni Muni Mahā Muni Śākya Muni Svāhā

Ritual is a way to remind yourself of what is truly important and to see more significance in the world you are in. Ritual certainly isn't the only way of doing that, but somehow you need to find a way to evoke more significance, so that the world no longer appears as cold, alienating and dimensionless as it can so easily seem in the modern materialistic, utilitarian world view.

Giving time

You can aid the process of deepening your appreciation of life by simply giving extra time to meditation. When it is going well and you can sit fairly comfortably, try meditating for longer periods. There are a number of benefits from extending the length of meditation sessions. Giving yourself a longer session may enable you to be more relaxed and better able to put aside distractions. It can often take a long time to become fully absorbed in concentration, and even to get in touch with feelings. Some people take ages to get going. Don't do this prematurely or force yourself beyond your limits. But when you do feel like it, meditate for a little longer; and over a period of time, gradually extend the duration of the sittings. If after a month or two you are able to sit and sustain your interest in the practice for forty minutes or more, you'll be doing well.

Practising day by day

If you have practised mindfulness of breathing, at some point it has probably given you clarity of mind, even if only for a split-second. So you know something of what it means to be undistracted, without all the distractions, images and thoughts that usually chatter away in there. The quality of a properly concentrated mind is happy. It is also clear, like a blue summer sky. As you become more concentrated, the sun comes out and the clouds of distracted thoughts disperse. In fact, when you are absorbed in meditation, there may be almost no thought at all. People usually identify mental experience with thoughts, as if thinking were the whole point of having a mind. But the experience of meditation shows that thinking is not necessarily the mind's most important activity. Your mental state can be at its richest and most refined when there is virtually no thought at all. Hearing this, people often conclude that meditation induces a vacuous, blank state.

A popular myth about meditation is that it involves 'making your mind go blank'. But your own experience tells you that being thought-free does not necessarily mean being blank. Take gardening or painting, for example, or simply looking at something beautiful. You can get so happily absorbed in an activity sometimes that thoughts simply don't arise, or at least there are very few of them. Your attention has withdrawn a little from the immediacy of the world, and you may not at first notice someone speaking to you, for instance. Thus awareness and thinking are distinct processes: you can be intensely aware of what you are doing yet hardly thinking about it. The same happens in meditation: you may be closely aware of the object of the practice without thinking about it at all.

A similar myth is that meditation is about getting rid of thoughts. It is true that irrelevant thoughts often distract people from concentration and that meditative absorption is relatively thought-free. But trying to get rid of thoughts as a deliberate method is usually ineffective. There are better approaches than aiming at the problem of distraction, even though you need to understand that as well.

It's more important to understand that the aim is to cultivate an absorbed, happy and concentrated state of mind. Just as, despite appearances, the sun is shining behind the clouds, so a calm, happy state of concentration is just waiting to show its face. You may not come across it all that often but concentration is always there. Even when you are distracted, *some* degree of concentration is still present: have a careful look sometime and check for yourself. If you remember this in your attitude to meditation, deeper concentration is much more likely to arise. Meditative work can be like flying a glider or surfing: you need to see the opportunity in every air current and wave. In the same way, you need to be sensitive to the positive potential of your existing mental states and to be ready to use them.

A good example is pleasure and enjoyment. Let's say you notice a pleasant peacefulness in the midst of a dull, distracted meditation. This is an opportunity, a fresh air current you can ride on. Use it subtly and enjoy it while focusing on the breath, making no more of it. Just letting in its beauty helps to keep the concentration from flagging. This is very pleasant, so the trick is to avoid hooking the pleasure on to some fantasy or harshly pushing it aside. Pleasure has a bright energy that you can learn to channel into the practice rather than letting it seduce you into diverting thoughts. It is akin to inspiration, the deep joy and excitement you can feel as a result of spiritual development, and this is sometimes experienced physically in the form of goose pimples and little rushes of pleasure. Pleasure is the aesthetic aspect of meditation – meditation is beautiful and you can learn to appreciate this, incorporating it as support for concentration.

Clearly recollecting how valuable it is to practise the Dharma, despite occasional difficulties, can arouse strong determination. After all, in your heart of hearts you really do feel deeply that you want to meditate, that you don't want to be distracted, that you do want to grow and develop. This kind of self-exhortation can be profoundly moving. There are also many traditional verses of reflection that you can read aloud before meditating, such as the 'Root Verses' from *The Tibetan Book of the Dead*, whose first verse was quoted at the beginning of this chapter. Here it is again in Francesca Fremantle's lovely, measured translation.

> *Now when the bardo of this life is dawning upon me,*
> *I will abandon laziness, for there is no time to waste in life,*
> *Enter the undistracted path of hearing, thought, and meditation,*
> *Making mind and appearances the path, I will manifest the Trikāya.*
> *Now that for once I have obtained a human body,*
> *This is no time to linger on diverting sidetracks.*[26]

Another aid is the sense of concentration itself: as they grow stronger, concentration and clarity of thought have their own distinct feeling-tones that one can learn to recognize and encourage. We'll look at this approach in detail later, particularly in Chapter 6. You need to get to know all these allies of meditation and to use them and benefit from their positive influence. The more you use them, the less you will be concerned with the next topic: the various hindrances normally encountered in meditation.

Hindrances to concentration

Paying attention to just one thing, as you do in meditation, is not always easy. There is usually resistance from parts of us that want to do something else. In his meditation teaching the Buddha identified five obstacles to concentration that are useful to monitor in daily life. Noticing their presence, understanding them and working to dissolve them outside meditation will not only make your waking life more focused but also substantially reduce their power when you meditate.

The five hindrances are 1) desire for sense experience, 2) ill will, 3) restlessness and anxiety, 4) sloth and torpor and 5) doubt and indecision.

1. Desire for sense experience

This is the most basic kind of distraction. You aren't really very engaged with whatever you are doing because your attention keeps getting drawn away towards some kind of sense pleasure. You haven't yet learned how to find beauty and pleasure in what you're concentrating on, so you can't help looking for pleasure and stimulation where you've found it in the past. In daily life, it helps to have confidence that finding deeper engagement will bring deeper satisfaction.

In meditation, it goes something like this: a quite ordinary sound suddenly seems extra interesting to your increasingly concentrated mind, so you start listening to it. Or you stop meditating, open your eyes and become fascinated by the colours and textures of the carpet. An excellent new idea occurs to you and you start exploring it. It is natural enough that interesting things to think about arise when the mind gets concentrated: there is what you could be doing this evening, what you could have to eat or events and ideas you've recently read about. These impulses are not wrong in any way, but following them when you're trying to meditate makes concentration impossible. It is choosing not to concentrate.

2. Ill will

This is similar to the previous hindrance, except that now your interest is captured by painful experiences instead of pleasant ones. In daily life, ill will (or any of the hindrances) can come up when the task you're engaged in looks as though it's not going to be easy.

In the meditation, you never really get started because something or someone is irritating you and you can't let it go. You can't stop thinking about the way you have been mistreated and about what you would like to say or do to even the score. Or maybe there is an external sound or smell that irritates you so much that you cannot stop thinking about it. Perhaps someone's idea or opinion has struck a wrong note and you feel that you have to analyse its faults and find counterarguments. All this can happen in daily life as well; but as long as it's going on, it will be impossible to concentrate fully on anything, much less to meditate. In this state, beauty can seem irritatingly irrelevant.

3. Restlessness and anxiety

These give no peace. It is impossible to settle down and concentrate. In both daily life and meditation, this is a clear signal that you need to slow down, that you are far too speedy. Either the body is hyperactive and fidgeting or the mind is anxious or both.

In meditation, a restless body and mind are usually the result of insufficient preparation. Maybe you began to meditate too soon after being very active or perhaps much is going on in your mind. There might be something weighing on your conscience. You need to work patiently with this kind of situation and find some rest. Sustained meditation practice will in time resolve conflict such as this.

4. Sloth and torpor

The hindrance to concentration with these is dullness of mind. You feel tired and heavy. There is vacuity in the mind (that's the torpor) and the body is leaden (that's the sloth). In daily life, maybe you need to change your activity or to stop and take a nap; or possibly you could do with some fresh air, an opened window or a walk in the park.

When physical sloth starts to dominate a session of meditation, it can be so overwhelming that your head nods and you start to snore. One way you can work with it is to focus attention on your posture. Its causes often lie in physical or mental tiredness or the effect of a large meal. But psychological factors can be involved too: certain emotions, if unacknowledged, can cause a deep feeling of resistance. Sloth or torpor can also be a reflex of the previous hindrance, restless mental activity leading to a depletion of energy. It is common to alternate between restlessness and dullness both in and out of meditation. This indicates the need to find a new balance.

5. Doubt

This speaks in an undermining tone and uses weasel words. It makes you hesitant and indecisive; you don't quite know what to do, where to go, what matters and what doesn't.

In meditation, the little raspy voice keeps picking away at our fragile attention. 'With all my problems, how can I ever hope to get anywhere with meditation? This kind of meditation is probably a swindle. Well, the teacher is OK, but the meditation doesn't work for me.' Or 'The meditation is OK but I wonder if this teacher really knows what she's talking about. She hasn't mentioned several things that I know from my extensive reading are crucially important for true meditation practice. I suspect she doesn't come from an authentic tradition ...'

How can anyone in this state of doubt possibly make up their mind, commit to what they are doing and absorb themselves in it? If all you can do is to prevaricate and sit on the fence, losing the power of your original motivation, doubt becomes a serious hindrance to meditation – and to your life more generally. It can badly undermine your confidence in both the practice and yourself.

There is nothing wrong with reasonable, sincere doubt about the value of your work or of meditation, its effects and the way it is being taught. Yet it is important to remember that no teacher is perfect in everyone's eyes. One must always accept some degree of uncertainty. Some things can be found out only from experience, so you have to take what you are told at least partially on trust and to discover the truth by your own experimentation. You are free to do that, but you can experiment only by giving yourself wholeheartedly to it. The doubting, oversceptical frame of mind often stems from self-doubt or a rationalization of it. So look into this trait and be as candid as you can. You can hardly expect to concentrate, or to meditate, without some confidence that you can eventually find your way into it.

These five hindrances are a useful checklist for assessing your general state of mind as well as how a session of meditation is going. Unless you are in a fully concentrated state, you can be certain that one or more hindrance is present. The most important thing is to recognize a hindrance as a hindrance. Once recognized, it is straightforward to take action and counteract it. Simple recognition weakens the hindrance, because it will contain a reminder that the aim of the meditation is to concentrate.

It is easy, however, to avoid recognizing what's going on, simply because you're naturally rather attached to your unhelpful habits. Most people have their own way of protecting their pet hindrances. For example, you may have succeeded in completely walling sloth and torpor off from recognition. This is similar to not wanting to get up in the morning: you keep finding good reasons for lying in for another five minutes. When you're taken over by ill will, you simply don't want to stop picking faults and running your mind over all the painful, unpleasant things that have been happening. And doubts prove themselves by immediately fulfilling their own prophecies: 'I don't see how I can do that.' 'There, I *knew* I wouldn't be able to do it!' Here you need to recognize clearly that you are nursing a hindrance to concentration.

Many instructions can, when rightly applied, help you to re-engage. But first you need to understand three basic principles for working against the hindrances.

Principles for working against the hindrances

The first principle for working against the hindrances is to **acknowledge that a hindrance is actually there**. It's no good carrying on regardless, trying to ignore it and wishing that it would go away. An ostrich-like stance will only create headaches and mental dullness. You need to take responsibility and accept that for the time being, this is *my* hindrance and *I* need to do something about it right away. Another way of expressing this principle is that to concentrate means meeting whatever mental states arise.

The second principle is to **have confidence in your potential**. Guilt and self-hatred are problems for many of us, and it's important in both meditation and daily life that you cultivate a kind and positive sense of yourself. Everyone has obstacles to their practice, but they can all be overcome. After all, you do have the power to understand and to choose how to act. So how can there be any real doubt that, with the right kind of effort, you can make spiritual progress? In sum, take heart and give yourself fully to the practice.

The third principle is to **work from the ground up**. You make progress only when you've established a basis for it. You need to establish a general awareness of yourself before you can generate a specific and more intense awareness of the meditation object. Then, if you lose your single-pointed concentration, you can establish it again by reconnecting with the more general mindfulness of body, feeling etc. So always work from the ground up; and if you lose your ground, find it again.

These general principles are a useful set of methods for working against the hindrances. [27] They are addressed mainly to meditation practice but they apply to the hindrances in daily life too.

Methods of countering the hindrances

There are five methods of countering the hindrances. The first method is to **consider the consequences** of allowing the hindrance to increase unchecked. What if you simply did nothing about your tendency to distraction, hatred or doubt? It would increase, and your character would become progressively dominated by that trait. If you reflect upon this, the importance of what you are doing may once again become clear and the mind may become more inclined towards concentration.

The second is to **cultivate the opposite quality**. If there is doubt, cultivate confidence; if there is sloth, cultivate energy; if there is restlessness, cultivate contentment and peace; if the mind is too tight, relax it; and if it is too loose, sharpen it. In other words, whenever a negative mental state gets in the way of concentration, try to cultivate a positive quality that overcomes or neutralizes it.

The third antidote is **a sky-like attitude**. Sometimes the more you resist a particular mental state, the stronger it seems to get. If the previous two methods don't work, you can try the sky-like attitude: imagine the mind as open as the space of the clear blue sky and the hindrances like clouds passing. In this way of working, you accept the fact that the hindrance has gained entry and simply observe it, watching it play itself out in the sky of the mind. Watch the fantasies, the worries, the images; watch whatever arises. It's the same as in the Just Sitting practice: you observe and feel closely, but without getting involved, for any involvement will feed the hindrance. If you can observe without getting involved, the mind-state will eventually lose its power and disperse, like a fire whose fuel eventually is used up.

Fourth, there is **suppression**, which is something of a last resort. Just say 'no' to the hindrance and ignore it or, if it still persists, push it aside. This is most effective when the hindrance is weak and you are quite convinced of the pointlessness of playing host to it. If the hindrance is very strong or if there is an element of emotional conflict, you may find that using this method creates unhelpful side effects. Tension, a lack of feeling and mental dullness commonly result from an overforceful approach. The best rule of thumb therefore is to use suppression only with weak hindrances. If you are in a positive, clear state of mind, it can be quite easy to turn such a hindrance aside.

Finally, there is **Going for Refuge** – when you recall that your practice is directed towards full Awakening and recommit to it. From time to time, everyone gets overcome by a hindrance and perhaps spends a whole session in a distracted state of mind. Such circumstances may occasionally even extend over several days. This can feel like failure; and when it happens, it is important not to lose heart. You need to see 'failed' sessions of practice in the perspective of your development overall. Unconscious tendencies are powerful in all of us, and sometimes they come up strongly and there is a struggle. All anyone can do in this circumstance is their best, and sometimes that is simply to maintain some kind of effort. Keep putting down that marker, making it clear that you are striving for the goal of the practice, even when you don't seem to be getting the results you would expect. That is enough; that takes you further. It is important to understand that the results of meditative effort do not always show themselves in the same session of practice. Good effects are certain to result from the effort; but it is uncertain how or where they will manifest, and often they will appear outside meditation.

Where the unresolved conflicts and other mental sufferings in your mind will resurface is also uncertain, but the space of meditation offers them a perfect place to play. In a way it is good that they appear there, as meditation is the best arena for their resolution. But then if a great deal of difficult material is surfacing, the ability to meet it appropriately can get rather weak. It is important not to be overwhelmed at such times; and when this happens to me, I persevere as best I can with a gentle and flexible (not to say ironic and amused) approach. I never feel I have been forced to give up. It is enough to remain mindful of what happens. It's this kind of situation when going for refuge is most useful. It's not so much a way of countering the hindrances as an attitude with which to reconnect after a challenging session. There may be a sense that you have lost your faith and need to reaffirm your commitment to the practice. In traditional terms you Go for Refuge to the development of the higher human qualities of Enlightenment symbolized by the Buddha, to his teaching the Dharma and to all those who practise it, known as the Sangha.[28]

These efforts in meditation should be made in a balanced way. You need to tread a middle path between too much and too little effort. If you are too easy-going and don't make a firm effort to become concentrated, don't encourage positive qualities and don't bother to avoid the hindrances, you will drift in a hazy, unfocused state of mind. That's one extreme. The other is when you force yourself so hard that you become rigid and inflexible, and later on there is some kind of reaction. Force often leads to dullness or headaches. A middle way between these two extremes can be found by ensuring that there is just enough tension, and just enough relaxation, in your approach. You need to sharpen your attention at some times and relax it at others, relaxing when the mind feels too tight and sharpening when it feels too loose. When you get beyond these hindrances and achieve steady and balanced concentration, you will become especially relaxed and especially energized, both at the same time. When bright, joyful energy and deep calm arise together, you enter a state of absorption known traditionally as dhyāna.[29] We shall explore that in Chapter 6.

Signs of progress

> *Those who accomplish such good things as these*
> *In every place unconquered do abide,*
> *Moving in perfect safety where they will –*
> *Theirs are the most auspicious signs of all.*

The Buddha in the Maṅgala Sutta[30]

If you practise regularly, you will soon notice the benefits of meditation. You will probably see some signs of progress during meditation itself, and perhaps feel unaccountably happy and peaceful. Ecstatic experiences of beauty may sometimes arise.

Outside meditation, you may find that you're happier and that life seems to carry on more smoothly. You will also probably find your thoughts and ideas coming clearer and your outlook more expansive and creative. Dreams may become unusually vivid and colourful. All these experiences are typical results of meditation, but progress may show itself in less definite ways too. You may notice that there seems to have been some kind of change. It may be the response of other people that brings this to your attention. For example, people may seem more attracted to you than before, perhaps sensing that you're relaxed and content.

Inner change may present challenges as well. Meditation can stir up a wealth of rich feelings and emotions that you're uncertain how to respond to. This is something you need to learn about, and I hope that what I am saying in these pages is of some help. The experiences of increased clarity, openness, happiness and beauty are to be welcomed; they surely indicate that you're breaking through some unhelpful psychological limitations. If in taking up meditation you were, say, just looking for something to relax you after work, that aim may be more or less the limit of what you'll get from the practice. But what you are actually exposing yourself to is a transformation that potentially is very profound. Through your practice you may start to see life quite differently, and to open up ways in which you could make fundamental changes in your life. Meditation has the power to change perceptions radically; and if you want to, you can participate actively in that process.

It seems a little hazardous to write about the enormous variety of experiences that can arise in the course of taking up meditation. As though thumbing through a medical textbook, you might find that you seem to have some of the worst symptoms and jump to rash conclusions. When you encounter something in your practice that you don't fully understand (as of course you will do sooner or later), it's best to consult someone who is more experienced in meditation. So as you read, please bear in mind that each person is unique and that general statements apply only in a general way.

What does it mean, for example, if you find yourself experiencing beautiful colours, marvellous patterns, voices or other sounds in meditation? The general term for such experiences, which are common, especially for new meditators, is *samāpatti*.[31] For those who have them, such experiences seem very mysterious and exciting, yet generally it is best not to attach any great significance to them. Many people don't experience samāpattis at all, but that doesn't mean something is wrong. What seems to happen is that you achieve a level of concentration in which you are no longer aware in the usual way of your body and sense impressions but in which the senses are still trying to operate. So you experience various distortions of sight, sound, smell, touch or taste.

Since there are many kinds of sense experience, there is a huge variety of samāpattis. You may feel as though your body has become enormous – as large as a house, a mountain or a galaxy. On the other hand, you may feel tiny, microscopic. You may feel as though you have been turned upside down or are now sitting facing the opposite way. Or your physical experience may be totally indescribable. Usually, because of enhanced concentration, these experiences are pleasant if rather odd.

A samāpatti experience is a good sign on the whole. At least it shows that your concentration has become independent of your sense experience. These signs will eventually pass and you'll enter a smoother, more integrated stage of concentration. Still, when they come up, it's natural enough for new meditators to think that they are about to gain some amazing spiritual insight. Perhaps it's Enlightenment! Actually, the experience is part of a fairly basic stage of concentration.

So the instruction is to enjoy the experience but to maintain some focus, at least, on the object of the practice. Apart from showing that a certain level of concentration has been reached, samāpatti is no indication of spiritual progress. It is neither to be encouraged nor discouraged. If you experience a samāpatti, it's wise not to get overattached: sooner or later it won't come any more. Don't meditate for the sake of samāpatti or you'll be in for a disappointment!

At times, and for various reasons, you are likely to lose interest in meditation. Even though the practice seems to be going well enough, certain things can make it seem boring. Let's say that your mindfulness of breathing meditation is relatively concentrated – you manage to count from one to ten every time and never lose the breath, even in the later stages. Yet you don't actually enjoy it that much and it's not inspiring. You practise harder but still nothing much seems to happen. You may feel sad, and even a little trapped, by this. The fact is, you really do want to meditate and make progress but it has become a chore, something you're making yourself do every morning. This sort of difficulty can occur when you see your practice narrowly, in terms of concentration. It has perhaps become just an exercise in 'staying with the breath'. Or it may be that your approach to meditation generally has become dry and lacking in feeling, concerned with getting results rather than with engaging in the moment-by-moment experience of the practice.

Probably you have lost appreciation of the emotional aspect of concentration. If so, the Mettā Bhāvanā practice is likely to help. The advice here is to practise both Mettā Bhāvanā and mindfulness of breathing regularly and to do the Just Sitting meditation as often as possible. A retreat will probably help to relaunch your practice; and if you haven't done one, now is almost certainly the time. It may simply be that you need to talk to someone about your meditation. But the essential feature that is lacking is inspiration, that sense of beauty. Once you realize it's lost, you have an opportunity to regain it.

A common difficulty occurs if you find yourself viewing the meditation object as though you were an outside observer, distanced from the felt process of meditation. Instead of the object itself (the tactile sensation of breathing, for example), you experience only a thought about it. If this becomes an established habit, it is definitely a dead end; and you need to cultivate the opposite by concentrating upon the actual breath experience rather than the mere thought of the breath. Have you somehow acquired a tendency to mediate your experience through thoughts? In itself, there is nothing wrong with thinking, but here thoughts seem to be obscuring other important aspects of experience.

So as you meditate, look for the more basic aspects of experience, especially body awareness, feelings and emotions. Outside meditation, a little physical exercise may be enough to establish a more harmonious and integrated state of mind, but certainly some adjustments need to be made. More contact with others, and Mettā Bhāvanā meditation, are likely to help. And generally, Just Sitting meditation is an excellent overall support. Just sitting with one's raw, changing moment-by-moment experience really helps to keep the mind fresh and open.

On the whole, this has been a practical chapter getting down to nuts and bolts, but meditation is not a 'set of dodges', in D. H. Lawrence's phrase. It is important to be clear about what meditation is trying to achieve, but you mustn't let the concepts that are necessary for clarity limit the imagination. Keep an open heart and mind. Newcomers to meditation often have a natural openness and faith that enable them to make rapid progress. They have few preconceptions about what they are likely to achieve. They don't know where they are going, and that's the best way to go! More experienced meditators need freshness in their approach most of all – that is the spirit of Dharma practice. Meditation is ninety per cent about remaining open to something new. Some of the rest is our own hard work, but something also comes, far more mysteriously, from the awakened space of the Buddhas.

> If your mind is empty, it is always ready for anything; it is open to everything. In the beginner's mind there are many possibilities; in the expert's mind there are few. ...
>
> When you have no thought of achievement ... you are true beginners. Then you can really learn something.
>
> Suzuki Rōshi[32]

Chapter five

....

On retreat: The conditions for effective meditation

What is meant by regulating and adjusting? It may be likened to the work of a potter. Before he can begin to form a bowl or anything else, he must first prepare the clay – it must neither be too soft nor too hard. Just as a violinist must first regulate the tension of the different strings – they must be in perfect tune before he can produce harmonious music. Before we can control our mind for the attainment of Enlightenment, we must first regulate and adjust the inner conditions … If these lessons are learned and applied, then samādhi can be easily attained, otherwise a great deal of difficulty will be experienced and our tender root of goodness can hardly sprout.

Zhiyi[33]

Meditation can vary greatly from one session to another: one day it's easy to concentrate, the next day you can't get started. You have a breakthrough on a retreat but when you sit again later, it seems that you're back where you were before. In the art of meditation it is important to understand what the main influences are and how they affect the mind. You may not always notice it but your mental states are strongly affected by the place where you are living, the people around you, what is happening in your love life and many other things. All these factors contribute to your ability to concentrate. Conditions for meditation can be simple, but they can also be as complex as the weather. If you can learn to understand them a little better, you'll be more able to create circumstances that help you to concentrate and reflect and to avoid what distracts and disturbs.

Perhaps the most basic condition is the physical environment. Almost everyone finds quiet, peaceful surroundings where there's no radio, TV or traffic noise more conducive to concentration. There is also, as you saw earlier, the mental and emotional setting of a session of meditation: what you do immediately beforehand can make all the difference between being able to concentrate in meditation and being distracted. In a way, your whole life is a preparation for meditation. Every action has made a contribution to the mental states you're experiencing at this moment. Thus the state of your mind as you are about to go into meditation is partly a product of your lifestyle. You might find that if you made one or two lifestyle changes, you would be more regularly in the mood for meditation.

Knowing clearly that actions performed now affect meditation later is in some ways more important than a willingness to concentrate in meditation itself. You may be very inspired and raring to get going with meditation practice, but it's the preparation you've done (or not done) that counts when you close your eyes and try to concentrate. If it's been done well, the mind will be flexible, interested and clear. If not, no matter how bright you feel when you first sit down, you'll rapidly become distracted and have no choice but to spend some of the session working on that unprepared state.

This point is often missed by people who have been meditating for years. Their practice often settles down over that time, so that they don't expect big changes any more. Gradually the assumption solidifies that since everything is going smoothly, there's no need to prepare. At the other end of the spectrum, keen new meditators set their sights extremely high, which is excellent, yet usually they don't see the destructive effect of their lifestyle. You need to be realistic: what's important is not thinking about results but checking where you are now and creating the best conditions for practice. In that way the results you want will arise naturally by themselves.

Conditions for effective meditation

You need to improve what Zhiyi called the 'external' conditions for your practice. Most of them involve making sure that practical arrangements, for example the place where you meditate, are helping the meditation. Skilful attitudes towards other people, which will tend to preserve a happy state of mind, are also included in this category. Then there are 'internal' conditions, an essential basis for anyone to develop higher, more absorbed states of consciousness. Effective meditation entails an understanding of how to create the best possible internal and external conditions.

Table 5: Conditions for effective meditation

EXTERNAL CONDITIONS	INTERNAL CONDITIONS
Relations with the outside world as preparation for meditation	Developing the dhyānas in ideal meditation conditions
Ethical foundation • acting ethically • freedom from guilt • positive stimulation	Speech
Place	Food
Material needs	Rest and exercise
Freedom to engage	Information
Communication	Activity

Before starting, it's important to bear in mind that in the conditions of meditation, perfection is more or less impossible. There is a limit to the peace and quiet available. You might think it would be perfect to live as a hermit on retreat in the wilderness; but in my experience of that, the mind can still find certain things distracting. There will always be a fly or an itch somewhere. In the end, you just need to acknowledge the reality of your situation and to practise as best you can. The impatience that usually comes if you expect perfection will make you feel compelled to force the concentration, disregard how you are feeling and ignore what is actually happening in your mind and body. This is the opposite of meditation. Getting caught up in these patterns is exhausting and frustrating, and you will fail to achieve any real calm or concentration.

External conditions

An ethical foundation

The first 'external' condition for effective meditation is your ethical foundation. It is possible to concentrate fully only when you are happy, and happiness comes from an ethical life. That is not necessarily a matter of doing the conventionally right thing. It is a sensibility based on the awareness that your actions have consequences, consequences that frequently appear as the thoughts, moods and mental states you deal with in meditation. Just as cause-effect relationships govern physics and chemistry, so a causal relationship exists between what you do and your state of mind. [34] Ethics is the creative, beneficial use of that relationship; you act to promote positive states of mind. Certain actions do affect your mind in certain ways. There are ethical or 'skilful' actions, such as ones prompted by generosity, and their great characteristic is their ability to make us and others feel happy. Many other actions – take malicious lying as an example – are inherently regrettable. Somehow you don't feel truly happy when indulging these 'unskilful', or unethical, actions: the malicious kind of satisfaction that results is inherently unwholesome and hardly counts as real happiness. The happier you feel, the more the capacity for relaxation, empathy and concentration increases.

Particular actions inevitably lead to happy states of mind, and are set out in five traditional Buddhist precepts: doing things that are of benefit to yourself and others; giving generously; sexual contentment; speaking the truth; and being clear-minded. The opposites of these – harming, stealing, sexual exploitation, lying and muddle-headed confusion – inevitably seed unhappiness.

The principle of *ahiṃsā*, nonviolence, means **doing what is of benefit** to you and others. Negatively it is the avoidance of causing harm. This is the basic principle, and underlies each of the other principles and the precepts.

The principle of *dāna*, generosity, means **developing a giving, sharing attitude**. Negatively it involves not taking others' property, energy or time unless that has been made freely available to you.

The principle *santuṭṭhi*, contentment, means **developing sexual self-control and contentment** with any sexual partner you have.

Negatively it means not harming through sex and trying not to have sexual matters as the central factor in your life.

The principle *satya*, truth, means **being truthful**. Negatively, it means not telling lies and correcting your wrong thinking.

The principle of *sati*, mindfulness, means **developing awareness** of your surroundings, your body and your mind, maintaining a bright, clear state of mind. Negatively it means working to avoid clouded, confused or intoxicated states. It also involves avoiding intoxication through alcohol or other drug abuse.

Freedom from regret

Your happiest times are when you genuinely feel no guilt, no regrets. No one is perfect, but when you do your best to live ethically, you feel a sense of freedom. You can be wholehearted, and no part of you is held in reserve. This is the essential reason why ethical living makes such a difference to meditation.

Yet this clear-heartedness takes effort to achieve. As you know of your failings (and may be confused about them), a natural sense of guilt remains, subtly holding you back from full, wholehearted action. So of course it shows up in meditation.

In certain ways you are preoccupied, tied in internal knots. The first step towards loosening them is honest recognition of what your behaviour is doing to you. You must be prepared to acknowledge that you do exploit others at times and can be selfishly mean and spin the truth to your own advantage. You need to become familiar with the subtle signs that tell you when, actually, you regret a particular act. There is no shame in recognizing your failings – it is normal to have them and wise to look for ways to change.

Recognition of guilt feelings now becomes an ethical tool that spotlights those areas you want to change and enables you to become happier. In this area, however, people are usually very complex. We are easily confused by guilt feelings; it is common to feel guilty even without having done anything regrettable at all. So if you are to benefit from using this tool, you need to discriminate between healthy and unhealthy guilt feelings.

It's very helpful to know that you can experience *invalid* guilt feelings. A classic example is when someone you see as an authority seems to disapprove of your action. You can then feel guilty even though there is nothing wrong with what you have done (i.e. there has been no harmfulness, meanness, sexual exploitation, lying or self-imposed confusion). This irrational guilt has a horrible feeling, quite different from having an uneasy conscience. It can help to ask whether this particular sense of guilt is reasonable or unreasonable. What action was connected with it, and do you truly and reasonably regret having done it? If it did seem regrettable and harmful (and here you might use the five precepts as a checklist), then why not acknowledge that you are responsible for its effects and try to learn from the experience. That's all that needs to be done. This is an example of recognizing 'rational guilt' or having an appropriate sense of regret. It's a very positive recognition which, though in some ways painful, can definitely help to change behaviours that cause even more pain.

On the other hand, if you realize that your actions have given you no grounds for regret (some person or group apparently disapproves of what you've done, but as far as you know, you've been truthful and harmed no one), then it is very helpful to recognize that *your guilt feelings have no basis in reality*. There is no cause for concern, and you are simply left with the irrationality of your emotion. If you persist with this kind of reflection, it will help you over time to dissolve the habit of harmful guilt. In general, the tone of negative guilt is often self-condemnatory. You need to bring more kindess and patience into the dynamic. That work will probably be difficult, because that habit is deeply ingrained and tends to confuse. But just consider how much you are affected by irrational guilt and the value of freedom from it.

Actions and their consequences
When in meditation you find negative emotions getting in the way of concentration, you may wonder where they come from. According to Buddhism, it is likely that your present mood, especially its emotional tone, has been conditioned by your behaviour in the past. Similarly, future moods will be conditioned by behaviour in the present. Sometimes this is obvious: if you shout in anger at someone, you're likely to get even more angry afterwards. Not all experiences

are conditioned in this way, as we'll see a little later, but emotional reactions generally come from a build-up of habitual responses.

Here is an example of how this might work in the case of a positive emotion. You give something to a friend, a gift they are delighted to receive. This act of generosity delights them, and puts you in a good mood too. Moreover, the memory of the action brightens your mental state for some time afterwards. You may even remember it years later and feel 'I'm so glad I did that.' Even if you never think about it again, the action will have had a good effect upon you.

Here is a negative example. In anger, you steal from a friend something of great value to them. Such a mean betrayal will deeply disappoint, depress and anger them. It will also have a profound effect on you. It is unlikely that you would ever forget it; it might colour the rest of your life. Without this behaviour between friends being confessed to and forgiven, one can only imagine the potential for twisted and unclear emotional responses thereafter.

The connections between your past acts of speech and your present feelings are often hard to discern, but a link certainly exists. The process of outer, relatively conscious action stimulating deep, relatively unconscious inner attitudes is basic in Buddhist psychology. It clearly distinguishes the result of this process, karma-vipāka (the effect of volitional action), from the initial *karma* (volitional action). Karma and *karma-vipāka* interplay ceaselessly and are an important condition for the mind states that arise in meditation.

None of us can be free from the effects of our past but we do have some freedom to initiate more skilful actions in the present, and we can develop that freedom further. In skilful living as in life, the more you do, the more you can do. Over time, and often it's a long time, you build confidence and learn to be kinder in your self-assessment.

The gates of the senses
It is fairly normal for people to go around in a mindless whirl of impressions, hardly aware of what is coming in through their eyes and ears. Yet all these sensations have the potential to affect you strongly. Everything you smell, taste, see, hear and touch can affect

your mental state, and that's important for a meditator trying to create good conditions for practice. And to some extent you can choose the objects you encounter, learn to monitor your sense experience and be more discriminating in your choices. You can look for the kind of stimulation that will help your meditation and avoid whatever confuses, irritates or unduly excites you.

This practice, known as 'guarding the gates of the senses', doesn't mean being fastidious, touchy and precious about preserving at any cost your fragile state of mind, fearful of putting your head out of doors in case you encounter something shocking. It simply means that you care about your state of mind and take responsibility for it. Naturally, people are affected differently by various kinds of input: what is helpful for one person can even be harmful to another. Many people would find that their meditation benefits from time spent in an art gallery (depending on the art) but others might not. One person is most inspired by contact with friends; another wants to spend much time alone – without those conditions, neither will easily settle into meditation.

As ever, the test is the actual effect of particular sense experiences on your mental states. You need to take responsibility for the consequences of your actions. It can take time to learn this, and the decisions are not always easy. Perhaps one weekend you start wondering whether you can attend a late-night party and meditate the next morning. Well, perhaps you could, though honest reflection might reveal that attending it could have a detrimental effect. You have to be careful of the tendency to rationalize weaknesses, to make apparently convincing excuses. The reasoning might be that going to the party will be an opportunity to put your Mettā Bhāvana into practice or that it will be a good test of your mindfulness. But do you genuinely need to test your mindfulness in such an extreme way, or do you simply want to go to the party regardless of the consequences? That would be a reasonably normal response, after all. For the sake of personal clarity (and this example overlaps with several of the ethical principles explored earlier), it's much better to be honest and avoid 'spiritual' justifications that merely obscure the real motive.

Nourishing the mind

Exposing yourself to the right sort of stimulation is at least as important as avoiding exposure to the wrong sort. The mind is always on the lookout for stimulation. It's a genuine need up to a point, but like children who will stuff themselves with sweets and junk food unless their mother provides regular nourishing meals, your mind will get interested in any old rubbish unless you take action and get some quality intake. If you choose to spend more time with people, paintings, movies, poetry, exercises, music and out-of-doors places that inspire you, your meditation practice will quite probably improve. Such activities counterbalance the dull, tense and noisy environments where most of us live and practise. You should also limit what you take in. If you don't simplify life, you can become saturated with experience and become overstimulated on the outside and dull on the inside. So counteract the symptoms by remaining mindful of the body, feelings, emotions and thoughts and don't let your attention wander here, there and everywhere as you walk. If you seek enjoyment from simple pastimes, foods and friendships, then by understanding your needs better, you'll become less enslaved by external things.

You can learn to employ this kind of simplicity in many areas of your life. The choice of leisure activity in particular needs to nourish you, otherwise a sense of dissatisfaction will spread into your working and domestic life. Practising meditation and mindfulness can reveal ways to manage your living and working environments skilfully. Many people have children or stressful working lives or both, and it's important to be realistic about their effects and to consider if there are ways you can change things for the better. The work you are doing in meditation and mindfulness practice offers special tools that can help you to see more clearly the habits you bring to your work and family relationships. How are you working, how are you relating to others and are you aware of the emotions that come up when specific events happen? If you look at these questions with mindfulness, rush into habitual patterns of thought and deed less speedily and find ways to discuss important problems with others, you will eventually find new ways of behaviour and useful insights into your situation.

On solitary retreat

I went to the woods because I wished to live deliberately.

Henry David Thoreau[35]

A good way to temporarily simplify your life is to go on a solitary retreat. A retreat of any kind will provide good meditation conditions. It's a most helpful way to escape the distractions of town from time to time and allow the peace of a retreat to revive your flagging practice. However, once you have established a regular meditation practice over a year or more, it may also be valuable to spend some time alone. A solitary retreat provides an undiluted experience of oneself and is something of unique spiritual value. How often in your life have you spent time completely on your own, without seeing anyone at all? Even to the extent that you have, it probably wasn't by choice. In the past, most of us have avoided solitude and associated it with loneliness. But that kind of loneliness probably results from a negative dependence on others. Now you are developing insights through your meditation that offer you freedom from such dependence.

In this new life centred upon good deeds and wisdom, solitude becomes a source of profound joy and a new depth of clarity. Imagine arriving at a remote country cottage and experiencing the thrill of knowing that you are going to be entirely alone for a week, a fortnight, a month or even longer. You are completely free to do and think what you like; and whatever you choose to do with your time, you can count on never being interrupted by others. Even your thoughts will be uninterrupted. What a rare and precious opportunity this is in our crowded, timetabled society for reflection, readjustment of perspectives and meditation.

> The (next) external condition that one must possess if one is to hope
> for success in the practice of dhyāna, relates to shelter. A retreat … to
> be satisfactory must be quiet and free from annoyances and troubles
> of any kind. [These kinds of place] are suitable for dhyāna practice: a
> hermitage in the high and inaccessible mountains, [or] a shack such as
> would serve a beggar or a homeless monk. These should be at least a

mile and a half from a village where even the voice of a cowboy would not reach and where trouble and turmoil would not find it.

Zhiyi[36]

Zhiyi singles out as an important 'external condition' for meditation the place you choose for your solitary retreat – a cottage, a caravan or even a tent. If it is to lead to a new depth of concentration, a retreat site must be quiet, and ideally silent: the fewer disturbances, the easier concentration will come. The main thing to avoid of course is people, who by talking, laughing, playing 'infectious' music and generally being themselves will constantly pull your focus away from the subtlety of meditation practice. That's the big advantage of solitary retreats. Though compromise is always possible, these considerations mean that your place of retreat should be in the country. Go and have a look at the place in advance if you can and be sure you are happy not only with its quietness but also its atmosphere – do you find the place attractive and feel inspired by the thought of staying there? That is important, because once you're settled into the practice you'll become more than usually sensitive to your surroundings.

Many Buddhist centres and individuals offer facilities for solitary retreats where everything, including food, is provided. However, you may be organizing the retreat yourself, so when choosing the location, check the availability of supplies. Walking several miles to get food may be acceptable to some people but personally, having established a meditation practice, I prefer to remain undisturbed for the whole retreat. Meditative states rely on a delicate balance of factors which, once upset, can take days to restore. It's a pity to have to break things up just because you've run out of oil or matches. The best solution is to plan carefully so that you can stay in one place.

Once these basic needs are provided for, you need to ensure that you really will be free to concentrate. If a bit of practical business has been left unfinished, it will plague you whenever you try to meditate. It is important to tie up loose ends before going away, if necessary asking others to manage your affairs. Similarly, you should avoid letters arriving on your retreat that might distract you.

Another factor that affects your ability to engage with a solitary retreat is communication. Away from people, you become far more sensitive to the state of your relationships. Just as with unfinished practical matters, it is wise to patch up any quarrels or misunderstandings before going away. Unresolved tension can play continually on your mind and could well obstruct your practice. Consider too the other people who live in the vicinity of the retreat venue. Even if you never meet or see them, there is some kind of relationship. Especially if you are starting a longer retreat (say, of more than a month), it can be a good idea to initiate a little communication. Speculation could be running rife in the area – what on earth can she be getting up to all on her own? – but it's more likely that this will come from your own super-sensitized, somewhat paranoid imagination. All you need to do is to introduce yourself to a friendly local and let them know, perhaps very generally, what you are going to be doing. In my experience, most people are well disposed towards those on retreat.

Internal conditions

Now you have set up all the external conditions for a retreat. You've been living an ethical lifestyle, you have found a quiet, isolated and inspiring place for meditation, your material needs are organized, you're on good terms with those you know and you've sorted practical matters and taken a complete break from day-to-day affairs. You are now well set up for meditation. Having arrived on retreat, you need carefully to create the kind of conditions that support concentration and insight. Zhiyi's 'internal conditions' consist mostly of methods of working in meditation and of those subtler aspects of preparation that can be created only on the retreat itself. You'll be meditating often now; and as you are never far away from another session of practice, you should keep up the preparation continually. The main thing is to be mindful between practice sessions. In that way, concentration will steadily accumulate. Instead of (as is common) taking a whole meditation period to reach the preliminary stages of concentration, you will now be able to start already in a concentrated state.

Over the years, I have spent much time on solitary retreat, as well as leading and participating in many meditation retreats. I've also known many others who have done these things, and it's always the same: after a few days on retreat you enter a timeless realm of experience. Everything seems so much more rich and alive. This is because life is simpler: time is not oppressive and you have no responsibilities apart from being yourself and thinking your thoughts. When you're less preoccupied by distractions, there is a light transparency of mind whereby you can appreciate much more than usual. You find it easier to maintain continual mindfulness and experience all your feelings, thoughts and motivations quite clearly.

When retreat life in itself almost becomes a meditative state, you'll want to keep it alive, and this is where it's helpful to understand the 'internal' conditions that support it. Very broadly, you need to regulate two areas of activity: that which tends towards dullness (sleepy mind) and that which tends to excitement (disturbed mind). On retreat, you'll find some conditions dulling the mind and others exciting it. So whenever you notice yourself going to one of those two extremes, find a way to start moving in the opposite direction. The most important 'internal conditions' requiring attention on a retreat are speech, food, rest, exercise and information.

Speech
You aren't likely to find speech upsetting the balance much on a solitary retreat unless you talk excessively to yourself. But on retreats generally (and many of these tips are just as applicable to a group situation) you may be surprised to discover how powerfully speech affects your experience. A good conversation may have an inspiring effect that strengthens your ability to meditate, but a disharmonious exchange can disturb you and prevent you from settling down and concentrating. So if you pay attention to what you say, how you say it and the effects of your speech on your mental state, you can maintain your inspiration and prevent unsettling disturbances.

Because words have so much influence over your state of consciousness, many meditation retreats incorporate silence into their daily programme. Verbal silence is something most people hardly ever experience, yet it can be deeply relaxing and a profound relief after the continual chatter that your mind normally has to cope with.

Your thoughts become clearer when not subject to interruptions, and so it becomes possible to experience yourself more deeply and continuously. Deliberately refraining from speech can be a very beneficial preparation for meditation, as well as a way of absorbing its effects. This can be useful for your practice at home too. For example, when you get up in the morning to meditate, silence beforehand definitely helps. Wash and dress silently, with awareness, and perhaps sit by a window for a few minutes. A quiet period after meditation also helps. Before meditation, silence helps to prepare the mind for concentration, and silence after meditation aids the absorption of its effects.

Food

Food is important: both its type and quantity will affect your practice on retreat. The type to choose depends on what you like to eat, your body's constitution and the local climate. As a general rule, it is best to avoid heavy, fatty foods while making sure that you have food you can enjoy. There's no need to make life difficult by enforcing an ascetic diet. Sometimes people attempt to combine a retreat with some kind of health cure, giving up smoking, fasting etc. This can be all right, and even a good idea, if you know yourself well. It's important to remember, though, that on retreat you'll find yourself becoming rather sensitive, that food usually influences your mood fairly strongly and that the shops may be miles away. Regarding quantity, it is best to avoid eating too much or too little. Eating too much is likely to result in dull and drowsy meditation; too little results in faintness, low energy and restlessness.

Rest and exercise

Rest and exercise are another important area. It's important to take sufficient rest and to maintain a degree of fitness. Needs vary. But once you have recovered from the upheaval of getting away and travelling to the retreat and have established a meditation programme, you'll probably need an hour or so less sleep than usual. This should come naturally, and it's also necessary to have as regular a sleeping pattern as possible. It can be tempting when you're on your own to stay up quite late or to overindulge in sleep. For the most part, it's best not to sleep too much or too little. Too little sleep results in sleepiness and dullness; so does too much, and it wastes precious time. But sleep and dreaming are also necessary and valuable activities. On retreat you're likely to experience deeper levels of dreaming, often very intense and colourful, reflecting inner changes caused by your meditation. So in terms of quantity of sleep, you'll need to experiment to see what 'too much' and 'too little' actually mean.

You'll need some physical exercise on retreat because there usually isn't much of a practical nature to be done; and that, in combination with lots of meditation, makes it easy to become inert and sluggish. Soon the energy available for meditation will run down. Most people need some kind of exercise, and a daily walk may be sufficient. If you like to exercise, beware of spoiling the meditation by overdoing it to the extent that the mind becomes restless and the senses coarse. For some reason, it seems easy to go to extremes with one's physical energy on retreat. Many people take no exercise at all for a week, by which time they are so sluggish that they are forced to do something about it. Then they go to the opposite extreme with an intense physical workout so stimulating that they lose their sensitivity in meditation. It is best to have a little exercise daily and to exercise more intensely when not on retreat.

Information

With the expansion of information technology, most of us have become a little addicted to a stream of new facts being delivered via our computers, phones and other devices. After a few days on retreat, it's normal to accumulate a good deal of extra energy. And with this 'addiction' still a bit lively, you may find yourself on the lookout for interesting objects of distraction. It is very easy to pick up a book or even an old newspaper that happens to be lying around and become engrossed in it for hours on end. This kind of reading squanders the emotional energy you would otherwise be putting into meditation.

New information always has to be assimilated, and that process seems to use a surprisingly large amount of energy. If you take in too much that's new, it can temporarily interfere with your ability to concentrate. The mind gets tied up in the assimilation. It is either consciously reflecting on the material or unconsciously digesting it, and is not free to be deeply involved in meditation. Instead, you stay on the surface experiencing restlessness or dullness. This is frustrating, which can lead you into a downward spiral of compensatory distraction. If there is a constant surfeit of information, you normally find yourself spending whole practice sessions just getting to a point where concentration gets slightly easier and never going deeper. So be warned: once in the precious space of retreat, experiment with the quantity of information intake. Try giving up reading for a while and see the difference in the quality of meditation. These remarks apply especially when you are meditating extensively and trying to develop the dhyānas. Ensuring that your intake of information is moderate will enhance the whole experience. The main point concerns reading distractedly, not reading in itself. Skilful practice entails establishing mindfulness at the gates of the senses so that you can judge the effects of whatever is allowed in.

Activity

On retreat you typically spend much time on your own with little to do, when normally there is plenty to do. Your energy will be looking for an outlet, so you may end up filling all your time with activity. You suddenly notice that several jobs need doing around the cottage. You remember several letters that you meant to write, start several writing or study projects, spend hours creating elaborate meals for yourself from a cookery book. Many of these activities are unnecessary, a waste of very precious time. Most of us nowadays have become attached to activity for its own sake. We are not used to doing nothing, and may find it mildly threatening simply to experience ourselves. So beware of retreat activity becoming a substitute for experience of yourself, a way of covering up or hiding from a new depth of self-awareness.

You may not be quite ready to do *absolutely* nothing, and of course it could be quite beneficial and therapeutic to do a little housework or gardening. However, you will benefit greatly from doing nothing at all for at least an hour or so every day. Your thoughts over the weeks will become stronger and more productive. By refraining from unnecessary activity, you can break through to a deeper level of mindfulness. Instead of doing this or that, simply sit in a comfortable armchair and relax, experiencing all the changes in your mind and body. It is right here, in doing nothing and simply experiencing yourself here and now, that some of the most important fruits of meditation may be realized. Your mind can become very clear and rich in these circumstances. You will find out what an enormous amount can happen when you are doing 'nothing' and will see how much significance there can be in small, everyday things.

Slowing down

The 'inner' conditions set up on retreat – monitoring speech, food, rest, exercise and reading – are a way to tune in to the higher state of consciousness that is developed in meditation. By regulating behaviour and attitudes in these areas, you won't waste energy needed for meditation or go to extremes such as too much or too little sleep. You will maintain a balanced, clear and often joyful state of mind. Maintaining the best internal conditions for meditation involves all the foundations of spiritual practice mentioned in the preceding chapters. You need awareness, positivity and purpose in order to accomplish this fine-tuning, this continual state of readiness for meditation. You need, above all, to be mindful. To establish yourself in mindfulness, it is a good practice, especially during the early days of a retreat, to do everything at a deliberately unhurried pace.

To summarize: when you go to a place of retreat with its inspiring location, quiet isolation and practical support, you place yourself almost automatically in good external conditions for meditation. But whether or not these good conditions have any effect depends on the preparation done or not done in the preceding weeks and months in terms of meditation, behaviour, reflection and study. And when on retreat, you also need to engage positively with the fact that, for better or worse, you are continually creating internal conditions that affect your mental states. So if you want to use the opportunity of the retreat to meditate deeply, you'll take extra care in your use of your time, attention and energy.

Chapter six

....

Integration and dhyāna

Oh now, when the Dhyāna Bardo upon me is dawning!
Abandoning the whole mass of distractions and illusions,
May the mind be kept in the mood of endless undistracted
samādhi,
May firmness both in the visualising and in the perfected stages
be obtained:
At this time, when meditating one-pointedly, with all other
actions put aside,
May I not fall under the power of misleading, stupefying
passions.

The Tibetan Book of the Dead[37]

This chapter explores the stage of integration in detail, especially in the context of the joyful, subtle and penetrating consciousness induced by the deep concentration known as dhyāna.

Sometimes when you meditate, blissful feelings may arise spontaneously. They can range from mild pleasure and joy to almost overwhelming ecstasy; the experience can be so beautiful that you shed tears. You may blush, find your hair standing on end or feel goose pimples. What is more, the ability to concentrate enters a new dimension of lucidity and calm.

In psychological terms, you are directly experiencing what is known in our system of meditation as the process of integration: disparate parts are combining into a whole. In terms of ethics, this is a skilful (*kusala*) mind-state. In terms of aesthetics, you are touched by the beauty of the imagination. In terms of spiritual progress, the meditator is able to let go of hindrances and distractions and is starting to enter a higher state of consciousness. These feelings are a typical beginning for the first of eight levels of dhyāna enumerated by

Buddhist tradition. It may not be actual, full-blown dhyāna, as there are pre-dhyāna stages too in which the experience is one of deepening inner harmony.

Before the nature of dhyāna is considered in detail, it may be useful to get a sense of the integration process from a psychological point of view and to see the connection between dhyāna and the day-to-day states of your mind. Those states often aren't blissful or peaceful at all: your mind resembles a battleground of contradictory likes, dislikes, hopes and fears.

Practising mindfulness often reveals all kinds of paradoxes and oppositions in your character. How different, for example, are your intentions from your actions? You make firm resolutions not to eat unsuitable foods, say inflammatory things, waste time on the Internet or buy items you don't really want. These resolutions no doubt have a tempering effect on your actions, but gaps remain between your intentions and what you actually do. Another example is when you sometimes show different behaviours at work, at home and with various sets of friends. This is natural enough. Indeed you presumably like particular activities and friends precisely because they allow you to express different sides of your personality. From a vipaśyanā point of view, this highlights the unfixed nature of your 'self'; and from the angle of śamatha, you are working to unify your experience of self. Imagine walking along with a friendly neighbour one weekend and quite by chance bumping into a friend from work. Both know you well but in very different contexts. The personality your workmate sees on weekdays is different from how you are at home, so each sees you differently and expects different behaviour of you. So the situation feels a little odd: you can feel the clash of expectations.

Things like that happen because you are not wholly aware of your emotions or even your thoughts; and as they build up, inner inconsistencies and tensions are created that can be very strong. When meditation brings up and releases them, it's no wonder that you experience blissful feelings and clarified concentration. When dhyanic feelings manifest, it is tempting to think that you have somehow made the grade and are now a real meditator. And when they stop, you naturally want them back. But it's disappointing when you try, for you can never truly recapture an experience. The clarity and bliss felt in dhyāna is a by-product of the process of integration, occurring as (increasingly subtle) inner conflicts are met, come to a head and are resolved in conflict-free states of absorption.

When such breakthroughs occur, it is only natural that the felt intensity lessens in subsequent sessions: the leading edge of your practice is returning to work on the remaining unintegrated aspects of your mind. The intensity of meditation goes more or less back to normal, even if the overall tone of concentration and emotional engagement is now established at a new level. Provided you keep practising, you should be able to maintain that new level.

Integration is a dynamic phenomenon. Your life used to happen in different compartments, but the momentum of practice is removing some separating walls, allowing contrary components in your character to integrate with the thoughts and emotions that formerly acted as hindrances to concentration. For a while, you have been able to see changes happening more or less at the 'horizontal' surface of the mind: you have more mindfulness, feel happier and have clearer thoughts and feelings. But meditation is now penetrating beneath the conscious surface; you are starting to become deeply absorbed in dhyāna and to go beyond the hindrances.

On entering into absorption at this deeper level, content from the subconscious mind will come into consciousness, a phenomenon that marks the beginning of a second, more 'vertical' kind of integration. You encounter previously unglimpsed capacities of the imagination that can then be integrated into the 'horizontal' conscious mind. These capacities are described in Buddhism in terms of the five *indriyas*: 'spiritual faculties' that, at a deeper level of spiritual progress, transform into *balas*, or 'powers'. These five are faith, wisdom, mindfulness, energy and concentration. And in them it is the role of mindfulness to balance the creative tension between faith and wisdom, on the one hand, and energy and concentration, on the other.

At this stage, you may experience previously unimagined emotions, thoughts and pictorial images released into your consciousness, perhaps connected with significant past experiences. Once the depth of the imagination is stirred, happy childhood memories or long forgotten painful experiences may come to the surface during meditation, over subsequent days or in dreams. These may well be vision-like: sometimes people encounter divinely beautiful or awe-inspiring forms such as gods, demons, Buddhas or symbolic images. They have a markedly different character to the samāpattis described earlier; they are more like archetypal images coming from the heights and depths of the imagination. As before, they are side effects of your deepening concentration. They are wholesome and helpful, but it is important not to cling to them as signs of success or to try to replicate them later on. In themselves, they are not especially valuable. Enjoy these ephemera with interest, but then continue to seek what is genuinely valuable.

Table 6: Sequential characteristics of ordinary consciousness, access concentration and the first dhyāna

Level	Characterized by	
Ordinary consciousness	Desire for sense experience	Mental factors in conflict
	Ill will	Energy blocked
	Sloth and torpor	Emotional clinging to hindrances
	Restlessness and anxiety	
	Doubt and indecision	
Access concentration	No gross hindrances present	Enjoyment
		Cooperation of mental factors
		Concentration easier
		More energy available
		No strong emotional pull towards hindrances
First dhyāna	One-pointedness, initial/applied thought, rapture, bliss (i.e. the dhyāna factors, described below)	

> Getting rid of these five hindrances is like having a debt remitted … it is passing from a famine-stricken country into a land of prosperity. It is like living in peace and safety in the midst of violence and enmity.
>
> Zhiyi[38]

Access concentration

The experience of dhyāna begins to emerge at the point in meditation when the five hindrances start to die away. This point is known as

access concentration,[39] as you now have 'access' to the dhyānas. It is also known as 'neighbourhood' concentration, because you're close to the territory of dhyāna. How do you recognize whether or not you've reached this stage? You will know you're there when concentration becomes significantly easier. At this point emotions and thoughts start cooperating with your efforts to concentrate instead of continually pulling you away into distraction. The few distractions you still do experience no longer exert a strongly emotional pull – you've emerged on the other side of the five hindrances. Venerable Sujivo has this to say about *upacāra samādhi*, as it is called in Pali:

> Access concentration is close to absorption, (but) it doesn't mean access concentration is weak. It can be very strong. Take for example a person, either he is watching the in- and out-breaths, or he is mentally chanting … , or he may be doing mettā, spreading loving-kindness to somebody. After some time of developing the practice with mindfulness, with mettā, with awareness, his mind will become calmer and calmer. When it becomes calmer and calmer he forgets about everything else. The mind becomes very soft, very quiet and very concentrated. It will at times become very light. And he forgets about the body, he won't feel his body at all. He won't be able to hear any sounds at all. He just knows the mind is very still and quiet either on the breath, or on sending loving-kindness to a person, or it might be a visualization, a light for example. The mind does not move. The mind is very still, very quiet, he cannot hear anything, he doesn't know where he is. But he still knows that he is concentrated on the object. And if he wants to think he can; if he doesn't want to think he can, too. Often, in this stage, the mind is like one who is floating. It is like being half-asleep. But it is not really sleep. This still constitutes upacāra samādhi, access concentration. [40]

This new situation provides a significant opening. As access concentration deepens, distracting thoughts have little power over you, making more energy available and allowing you to notice distractions before they fully take hold. You thus disengage from distraction more easily, which frees even more energy and further sharpens the capacity for awareness. You enter an expansive, progressive phase. As Sujivo suggests, the term 'access concentration' doesn't just mark a crossing-point between the ordinary mind and dhyāna. It describes a broad band of consciousness that ranges from the point where you are concentrated but still frequently slip back into distraction (that is, almost in the hindrances) to a state in which concentration is extremely easy (almost in dhyāna). This is within the reach of anyone who meditates regularly; it's not really so very far away from most people's ordinary state of mind. If you know how to recognize this 'access' point, you can learn how to encourage it and to dwell in it for as long as possible. And then, the longer you can sustain it, the greater is the possibility that you can move on to full concentration (the first dhyāna). This is again within relatively easy reach of anyone who meditates regularly. You are likely to experience at least a taste of it within the first few weeks of taking up meditation – particularly if extra time is spent on practising, say on a retreat.

Dhyāna

Some people feel that teaching in terms of ever-higher levels of concentration introduces something competitive, like marks at school. Of course, it's not intended that way. It's just that some states of mind are much more preferable to others, and Buddhist tradition holds that the happiness of dhyāna is especially helpful in facilitating spiritual development. Discovering that non-sensual pleasure is very helpful for the path of Awakening was a key moment for the Buddha – when he remembered that as a child he had spontaneously become absorbed in dhyāna under a rose-apple tree.[41]

The practical details of actually meditating in the dhyānas come from the experience of meditators down the ages who, like Sujivo, practise and teach orally within their own culture. There have been countless lines of oral transmission since the Buddha's time, many of which remain fresh today, and there are some variations in terms of the particulars of meditation practice. Yet generally, there is great unity of principle across all the long-standing Buddhist cultures, and that understanding is now establishing itself in the contemporary world. So teachers in all traditions, using their own meditation experience as a basis, will interpret the signs of dhyāna in ways they find helpful for their students while looking to the scriptural accounts for clarification and guidance. Though it is useful to acquire an understanding of the technical differences between the dhyāna stages, it is not absolutely necessary.

The Buddha sometimes found it sufficient to teach with images, which can communicate directly aspects that may not otherwise come across.

> [A] skilful bath man or his apprentice will scatter perfumed soap powder in a metal basin, and then besprinkling it with water, drop by drop, will knead it together so that the ball of lather, taking up the unctuous moisture, is drenched with it, pervaded by it, permeated by it within and without, and there is no leakage possible …
>
> His very body does he so pervade, drench, permeate, and suffuse with the joy and ease born of concentration, that there is no spot in his whole frame not suffused therewith.[42]

In this ancient image, the experience of the first dhyāna is said to be like soap powder and water being mixed thoroughly together until the water completely saturates the dry powder and the water is pervaded by the soap powder.

The Buddha continues his set of comparisons in which water, a universal symbol for the unconscious mind, is the link. Being in the second dhyāna feels like a calm lake being fed by an upwelling underground spring. The third dhyāna feels as though lotuses and water lilies are growing in that lake soaked and saturated by its water. The fourth is like relaxing in a white towel after bathing in a cool lake on a hot afternoon.

In the **first dhyāna**, water is mixed perfectly with its opposite element, dry powder. The image of mingling opposites together expresses both the vertical and the horizontal integration of unresolved differences in consciousness. Emotionality versus rationality, masculinity versus femininity, consciousness, unconsciousness, introverted and extroverted tendencies all shift and melt into more creative and harmonious coexistence. Dhyāna is a state of mental purity in which you feel more truly and deeply yourself than ever before. After meditating in the first dhyāna, you may feel the happiness from it for hours and even days or weeks after.

In the **second dhyāna**, concentration is so pure that you experience no thought whatever. There is thought in the first dhyāna, but it's very subtle and is settled on the meditation object. Crossing from the first into the second dhyāna is to drop into a more lucid absorption which, apart from a subtle mindfulness of the state you are in, is thought-free. The second dhyāna is a state of very great inspiration in which you are sustained by blissful mental and spiritual refreshment that wells up inside, like an underground spring flowing into a calm lake. It is unusual for this degree of inspiration to arise spontaneously outside meditation, but there are rare individuals, naturally blessed with vast and elevated minds, whose experience is just this. There are bound to be individuals in the world who at times dwell in this sort of state without even hearing about meditation. In classical times, artists and poets called to the Muses, goddesses who bestow inspiration. The person in a state of deep inspiration is united with higher forces of the imagination, and they are experienced as outside the conscious personality, as when prophets or yogins receive instruction from a deeper level of consciousness.

The **third dhyāna** is compared to lotuses growing among the waters of a lake, completely surrounded and soaked in the medium of water. In your progress through the dhyānas you become more and more integrated with the higher element of inspiration. In the second dhyāna, it is experienced as just trickling into your consciousness. By the time you reach the third dhyāna, the stream has greatly expanded until it has become your whole environment; it is a very rich experience of vertical integration. In this dhyāna, you feel as though you are part of something much greater than your conscious self. You may need to remind yourself that it is still a mundane state of mind, one unawakened to ultimate reality, because it feels like a 'mystical' state in which you experience yourself surrounded, pervaded and unified with this higher element.

The **fourth dhyāna** is an experience of complete mental health and happiness. Like the other dhyānas, it doesn't endow anyone with ultimate wisdom or compassion – you could still conceivably act unethically and fall back in your progress. But even though you don't possess the fullness of insight, you are in the best possible state of mental health, which makes a moral fall far less likely. In the fourth dhyāna, all the powerful energies that have been tamed and liberated through previous meditation coexist in perfect, harmonious peace. The Buddha changes his style of imagery at this point, introducing a human being who seems to have mastered the water element. He is sitting in the sun by the side of a lake, radiant and at perfect ease, having bathed and wrapped himself in a pure white cloth. The inspired state of consciousness, generated through the other dhyānas, has become yours to wear and to take into the world as a protection and an outgoing influence. Your deep happiness radiates outwards, counteracting harmful influences and affecting others too, so that you may become charismatic and even 'magical'. This is why the fourth dhyāna is regarded as the basis for the development of magical powers (such as walking on water, passing through walls and so on, as attributed to practitioners of many religions) and amazingly acute faculties of perception.

Dhyāna factors

As a more precise aid to recognition, it's helpful to look in a more technical way at the various parts of the dhyāna state. Like a rainbow of higher consciousness, dhyāna consists of a spectrum of positive mental states with different hues and shades. Tradition enumerates five dhyāna factors (*dhyānāṅga*) plus a sixth, equanimity, which emerges in the fourth dhyāna. You should not think that dhyāna comprises only these factors, for it can also include many other positive qualities. In other words, dhyāna comes in different aspects, but the six dhyānāṅgas are constants that define its essential nature. You can imagine them as bands of red, orange, yellow, green, blue and indigo light. Dhyāna is a synthesis of both positive emotion and deep concentration, of both the warm and the cool ends of the spectrum. Three dhyāna factors are predominantly emotional and three are predominantly cognitive.

Table 7: The spectrum of dhyāna factors

Cognitive (cool)	One-pointedness
	Initial thought
	Applied thought
Emotional (warm)	Rapture
	Bliss
	Equanimity (in the fourth dhyāna)

The 'cool' part of the spectrum shows the faculties of one-pointedness (*ekagattā*), initial thought (*vitakka*) and applied thought (*vicāra*). **One-pointedness** is the ability to pay attention, and is especially strong in the dhyāna state. Initial thought and applied thought are aspects of clear thinking. **Initial thought** is when you think *of* something. For example, out of all the millions of possibilities, you might think of your friend Jules. As you call him to mind, some kind of thought or image representing Jules arises in your mind's eye. **Applied thought** is when you think *about* him: you explore your general idea of him more and perhaps wonder how he is and what he might be doing now. Initial and applied thought are a simple analysis of the way you think. Like one-pointedness, they occur outside dhyāna too – you are thinking of and about things all the time. But in dhyāna, thinking is wonderfully lucid and almost entirely under conscious control.

In the 'warm' part of the spectrum are the feelings of rapture and bliss mentioned earlier. **Rapture** is when you experience the process of integration as expressed in body pleasure. Though predominantly physical, it is not entirely so – you are physically thrilled and happy. Traditionally there are supposed to be five degrees of intensity of rapture.[43] You'll recognize the first stage: the sensation of goose pimples as the hairs on your body become erect with pleasure. The second is even more intensely enjoyable: rapture descends upon you in little shocks, like repeated flashes of lightning. In the third, it washes over you again and again, like waves breaking on the shore. In the fourth, it quickly floods every part of your body, like a huge volume of water suddenly entering a sea cave, according to a traditional simile. In the fifth, it is so intensely joyful that it is said to transport you bodily into the air in the miraculous phenomenon of levitation.

Bliss is gentler and subtler. But though less dramatic, it is in its quiet way actually more intense. Rapture is traditionally compared to the delicious feeling of anticipation when you know that you are about to get the very thing you've always wanted. Bliss is more like enjoying the satisfaction of actually possessing it. Bliss is thus a deeper stage of integration in which the mind has begun to absorb the wilder and less refined sensations of rapture. With experience, you become less attached to these relatively coarse feelings and move towards a deeper, stronger state of happiness. The occurrence of rapture and bliss show that increased concentration is an intensely satisfying experience.

It is interesting to see how bliss arises from rapture. As absorption takes a firmer hold, the experience of bliss becomes, as it were, larger, and it increasingly contains the feelings of rapture. This process of containing is sometimes known as *praśrabdhi*, and it is through increased praśrabdhi that the concentration deepens further. The deepening bliss gradually assimilates the bubbly, thrilling energy that is released through rapture. Praśrabdhi makes the mind pliable, flexible and very easily worked. It is a maturing and strengthening quality that is very characteristic of higher states of consciousness and is important in meditation generally.

Table 8: Moving from the hindrances to the dhyāna factors

This dhyāna factor	arises through developing this quality	by engaging in this kind of activity	and transforms this hindrance
One-pointedness	Interest	Be curious: what's happening here?	Sense desire
Initial thought	Energy	Accept responsibility for this state of energy and engage more – or try relaxing.	Sloth and torpor
Applied thought	Commitment	I can, and so I will, engage with this.	Doubt
Rapture	Enjoyment	Enjoy the positive, wholesome pleasure.	Ill will
Bliss	Peace	Relax and appreciate the beauty and serenity.	Restlessness and anxiety

From the hindrances to the dhyāna factors

Since each of the five factors of initial thought, applied thought, one-pointedness, rapture and bliss is a component of dhyāna, you can encourage the dhyāna state to manifest by focusing on those factors missing from the experience. By developing a dhyāna factor such as one-pointedness, you will be simultaneously counteracting one of the five hindrances – sense desire in this example. This correspondence is shown in Table 8 along with some pointers for arousing the relevant factor.

How does this work in practice? Developing **one-pointed concentration** causes interest in objects of sense desire to diminish. It is certainly more satisfying and enjoyable to be one-pointedly meditating than to be sitting there supposedly meditating but with your mind tossing here and there, propelled by sense desire. Likewise, ill will has no choice but to subside when through your efforts **rapture** starts to arise. It is simply not possible to be angry and at the same time to feel so happy. There is less possibility of restlessness or anxiety taking hold if you have some intuition of **bliss** in the meditation: it introduces at least the mental image of contentment, which is a seed that can grow. As it spreads, you will feel increasingly calm and the hindrance will gradually subside. If you attempt to clarify the objects of your thinking – if, in other words, you start arousing clear **initial thought** in meditation – any mental torpor, and even physical sloth, will begin to lose its hold. In meditation, your thoughts can sometimes acquire such an abundance of energy and clarity that their inspirational power can eventually cut through the heaviest resistance.

All these processes sometimes work only very slowly, so patience is required. Any stubborn doubt can eventually be dissolved if you introduce an element of applied thought – not just any old distracted thought but perhaps by reflecting on the value of the practice or on the fact that actions, whatever they are, always have consequences. If you apply your thinking truthfully, you can put irrational doubts in clearer perspective. It is the nature of this more investigative thought not to allow any 'sitting on the fence' but to demand a clearer examination of the meditation object.

In practice, it may take some time to move from hindrance to dhyāna factor. It depends upon the strength of the hindrance. But if you know that there is a path that leads from one to the other, you can have more confidence in making the effort to establish the relevant factor of dhyāna. And as you work, you may be able to find intermediary factors, such as those suggested in the middle column of Table 8. For example, trying to arouse interest in the practice itself rather than in the objects of sense desire could be a first step towards shifting the emphasis of your attention more towards one-pointedness. The inability to pay attention usually depends upon some emotional factor. You certainly have an emotional investment in the particular hindrance you are stuck in, otherwise you could simply drop it and forget about it. If you first allow yourself to experience what this investment feels like, experiencing its character, and then recall the character of the dhyāna factor, it may be possible to detach the emotional energy from the hindrance and rechannel it in the direction of that aspect of dhyāna.

This may seem a rather technical way of working in meditation but it is a useful training in getting closer to the truth of experience. It can be helpful as an approach at times, if not all the time. For keeping the general sense of practice fresh, at times do Just Sitting and/or Mettā Bhāvanā.

Table 9: Progress of the dhyāna factors through the first four dhyānas

	First dhyāna	Second dhyāna	Third dhyāna	Fourth dhyāna
Cognitive dhyāna factors	One-pointedness	One-pointedness	One-pointedness	One-pointedness
	Initial thought			
	Applied thought			
Emotional dhyāna factors	Rapture	Rapture		
	Bliss	Bliss	Bliss	
				Equanimity

As soon as each of the five factors is strongly present, you enter the first dhyāna. If concentration deepens further, you gain access to further dhyānas. Each progressive stage of dhyāna has a different ordering of dhyāna factors, as shown in Table 9. As concentration deepens, the cognitive factors tend to drop away and the emotional factors are progressively contained, as described above. This process continues until in the fourth dhyāna a new emotional factor, equanimity, arises. The fourth dhyāna is also the basis from which a further four dhyānas, known as 'formless' dhyānas, can be developed.

The traditional classification of dhyāna levels is useful for defining higher consciousness in the abstract, but it is an artificial way of looking at experience. The dhyāna factors provide a more experiential framework. They become stronger; and then, as you enter further into the meditation, thinking (first initial thought, then applied thought) is left behind. This is because discursive thought takes place only in a comparatively unrefined state of mind. It also takes up a considerable amount of energy. As concentration deepens, all thought dissolves and the energy previously taken up with thinking becomes free to flow directly on to the meditation object. At this point you find yourself immersed in a state of lucid, conceptless concentration: the second dhyāna. From this stage onwards, you experience vertical integration more and more strongly. In terms of the Buddha's simile, this is the point when an underground spring begins percolating up from the depths.

The spring of inspiration expands and broadens until, in the third dhyāna, it becomes the entire medium in which you experience yourself. This completes the process of absorbing or integrating the wildness of rapture into bliss (a progression known technically as *passaddhi*), so that the only dhyāna factors remaining are this peaceful bliss and one-pointedness. The process of purification continues into the fourth dhyāna, at which point bliss is transformed into equanimity (*uppekkha*). At this stage the mind goes beyond any possibility of conflict and reaches a peak of emotional stability and purity. Your one-pointedness of mind becomes unshakeable: you can maintain the concentration undistracted for as long as you wish.

Table 10: Progressive changes in experienced meditation object

Level of consciousness	Type of object (nimitta)	Experience of object
ORDINARY CONSCIOUSNESS On first taking up a meditation object, concentration is characterized by the five hindrances.	Preparatory image (parikamma-nimitta)	The basic object of the meditation experienced as separate
PREPARATORY CONCENTRATION (parikamma samādhi) Some continuity of concentration has been established. The object becomes more internalized as the hindrances are weakened.	Acquired image (uggaha-nimitta)	A subjective mental impression of the object, experienced internally
ACCESS CONCENTRATION (upacāra samādhi) Concentration is settled easily upon the acquired image but is not fully stable. The object acquires an image-like quality.	Reflex image paṭibhāga-nimitta	Indescribable (see text)
FULL CONCENTRATION (apana samādhi or dhyāna) Concentration is very stable. The dhyāna factors, which appear weakly in access concentration, become strong and constant.	Reflex image (paṭibhāga-nimitta)	Indescribable (see text)

Signs of higher states of consciousness

Another approach that helps you to become familiar with higher states of consciousness is noticing how the object of meditation changes at different levels. As you progress into dhyāna, the way you experience the breath or mettā – whichever object you happen to be concentrating upon – will undergo noticeable changes, as Table 10 shows. It may seem that the object itself changes, but of course you are witnessing a transformation in your own imagination. Any change in your subjective state is reflected in how you experience the outside world: when you're in a good mood, you perceive it as beautiful etc. It's the same when you meditate. The various ways you perceive the meditation object are affected by your changing state of mind. You naturally perceive the meditation object, the breath for example, as some kind of image. The technical term for this image-object is *nimitta*, meaning a sign. The table shows how it changes as you progress towards dhyāna.

It is interesting to wonder to what extent the nimitta is a true perception of the object and also what that might mean, but the point is that this is how the object is currently appearing in the mind. The nimitta changes in the course of every kind of meditation, including mindfulness of breathing and Mettā Bhāvanā, but you'll learn most about its nature by exploring the phenomenon in the context of meditations that entail concentration upon an external physical object. The classic example is the *kasiṇa* visualization method taught by the Buddha.[44]

A kasiṇa is a coloured disc set up in front of your meditation seat. You gaze at it for a long time until its qualities are so well impressed on you that you can close your eyes and visualize it as an internal image. So at once there is a clear change in the experience of the nimitta. As concentration upon the disc deepens, it will eventually pass through the three levels of consciousness: ordinary sense-based consciousness, then access concentration and then into full concentration, dhyāna. At each level of consciousness, there is a significant change to the nimitta.

The most effective kind of kasiṇa is one with a really bright colour that impresses itself vividly on the mind. Traditionally a disc is supposed to be made of flowers in order to achieve that quality, but you can experiment. Nowadays a disc of bright coloured light can easily be created on the screen of a computer or a smartphone. Other ways to create nimitta discs are used too, for example in the fire kasiṇa meditation in which you gaze through a round hole at flames.

Begin by positioning a kasiṇa disc in front of your meditation seat; then simply look at it. With eyes open, do your best to maintain attention continuously upon the kasiṇa, returning to it every time you become distracted. Whatever you perceive while looking at the physical object with the eye is called the preparatory image, *parikamma-nimitta*. Having gained a relatively undistracted perception of this, you have reached the first stage of preparatory concentration, *parikamma samādhi*.

At that point, close the eyes and visualize a replica of the preparatory image. This may take many attempts, but eventually you will get some perception of the coloured disc in your mind's eye. A tip for getting into this is to single out the memory you have of the kasiṇa you've just been looking at. What does that look like, how does it feel, what is its felt sense? The perception may not be 'visual' in the way you expect. The perception of an inner object is known as the acquired image, *uggaha-nimitta*. Now place your attention on this visualized image. When, after much practice, you manage to establish your attention stably upon the acquired image, then the level of access concentration, *upacāra samādhi*, will eventually arise.

In access concentration, there is a subtle but significant change in the appearance of the object: it becomes lighter and, as it were, transparent. The new quality is not easy to describe and may vary much from person to person. For example, there is often a numinous, otherworldly aspect. Buddhaghosa, an early writer on meditation, describes the new nimitta as being 'like the moon's disc appearing from behind a cloud', as 'cranes (silhouetted) against a thunder-cloud' or 'like a crystal fan set in space'.

The images give a feeling for the kind of thing that happens rather than literally representing the experience. You should not necessarily expect to see anything like this, though the nimitta may well have a visual aspect or a quality deriving from another of the senses. In terms of the different levels of nimitta, at this point your perception of the meditation object has reached a stage at which it is much subtler. It is now the *paṭibhāga-nimitta*, the reflex or counterpart image. You should now concentrate your full attention upon that. As you sustain access concentration with the reflex image as your object, the dhyāna factors of rapture, bliss and so on will arise and you will enter the stage of full concentration, dhyāna.[45]

The mind naturally creates images, though these are often unclear and unnoticed. So in any meditation practice where there is strong concentration, some form of nimitta will be clearly perceived. As I have said, it may not have a visual appearance at all. There can be a tactile type of nimitta, as when the breath you are concentrating on acquires a special subtlety at the stage of access concentration. It may be simultaneously visual-aural-tactile, like an image in a dream. It is difficult to describe reflex images satisfactorily because they are not experienced through the physical senses. Similes or poetic images work best, such as those of Buddhaghosa or the Buddha, whose image of mingled soap powder describes this kind of experience well.[46] In access concentration you are entering a realm of pure mind, moving from the realm of the senses (known as *kāmaloka*) into the realm of purely mental form (*rūpaloka*).

The 'Formless' (Arūpa) Dhyānas

Four more dhyānas, called 'formless' absorptions or *arūpadhyānas*, may be developed on the basis of the fourth *rūpa*-dhyāna. That is the high point of conditioned existence, a complete attainment of integration that enables a total experience of the natural world, especially in terms of the infinities of space and consciousness. The arūpadhyānas could therefore be described as special extensions of the fourth rūpadhyāna.

Ayya Khema offers some useful advice for gaining access to them.

> When you come out of fourth jhāna [dhyāna] and want to reach 'the infinity of space', you can notice the boundaries of the body, wherever they may be at the moment, and start stretching its limits further and further. The contemplation on the four elements … gives some inkling of this process.[47]

In the first arūpadhyāna, **the sphere of infinite space**, the boundary between the subject meditating and the object of meditation has become so subtle as to be almost indistinguishable. The nimitta or meditation object now expands to fill the whole of space and the meditator transfers his or her attention from this infinitely large nimitta to the infinite space it is occupying. This may produce a further degree of concentrated harmony and tranquillity, which is what provides access to the first formless dhyāna.

The sphere of infinite consciousness arises when you give attention to the fact that you are experiencing infinite space. This implies that in some way your consciousness has also become infinite: if you are aware of an object of infinite space, then there is a corresponding subject of infinite awareness. Experiencing this, you then withdraw your awareness from infinite space, concentrating entirely upon infinite consciousness. This is the point at which the second formless dhyāna arises.

At the stage of **the sphere of no-thingness**, you concentrate your attention upon the fact that within the context of your infinite consciousness, there are no specific things that can be distinguished. In this expanded state you cannot identify any one thing as distinct from another, even though your mind is unprecedentedly clear and bright. Focusing upon this produces an even more exalted state of consciousness, the third formless dhyāna.

When **the sphere of neither identification nor non-identification** arises, you go almost completely beyond the distinction between subject and object. You now concentrate your attention upon the way that you are identifying, or recognizing, the experience of infinity, and this causes a final stage of dhyāna to arise. At this point you are hardly separate from the experience. There is, in a certain sense, no subject who identifies, so that the process cannot be described either as identification or as non-identification.

The dhyānas of the formless plane are subtler than the highest experience point in conditioned existence as marked by the fourth dhyāna, and in them the distinction between subjective experiencer and objective experience becomes ever more subtle. Yet these higher states of consciousness are still conditioned; they do not indicate or encourage any insight into the ultimate nature of reality. Being conditioned, they are also impermanent – you can still fall back into lower states of being and consciousness.

> *Here perpetual incense burns;*
> *The heart to meditation turns,*
> *And all delights and passions spurns.*
>
> *A thousand brilliant hues arise,*
> *More lovely than the evening skies,*
> *And pictures paint before our eyes.*
>
> *All the spirit's storm and stress*
> *Is stilled into a nothingness,*
> *And healing powers descend and bless.*
>
> *Refreshed, we rise and turn again*
> *To mingle with this world of pain,*
> *As on roses falls the rain.*
>
> Sangharakshita[48]

Chapter seven

....

Consciousness and world

The path to full Awakening doesn't really consist of stages, even if it is helpful to have them. That's because *you* are the path, and what you are is not so easily expressible. But then what are you? A quest for vision and insight opens up when the big, existential questions start nagging at us, saying, 'Listen, life is here and now. Death will come, and maybe sooner than you expect.' *The Tibetan Book of the Dead* earnestly reminds us of this possibility:

> *Oh now, when the bardo of the moment of death upon me is*
> *   dawning!*
> *Abandoning attraction, and weakness for all worldly things,*
> *May I be undistracted in the space of the bright (enlightening)*
> *   teachings,*
> *May I (be able to) transfuse myself into the heavenly space of the*
> *   unborn:*
> *The hour has come to part with this body, composed of flesh and*
> *   blood,*
> *May I know the body to be impermanent and illusory.*[49]

One day you may find yourself asking, 'What was this experience I called "life"? Does it have any point?' Right now, you may ask, 'What am I, what is my humanity? Does it have any meaning or is it all some kind of dream? Why do people suffer? Does anything determine our future? What happens when I die? And how did I get here in the first place? How is it that I was born in my particular set of circumstances and someone else in another?' Curiosity about the nature of human existence steers life into profound waters, even in early childhood, though most parents' answers give little satisfaction. Since you have been lucky enough to encounter Buddhism, you have both access to some amazing tools for exploring reality and the chance to gain confidence from your findings. Methods such as meditation, developing awareness, spiritual friendship and ethical sensitivity enable you to cultivate your mind until you see right into the above questions for yourself. The key, again, is mind.

Let's go back once again to the verse quoted right at the beginning of this book:

> *Experiences are preceded by mind, led by mind, and produced by mind. If one speaks or acts with an impure mind, suffering follows even as the cart-wheel follows the hoof of the ox (drawing the cart).*
>
> *Experiences are preceded by mind, led by mind, and produced by mind. If one speaks or acts with a pure mind, happiness follows like a shadow that never departs.*

The Buddha in the opening verses of the Dhammapada[50]

The Buddha's teachings offer a useful view of reality: that of universal conditionality. Where has your present experience come from? It has come from your own mind, from the attitudes that have conditioned all the actions that have helped to make you what you are now.

Conditionality offers a framework for reflection, a way to consider and wonder about the nature of existence. It's not too hard to get some understanding of how your particular attitudes, responses, likes, dislikes and ways of speaking, moving and looking at things have developed and how your nationality, religion, class and gender predispose you to act in certain ways.

In other words, your interests and emotions get you into particular situations. Everyone, despite perhaps wishing otherwise, tends to get into similar situations again and again – the same decisions, the same social patterns, the same feelings, the same issues, the same pleasures. The Buddha spoke of our lives as a process of becoming now this, now that. We're all subtly re-conditioning ourselves every second: even when apparently doing nothing, you are thinking and making semi-conscious decisions, and they all have some effect. In the space of a single hour, you perform hundreds of minute physical acts and react to circumstances with countless thoughts and emotions. Perhaps many of these are insignificant, but even trivia add up. As when different currents combine into a river, a momentum builds that propels you in a particular direction – at least for a while.

Luckily, your life is not completely determined by previous conditioning. It is possible to make changes; and if you apply all your effort, you can get completely free from this conditioned existence or *saṃsāra*. This freedom is called Awakening or *Bodhi* (from the same root as Buddha, the Awakened One). This is no doubt some way off, yet its first glimmerings are contained in the initial realization that you are not separate from the process of becoming. You are no more, no less than the momentum of that process: a self-modifying flow of actions you can choose at any time to redirect. You have only a degree of moral choice, but you always have some. Though individuals vary enormously in the degree of choice available to them, all self-conscious beings partake in a dynamic of moral action and consequence.

The *Avataṃsaka Sūtra*, inspired by the extraordinary potential that this holds for us, describes our mutual environment in terms of innumerable beams of coloured light, all criss-crossing and penetrating one another. In this vision the universe consists of the currents and counter-currents created by all the actions beings perform as they simultaneously influence and are influenced by one another.[51]

This is of course not how people normally experience their lives. The true nature of the same reality, viewed from a more human-centred vantage point, is that our existence is transient: nothing lasts, and we feel that it's a problem. The constant changes of life are often difficult for us to accept, and this is what, in the end, makes our lives frustrating. People never want things they like to come to an end, or even to change in any way, yet they always do. Being out of step with what actually happens makes frustration inevitable. When fundamental things change, people feel insecure, angry and cynical – painful emotions that unfortunately create conditions for even more pain.

The only way this challenge can be resolved is by learning to sit more easily, and eventually more joyfully, with the fact of impermanence. Ending, changing, renewal, death, birth and change are simply how things are. Indeed, that's very good: all the creative possibilities of life also depend upon impermanence, and so does spiritual transformation. Precisely because life is so changeable, you can change yourself. With that understanding you hold the key to happiness. That insight enables you to participate creatively in reality instead of being a passive victim.

As a practitioner engaged in transformational practices such as meditation, it helps if you can understand your place in the vast universe of being and consciousness and what potentials exist for you. You are changing your consciousness in a number of ways, and that will change the way you perceive the world. According to Buddhist tradition, the quality of any being's state of existence reflects the quality of their consciousness. As you improve the quality of your consciousness, your state of being will reflect this. As your consciousness becomes more harmonious, clear and happy, your experience of the world will, on the whole, be more beautiful. In other words, you will see beauty in more ways and in more things, and that will affect your exchanges with others too. Gradually your social interactions and friendships will become more creative and satisfying.

Does Buddhism say that if you meditate, you're going to be reborn in heaven? As John Lennon knew when he wrote 'Imagine', many people nowadays cannot accept the idea that there literally is a place somewhere up in the sky where everything is perfect and that far below there is a hot and horrid hell realm.

> *Imagine there's no heaven |It's easy if you try*
> *No hell below us |Above us only sky ...*

But it could be that life will become more pleasant through the deepening awareness and understanding that comes from meditation practice. This less literal understanding of heaven and hell is what traditional Buddhism intends to communicate in the wheel of life. This graphic image portrays the demon impermanence gripping a wheel containing six typical realms of existence. These are the likely outcomes of various kinds of 'becoming', as we and all other beings are reborn in different realms of existence according to the habits we build up over our lifetimes. It is expressing (for Indo-Tibetan culture, using examples that are somewhat caricatured) the principle that your behaviour has the conditioning potential to create different worlds. In view of the long-term habitual repetition of one or another type of behaviour, we humans could even change mode and become, for example, an animal owing to wilful stupidity, a hungry ghost because of intense craving, a competitive titan through envy and jealousy, a suffering hell-being as a result of hatred and deep resentment or a divine being thanks to good deeds. These are indeed like cartoon images: look at an addict in need of a fix, for example, and you'll understand the appellation 'hungry ghost' immediately. Look around some more and you will see objective worlds in which these states of being are very real. Some of us are indeed born as actual animals (next door's Siamese cat, for example) and others actually do come to inhabit hellish realms (life in one of the world's many war zones). People are also born into happy lives of almost incredible privilege, but others resent them so much that their entire lives are twisted with envy.

It is not beyond the bounds of possibility that divine and demonic beings actually do exist in some dimension invisible to normal perception. According to the Pali scriptures, the Buddha spent a significant part of his time teaching divine beings (*devas*).[52] Traditional cultures universally recognize deva-like beings; ours is the only society in history that does not. Practitioners exploring the big perspective of the imagination should at least be open to the possibility of such existences. But if you're not able to go that far, the six realms may also be regarded as the mental states predominating in a concrete human situation. Viewed in those terms, it's not hard to imagine life conditions in which your mental state eventually becomes fixed in animal sensuality, tight-fisted meanness, jealous competition, paranoid hatred or proud, intoxicated happiness.

More relevant to this discussion is that devas are said to experience dhyanic consciousness: when you enter the dhyānas in meditation, you are temporarily elevated to a divine state. That is pretty much how it can feel. The principle here is that your consciousness determines the level of your being – body form, mental capacity and experienced world. In the familiar 'real world', you can see all this in a grumpy mood. Your face looks unpleasant and your body is tightly held; the world feels irritating, your sensitivity to pain is heightened and your patience is limited. Naturally this state of consciousness affects your physique, capacities, sense perceptions and thinking (which during an attack of the grumps may become narrow, paranoid and self-blaming). The principle also applies in the longer term, as tendencies become habitual and fixed. Grumpiness can become someone's normal characteristic, the confirmed disposition getting permanently etched upon the face and paranoid anxiety becoming a settled state. Buddhist tradition holds that in a subsequent existence, such tendencies are likely to be expressed in an unpleasant body form and mental disposition.

According to the processes of nature, many kinds of consciousness find collective embodiment in a mutually visible world such as ours. Buddhism allows for the possibility of many different kinds of world, but all of them will contain at least three levels (*loka*) of being and consciousness: kāmaloka, the realm of sensuous enjoyment; rūpaloka, the realm of pure (or subtle) form; and arūpaloka, the realm of no (i.e. exceedingly subtle) form. As each of the two higher lokas may be experienced by developing the dhyānas in meditation, these parallel the change in nimitta (perceived meditation object) noted earlier. This may be seen in the planes of conditioned existence given in Table 11, which correlates different kinds of being, including our own, with their range of mental states and levels of consciousness.

Table 11: The three planes of conditioned existence

Level of consciousness	State of consciousness		Embodiment
Kāmaloka Plane of sensuous enjoyment	Ordinary mind	Five hindrances	Hell-beings
			Hungry ghosts
			Animals
			Asuras
			Humans
		Access concentration	Kāmaloka gods
Rūpaloka Plane of subtle form	The four rūpadhyānas		Gods of subtle form
		First dhyāna	
		Second dhyāna	
		Third dhyāna	
		Fourth dhyāna	
Arūpaloka Plane of exceedingly subtle form	The four arūpadhyānas	Infinite space	Gods of exceedingly subtle form
		Infinite consciousness	
		No-thingness	
		Neither identification nor non-identification	

Consciousness and world

Apart from most gods, the human and non-human denizens of the wheel of life are habitually dominated by the self-referencing and materialistic concerns of the kāmaloka. Sense needs and enjoyments largely prevail, and the world we humans create together reflects this. If you consider what you ordinarily think about and how you prefer to use your time, you'll probably have to agree that this is indeed your usual state of consciousness. Things change dramatically, however, on entering the first dhyāna and the rūpaloka. Desire and preoccupation become far less important, and all forms, whether feelings, ideas or sense perceptions, feel as though they are composed of fine material or are made of light. The perceiving mind itself feels light and transparent. An example described earlier was the process by which, as concentration deepens, the object of meditation alters and appears as a subtle counterpart of the original. The Pali word 'rūpaloka' may also be rendered as the realm of archetypal form or the Imagination, as this new opening of the mind provides a portal into the rich realm of image and mythic symbolism – a world of less-defined meanings and full of gentle marvels, colour and light.

The five conditioning natures

The world you experience is a product of your consciousness, which itself is a product of conditions some of which are ethical attitudes. However, many other factors also play a part, such as your environment and your body. To complete the picture, another Buddhist teaching of universal conditionality, the doctrine of the five niyāmas,[53] shows conditionality operating at five different frequencies or natural realms.[54]

Table 12: The five conditioning natures

Niyāma	Realm of conditionality	Stage of system of meditation	Śamatha / vipaśyanā
Utu	Nature of inorganic matter	Integration (and mindfulness)	Śamatha
Bīja	Nature of organic matter		
Mano	Nature of automatic mind functions		
Karma	Ethical nature	Positive emotion	
Dharma	Nature of reality beyond self-identification	Spiritual death	Vipaśyanā
		Spiritual rebirth	

1) First, there are the conditions operating in the realm of **inorganic matter**. Inorganic entities, for example constellations, planets, oceans, clouds, solids, chemical compounds and atomic particles, are affected by conditions such as gravity, chemical reactivity and atomic structure. This is *utu* niyāma. It comes from a Pali word meaning 'seasonal'. You can also call this the elemental or environmental nature.

2) In the second realm, of **organic matter**, is found our own flesh and blood and the bodies of organisms, gross to microscopic, that fill the biosphere – all subject to the conditioning of botanical, biological, physiological and other ecological forces. This is *bīja* niyāma, the biological nature.

3) The third realm is that of the **automatic mental functioning** that all sensing organisms possess. Perception, response, instinct and reflex are all active at this level. The various forces by which this kind of functioning is conditioned are explored by neuroscience, genetics and behavioural and cognitive science. This is *mano* niyāma, the perceptual nature.

4) The fourth realm is **volitional action**, which comes about when individual life forms acquire self-awareness. For Buddhism, with its special concern for spiritual evolution, this stage is crucial. Self-awareness bestows individual

choice, and individual choice offers the possibility of ethical action. This possibility allows the individual to redirect their personal evolution towards higher levels of being and full Awakening. This is karma niyāma, the ethical nature.

5) The fifth is the realm of **total reality**, governed by the forces that come into play once individuals see through the illusion of substantial existence and start to touch the true nature of things. This aspect of conditionality, that is the *Dharma* niyāma or ultimate true nature, shapes how realizations of the truth of things have their effects on each individual and their world.

Over some of what affects your life you have no control, some of it you can change and some comes into play only with insight. Your susceptibility to physical laws and your body, senses and perceptual processes are given, but you can change the way you react to things – this is the conditioning realm of ethics. Then, after the point of insight, a new kind of creative conditioning can start to influence your life. The practice of meditation and mindfulness has its effects largely in the ethical realm, in creating the increasingly positive states of mind shown in Table 12. These, as śamatha, are a condition for insight (vipaśyanā) meditation. And with insight, reflection and direct seeing, the fifth realm of the fruits of insight, the Dharma niyāma, becomes more established.

In terms of the system of meditation, the stage of integration works especially with the first three niyāmas. In learning how to be mindful of your body and your feeling responses and of all the perceptual and instinctual reactions that make up your changing mind states, you acquire the strength of basic integration. The stage of Positive Emotion works in the fourth realm, ethical conditionality, as you develop increasingly helpful and harmonious responses to experience. The stage of spiritual death entails letting go of the idea of a fixed self, something that gets in the way of the new creative conditionality. The more room allowed for that creative element in your life, the more you enter the stage of Spiritual Rebirth.

Chapter eight

....

Seeing

Oh now, when the bardo of Reality upon me is dawning!
Abandoning all awe, fear and terror of all (phenomena),
May I recognize whatever appears as being my own thought-
*   forms,*
May I know them to be apparitions in the intermediate state;
(It has been said), 'There arrives a time when the chief turning-
*   point is reached;*
Fear not the bands of the Peaceful and the Wrathful, who are your
*   own thought-forms'.*

The Tibetan Book of the Dead[55]

Vipaśyanā, the insight method of meditation, reveals our self and our world as they are beyond our assumptions and self-referencing emotions.[56] It is direct experience, not abstract understanding, and contrasts with śamatha methods such as mindfulness of breathing that prepare the mind for vipaśyanā by cultivating profound concentration and strong, positive emotional integration. Vipaśyanā is generally preceded by śamatha practice, because if concentration is wavering, the mind will be unable to rest in the special object of vipaśyanā meditation. And when insight comes, a stock of calm, strength and happiness is needed in order to absorb its revelatory, visionary impact.

In revealing the true nature of the self and the world, vipaśyanā has a penetrating, sometimes surprising quality, and occasionally it is shocking. It is also, as Zhiyi tells us, 'rich'.

> Śamatha is a refreshment of the lower consciousness, while vipaśyanā may be compared to a golden spade that opens up a treasure of transcendental wealth.

....

Śamatha is an entrance into the wonderful silence and peacefulness of potentiality; while vipaśyanā is an entrance into the riches of intuition and transcendental intelligence.[57]

The vipaśyanā method

The vipaśyanā method uses receptive attention to penetrate the veils of habitual emotion and rigid views and see the real nature of all the phenomena of experience. There are direct and indirect approaches, which can be used at different times and circumstances.

Direct seeing is simply that: you look directly into the nature of things. You need to learn how to do it, of course; and the indirect method, called insight reflection or contemplation, can teach you to some extent. This involves reflecting upon an idea, image or phrase in the light of certain topics and opening to the truths that the reflection arouses.

The core reflection topics are impermanence, unsatisfactoriness and insubstantial selfhood – the three *lakṣaṇas* (universal characteristics of existence identified by the Buddha). You must have strong confidence in the truth of these ideas if you are to allow them to change you in any depth, so it is important to study and understand them. Other necessary supports are concentration and mindfulness. To penetrate deeply into vipaśyanā, you'll need to generate mindfulness in daily life and to learn to recognize thoughts, feelings and so on as they arise. This enables you to look into them more deeply during reflection (the direct seeing) meditation. Generating that degree of śamatha and self-awareness will require a substantial daily meditation practice, and probably retreat conditions.

Because of the need for fine concentration, vipaśyanā meditation is done either in access concentration or in dhyāna – ideally the first dhyāna, since that allows for some thought. For example, to meditate on impermanence you enter a state of concentration, and then within that tranquil state you either reflect on the notion of impermanence or look directly at the impermanence of the sense contacts and feelings currently arising and dispersing. Ordinary awareness isn't much good for vipaśyanā: it is plagued by the hindrances, which make thought either vague or rigid. In access concentration and dhyāna, however, the thinking faculty is sharp, pliant and easy to direct. It is hardly 'thought' at all in the usual sense. The mind is so receptive and absorbed that you may need to attend to impermanence only for an instant for its significance and meaning to reveal itself. You don't try actively to understand anything but simply allow yourself to be affected by the truth. It's enough just to lay the image of impermanence within your receptive mind and to remain with the experience as it unfolds. If, by analogy, you placed a diamond or an amethyst on dark velvet, you wouldn't have to make an effort to see its beauty. That would naturally reveal itself as you became accustomed to looking at it.

However, you do need to continue looking, to remain constantly with the experience. That is the work. Its cumulative effect may not always be visible, and the transformation it brings may sometimes take you into difficult areas of experience.[58] But if you can remain open, maintain contact with mentors and peers and develop a patient understanding of the process of insight, you will be able to maintain the necessary perspective and the inspiration to keep practising.

The three prajñās

Buddhist teaching distinguishes three phases of deepening insight. They are known as the three *prajñās*, often called 'listening, reflecting and meditating'. These are the phases of 1) receptively taking in information about the nature of reality, 2) actively clarifying, understanding and digesting the implications of that information and 3) receptively allowing the reality of those implications to transform you and bring about full Realization.

Listening

The first stage is reading, studying or simply **listening** to the teaching. It is known as *sutamayiprajñā*, the wisdom of hearing. It is the preparatory stage, not wisdom proper. The following verses from Gampopa illustrate how your ability to learn depends to a large extent upon attitude: the traditional model is that of a clean, empty receptacle, ready to be filled.

Not to listen is the defect of a pot turned upside down; not to bear in mind what you have heard is that of a pot with a leaky bottom; to be affected by [negative emotion] is that of a poisonous pot.

… When you listen to the explanation of the Dharma, you must listen to the voice of him who explains it without the perceiving faculty of your ears straying to some other sound. When you do not listen in this way, it is as though juice is poured on a pot [that is upside down], for though your body is present in the teaching room, you do not hear a single word of the Dharma.

… When you do not bear in mind the Dharma … though the words have reached the perceiving and hearing faculties, it is as if juice is poured into a pot with a leaky bottom – however much you may pour, nothing will remain there; and however much of the Dharma you may have heard, you do not know how to instil it into your mind and how to take it to heart.

… When you hear the explanation of the Dharma, but listen to it with … thoughts affected by the five [mental] poisons … not only will the Dharma not become beneficial to your mind, it will even turn into its very opposite, and this is like healthy juice poured into a poisonous pot.

Gampopa[59]

If you want to absorb something new, it is essential to take an active interest. As the verse amusingly points out, to take in a spiritual teaching you need to be more than just physically present when it is delivered (or encountered in a book). To really have an engaged interest, you need to see its vital importance in your life – something that may well require further reflection. It is also important to put aside your immediate reactions to the information, so that you don't become a poisonous vessel in which personal prejudices contaminate the teaching. The meaning needs to be understood as it was intended: someone's words may be unclear or offensive, yet you can't justify dismissing them unless you're sure you really know what they meant when they said or wrote them.

Reflection

The second stage, **reflection**, is considering in depth the material already taken in through study, reading or listening. It is a long-term process of digesting received ideas into the body of your thinking and feeling, which makes them your own. To some extent, this happens naturally once the original ideas have been taken in. But the process also needs some active direction. Once the original ideas have been well understood, reflection can then go deeper and be employed in insight reflection, i.e. the 'indirect method' of vipaśyanā.

Meditation

In the third stage, meditation, which is vipaśyanā or direct seeing, you attempt to look directly into the nature of things and see reality as it truly is. You open yourself up to a radical transformation through seeing the realities of unsatisfactoriness, impermanence and insubstantiality.

Insight is direct experience of the real, ultimate nature of existence, not the abstract understanding that burdens unawakened beings. On this side of Realization, all you have are *ideas* about the nature of reality. You can't help having certain views. You couldn't function without some kind of working explanation of what the world is and why you are in it. Yet if you really look into them, the explanations remain endlessly vague and unsatisfactory. You may have tried hard to think them through but you haven't been able to do so satisfactorily. Though there are moments when you think you've understood it all, questions arise at other times.

In short, however educated and intelligent you may be, you simply won't be equipped to fathom this through rational processes alone, because rationality cannot fully apprehend the nature of existence. This is why spiritual practice, which employs methods not limited to rationality alone, is so valuable. Spiritual practice doesn't bypass your rational faculty. On the contrary, its energy depends on you using reason as much as you can in order to clarify and question the views you hold and to come up with sounder ones that point you in the direction of a fuller truth. This is called developing Right View (*samyagdṛṣṭi*), and study to that end is an important prerequisite for vipaśyanā.

Right now you almost certainly hold many views about yourself and the world that are unhelpful. These are known collectively in Buddhism as Wrong View (*mithyādrṣti*). They are attitudes at least as much as intellectually held views about reality; indeed the rational content may be practically non-existent. Often completely unconscious, such views are typically clung to as part of the way people insist on seeing themselves. For example, there is the widespread view that people actually do understand the nature of human existence, that it's just a matter of common sense. A majority of people believe that 'I am just me' and that the world is as it appears in the media. It is a view that is often rigidly held, promoted defensively (even aggressively) and based seemingly on fear of change. The rigidity deepens the lack of understanding and stifles the curiosity that could have led to positive change. But of course notions of 'me' and 'the world' are not easily understood. It is very hard for anyone to see that such basic components of life could be subjective constructions. But unless you can become aware of your ignorance about the fact of existence, you can hardly begin on the spiritual path.

In fact, your ignorance must move you. If you're really going to find the truth, you need to be emotionally aroused. I don't mean that you should panic, but you do need to stir up a strong spiritual determination, which Buddhism calls *saṃvega*. A translation of saṃvega I like is 'the oppressive sense of shock, dismay, and alienation that comes with realizing the futility and meaninglessness of life as it's normally lived; a chastening sense of one's own complacency and foolishness in having let oneself live so blindly; and an anxious sense of urgency in trying to find a way out of the meaningless cycle.'[60] The upshot of this is that strong engagement is essential: you must really want to know. You need to feel a kind of hunger for the truth. As Gampopa says:

> When hearing the Dharma you must be like deer listening to the sound of music.

> When thinking about it, you must be like a man from the north shearing sheep.

> When making it a living experience, you must be like a man getting drunk.

When establishing its validity, you must be like a Yak eating grass hungrily;

And when you come to possess its fruition you must be free from clouds like the sun.[61]

As I have mentioned, vipaśyanā meditation depends on a well-grounded ability to recognize individual thoughts, feelings and sensations as they arise. That, for most people, will require several hours of meditation practice each day, including plenty of śamatha meditation. It's a major commitment, I know; but if you don't slow down and open up your awareness, you will never see outside the net of your habitual assumptions.

Thoughts and thinking

In both vipaśyanā methods, insight reflection and direct seeing, you look into the nature of *process* generally, especially the thinking process. You see into its fundamental lack of substance and observe that, contrary to intuition, this experience does not add up to a self. Really seeing through this delusion that 'I am my thinking' frees the considerable energy that you've burdened with the task of maintaining it.

To enter into your experience of thinking, it helps to notice the difference between your associative thought processes and those thoughts you deliberately direct. It is normal for thoughts to proliferate, just as conversations do – as when you're talking with a friend about something that happened last week; and by the time ten minutes have passed, you're deeply into a different topic. Neither party recalls exactly how the conversation got there, so you have to reconstruct the sequence of links in the chain of ideas.

The same pattern happens continually in your thoughts. Perhaps you're sitting in meditation, and not with much concentration. You gradually become aware that you've been thinking for at least five minutes about how to make a specific sandwich. As your self-awareness suddenly peaks, you wonder, wherever did *that* come from? Trying to recall, you remember the chain of associations that eventually triggered it. One came quite soon after sitting down, as drifting through the open window came the jolly jingle of an ice cream van. But the thought of ice cream was not what sparked the connection with food (and thus the sandwich). It was the association of the sound with the time of year. Now it's spring, and it's the first time this year that those chimes have rung out. Hearing them made your memory drift far back to a former springtime when you were very small and you were taken for tea and cakes with an amazing old aunt. The daydream persisted, and eventually mutated into a reverie about sandwiches.

This is a typical kind of what the Buddha called *prapañca*, proliferating thought. The extent to which it occupies the mind varies from person to person and from day to day, but the associative style of thinking is the way our mind seems to work for much of the time. The majority of ideas come into our mind unbidden, usually through some kind of association, much of it dream-like, but there is also a richness and creativity to it. It is natural to pursue mental objects and to associate one with another, and the mind is constantly throwing up associations that are often extraordinarily meaningful. Creative and original ideas often arise this way: a particularly evocative set of associative thoughts sparked Einstein's relativity theory. The distracted mind can seem like an internal Internet in which you endlessly click the links in your life history. But that mechanical model should not blind you to your mind's spontaneous, organic and essentially mysterious nature. Prapañca, associative thinking as well as proliferating thought, may be chaotic and 'proliferous', yet it is alive – it is not software, and it is not operating at random. Despite appearances, your mind is vividly awake and contains extraordinary potential.

Directed thought is what people usually mean by the word 'thought': the deliberate creation and direction of ideas, as when you plan your day or analyse a problem. There is a more or less definite purpose to it: you keep your mind on a particular issue and seek some kind of a conclusion. You look into the implications of a certain idea and wonder what it means. In such deliberations you employ logic, at least your own kind (perhaps jumping to conclusions, making rash generalizations and avoiding obvious truths). The direction your thoughts take will probably be fuelled by some emotion – it could be compassion, hatred, fear, anxiety, love or a professional determination to achieve a good solution.

Most people spend only a small proportion of time actually directing thoughts, and even then associative thinking plays a role. You can notice it while reading: very often, once attention has been one-pointedly directed upon a topic for a while, your thinking again spreads out and engages with various associating ideas. Other, less conscious yet relevant considerations are taken aboard and reorganized by the directing attention. Then, yet again, you focus your thinking in a chosen direction. All this tells us how organic and highly complex thinking is, and hints too at W. B. Yeats' observation that

> Wisdom is a butterfly and not some gloomy bird of prey.[62]

It is important also to watch out for vague and unclear thinking. The soundness or cunning of your reasoning may reflect your ethical sensitivity too, as it is easy to come to conclusions that support your own interests. It is important therefore to check your reasoning in case it is lacking in cogency, or simply lacking. When they look, most people will find that much of their thinking is half unconscious. What, for example, is your present notion of spiritual development? Almost certainly it will be just that: an idea. Or it's some kind of image – one that strongly motivates you, configuring in detail your view of yourself and your world. To work positively, the image needs to be mapped closely on to your actual experience of life. Without that connection, it is easy to become trapped in disconnected, abstract views of the nature of spiritual potential, which will inevitably be 'wrong' to some extent. Thus the down-to-earth concerns of mindfulness practice: what are you doing now, what's really happening? How does the activity you're engaged in now connect with the spiritual path you're hoping to embark upon? Your ideas and views need constant examination in this light.[63]

Insight reflection

The three levels of wisdom outline an increasing clarification of views that relate to the path of liberation. Crucial to this is the second level, reflection. We'll look shortly at some standard frameworks for this, for example reflections on the *lakṣaṇas*, the ultimate characteristics of existence. But in the spirit of Yeats' butterfly, let's not overspecify the way it all works. Once introduced into the labyrinth of your habitual mind, reflection topics become less easy to track. That's fine and to be expected; the main thing is to take them in. After you've done that, you'll find yourself rambling around them for ages in all kinds of strange ways. But the rambles are always connected to the nature of things, to the great existential mystery vipaśyanā opens us up to. As already noted, that process is organic and beyond the rational, even though rationality is included.

To give several images: reflection is like sitting at a warm fireside on a winter's night gazing into the flickering glow of thoughts and ideas. It is like looking out of the window on a train journey: your eyes take in both the changing scenery and the reflections in the glass. The glass surface holds the gaze, occupies the senses and frees the thinking mind to engage in deeper concerns as ideas arise and disclose their previously unnoticed layers of meaning. Reflection is a subtle activity that needs to occur within an expanse of receptivity. You need to allow the mind space to relax and be itself and then to deliberately choose an object for contemplation. But the contemplation will be at least partly associative. Your deliberations may be laser-sharp and penetrating, cooly separating unwanted matter like a surgeon using a scalpel. At other times you'll need to seize on ideas hawk-like, hotly challenging and testing them, perhaps making yourself face unexpected conclusions. All along, you need to find a place for the gently musing butterfly style too. That's because you need both the activity and the receptivity, the musing and the deliberation. Indeed, the word 'reflection' implies a mutual, cooperative relationship between a subject and an object.

When you next have some free time, even as little as twenty minutes or half an hour, resist the impulse to play with a gadget or to pick up a book. Engage in reflection instead. Put everything else aside, sit in a comfortable chair, relax and do nothing – except one thing: connect with your body and feelings. Notice your already running thoughts. In order to think deliberately, you must free energy by withdrawing the attention escaping into all kinds of interests. Thinking is an introvert: it needs time to itself. Often the reason why meditation is wasted in distracted thinking (or you have sleepless nights filled with intense thoughts) is that you don't allow your thoughts any other time for play.

So don't hesitate to spend time doing 'nothing'; it isn't a waste of time or an indulgence. Nor, in seeking clear thought, are you pretentiously viewing yourself as a 'thinker'. Giving time for thinking will make a big difference both to the quality of life you experience and to your relationships with others. Many emotional problems are caused or made worse by neglecting thought. To some extent, reflection is a human need, a faculty that wants to be exercised. It is something we all have deep in our nature.

In his *Jewel Ornament of Liberation*,[64] Gampopa lists numerous topics for reflection at this (more or less conceptual) level, some of which might work for you if you try them out.

The first is that you have a **potential for Enlightenment**. The historical Buddha and many other practitioners of his teachings have all gained a state of complete spiritual freedom. Anyone can do this by making the appropriate effort. This is really something to ponder!

Then comes the **preciousness of human life**. Life is not always easy, and sometimes it can be very painful and difficult. Yet we humans are uniquely free, especially if all our mental and physical faculties are available. You have heard about the Dharma, and I hope that, like most readers of this book, you have the freedom to practise it openly. However, many do not; and many simply have no leisure to practise – they must work hard just to sustain life or their present situation gives them no personal space. Do you really understand how lucky you are when, for example, you have time to meditate in the morning?

You live in a universe characterized by **impermanence**. Nothing lasts for very long, if it lasts for any time at all. This day is passing, its unfolding events never to be repeated. The changing thoughts and feelings in your heart and mind will never be quite the same again. Things you like are changing and will disappear, and it's the same with everything – your body, friends, relations and possessions. How amazing this is! – even if you sometimes find the intensity of it difficult to bear.

And it's clear from this that life, at least in the way most people want it to be, is very **unsatisfactory**. Everyone suffers when their experiences are other than what they want. And yet it isn't possible to find any real, lasting or complete satisfaction: all sources of satisfaction are temporary and usually leave you wanting more. If you chase satisfaction too urgently, you step into a spiral of addiction. But you care about satisfaction of one kind or another more than anything else. You need to learn to take pleasures lightly and to enjoy them for their transient beauty as well as for their content. This is something worth reflecting on.

Then there is the realm of action: all **actions have consequences**. If you look back on the things you've done, you'll be able to see some of their effects in your present circumstances. Then you can look at what you are doing now and consider the likely consequences for your future. You can look at the chain of the links of dependent arising taught by the Buddha (see Chapter 9). How profound and mysterious it all is!

Spiritual influence and inspiration is another profound topic. Who are your spiritual ancestors – those in the past who helped you to gain your present perspectives on life – and who are those helping you right now? Come to appreciate what their influence has been and the effect it still has. This affects your influence on others. Having an influence in the world is something no one can avoid, even if they want to. It is, moreover, a responsibility that you can learn to embrace and that can teach you to stand more confidently on your own feet and act in a helpful, generous and truthful way.

Finally, you can reflect on the value that **spiritual development** brings into the world – the clarity and positivity that eventually flowers as bodhicitta, the attitude that holds Enlightenment for all as the supreme value. That is the basis on which people grow towards the state of Buddhahood.

All these topics bear endless reflection. You can relate easily to some, whereas others may arouse difficult emotional responses. That's to be expected – facing such difficulties is essential to your work. And your work usually benefits from discussion. Talking, even argument, can breathe fresh air into stale, habitual thoughts and reveal unclear or wishful thinking you wouldn't even notice otherwise. Formal discussion or study groups can help you to test out your views. If you know a topic well, it's a great idea to present it to others. The feedback evoked through having to account for your ideas makes excellent nourishment for reflection. Your listeners will act as mirrors, showing exactly how much you have made the teaching your own and how much it is still theory.

Sometimes it is helpful to walk up and down with your thoughts. Walking meditation, described in Chapter 3, is as good a way for reflection as sitting meditation, and can be more practical. You can even do it when you are not in an especially concentrated or even positive state of mind, for the walking itself has a calming effect that eventually brings your thoughts together.

A well-nourished practice of reflection will develop potent understandings that you can return to again and again and that seed further refinements. These understandings are ideal for vipaśyanā reflection. Somewhat like real seeds, they are tasty, concentrated nuggets of truth. Indigestibly big and abstract concepts such as 'impermanence' or śūnyatā aren't much use. You need living Dharma seeds that accumulate over years of reflection many facets of meaning as they live and grow in your imagination.

It's not just ideas that do this: many forms of vipaśyanā meditation employ symbols, mantras and what are known as seed-syllables, all of which can come to embody the results of reflection. A classic example is the mantra or sound syllable OM MAṆI PADME HŪM. It is repeated in the meditation practices of Tibetan (and other Mahāyāna) traditions connected with Avalokiteśvara, the Bodhisattva of Compassion, and is seen revolving on prayer wheels or fluttering on flags. It is wrong to think that these expressions show a mechanical approach to spiritual development, as if the more they are repeated, the closer you would be to Awakening.

A mantra is a word or a sound that holds a set of meanings, as complex as synapses extending in the brain, which then evolve as you meditate on them. As it has no definable meaning, a mantra is a useful hub around which families of ideas, understandings and mini-insights naturally cluster. The point of repeating a mantra is the same as that of repeated reflection: it holds the attention there, allowing the accumulated meaning to percolate beneath the surface of the conscious mind and enabling deep transformation to take place. Mantras are therefore essentially about generating an atmosphere of calm receptivity. The same principle also applies to all the many kinds of symbolic representation found in the traditions of Buddhism, for example statues or paintings of the Buddha, Bodhisattvas and other awakened beings. For the practitioner, these images hold the potential living reality of enlightened wisdom and compassion in a way that words cannot. Images, ideas and symbols of this kind continually grow in significance in the meditator's mind. Reflection on them feeds insight meditation and the results feed further reflection, initiating a spiral of growing insight into reality.

You can now see how the three levels of insight, or *prajñā*, work together. As it goes deeper, reflection can become the imagination's central core. It absorbs whatever information it has 'listened' to by continually winding round the idea, turning it upside down and inside out in a quest for its inner meaning, then from time to time addressing that inner meaning directly, in a way beyond words. Finally, it allows the fruits of that work to nourish even deeper reflections.

Like meditation, all three levels of insight require certain conditions in order to be fully effective. Perhaps the most important one is your sense of motivation, the 'hunger for truth' mentioned earlier. Unless you strongly want to gain insight, it won't happen. Then it is important to exercise the intellect and to nourish it, using every opportunity to read well-written, well-thought-out material. This can be whatever takes your interest, but includes novels and poetry as well as original Dharma texts. It also helps to read the books you have found valuable again and again. Once more, repetition is vital for taking understanding deeper: you rarely comprehend every aspect of an idea in the first moment you encounter it.

The practice that will tie these conditions together, and allow you to focus your energies in one-pointed reflection, is mindfulness. Mindfulness supports the development of insight, just as it supports concentration in meditation. If you continually maintain a breadth of awareness of body, feelings, emotions and thoughts, you can focus more easily on your most important thoughts in deep reflection, forming the Dharma seeds that may flower later on into full-blown insights.

Finally, taking your thought deep requires a measure of inner solitude. My teacher once wrote: 'Without some degree of solitude reflection is impossible, and without prolonged reflection no great work of art was ever brought forth. The poet needs solitude as the lungs need air. By solitude is meant not so much physical loneliness as inner isolation, for the time being at least, from all that does not directly concern the process of poetic creation.'[65] He was talking about creating poetry, but Sangharakshita very reasonably sees that as a form of insight reflection. Reflection provides a context for your practice of Buddhism. If you reflect often, your understanding will remain in touch with the flavour of Dharmic ideas and will always be ready to take them further. All your experience will be seen in the light of the Dharma, so that the liberating flavour or taste of the Dharma is with you all the time. Then you tend to put the Dharma more into practice.

> Just as, monks, the great ocean has but one taste – the taste of salt – so this Dharma-discipline too has but one taste – the taste of freedom.

> Gautama Buddha[66]

Direct seeing

The fundamental topics for the direct seeing method of vipaśyanā are the three universal characteristics of existence: impermanence, unsatisfactoriness and insubstantiality. Impermanence is the truth that nothing lasts and everything changes. Unsatisfactoriness is the truth that because everything is impermanent and no source of satisfaction can last forever, you cannot expect full, lasting satisfaction from anything. Insubstantiality is the truth that in the light of universal impermanence, no individual things exist as fixed entities because from one moment to the next, there is always change. This applies to material objects such as mountains and rivers and hats and coats; it applies to people like you and to something you are fond of and like to call 'me', which has such a momentary existence that it can hardly be said to exist at all. This is why insubstantiality is also often called non-selfhood: nothing has stable, abiding 'thingness'. No thing has abiding substance. People don't usually find these three characteristics very palatable. Indeed, reflection on the nature of reality necessarily involves an encounter with challenging truths. Vipaśyanā practices draw attention to aspects of life that most people manage to ignore, facts that are difficult and confusing. It is another reason why śamatha meditation is a necessary basis for vipaśyanā: emotional integration acts as a buffer for vipaśyanā's challenges to the sensitive ego.

The present time has been called the age of anxiety, but it is triggered by the same old reality: the impermanence that sits in the background of people's experience in all times, places and cultures. It is the obvious fact that because everything always changes, you must eventually be separated from all that you love. Your grasping to keep what you like, your efforts to avoid what you don't like and your attempts to make painless all the inevitable changes in your life all provoke anxiety: in your heart you know that these strategies are doomed.

Buddhism teaches that an even deeper insecurity arises because people misunderstand the nature of impermanence. If you only looked it in the face for once and understood its positive significance, you would be liberated from anxiety and unlock a fuller, more enjoyable experience of life. This looking is direct vipaśyanā meditation. If sustained, it will enable you to accept the nature of impermanence and to embrace the fact of change in a creative way. Its fruition is a life of freedom from all hope and all fear, a gateway to a new kind of existence. It is expressed in Tibetan Buddhism, for example, as the ḍākinī[67] who dances joyful and naked wearing human bone ornaments and a necklace of human skulls. With her dishevelled, waist-length hair and her skin flushed with excitement, she drinks deeply from a skull. This disturbing image, both attractive and frightening, conveys something of the nature of insight. Imagine yourself in her place – decorate yourself with bones, laugh, dance and drink intoxicating juice from that cup – and you'll feel how totally fearless she is. Fear in all ages is conditioned by anxiety about death, by fear of that which cannot be known by the conditioned and reasoning mind. The Buddha, who wanted his disciples to achieve this insight into impermanence, said to them calmly as he passed away, '(Just like my life) all conditioned things are impermanent – so practise diligently with mindfulness.'[68]

To meditate on impermanence means constantly noticing the quality of impermanence in your experience and constantly placing your attention on it. This sounds as simple as anything can be, and it is. But since impermanence is a feature of every experience without exception, actually doing it is quite challenging. Assessing every experience takes effort and persistence, especially at first. This is partly because the activity of recognizing impermanence in everything is not what you are used to doing. It will probably feel very counter-intuitive; and as it may also seem very challenging to see dissolution everywhere, there may be much emotional resistance. Furthermore, impermanence itself is multidimensional: things are not simply impermanent – they're impermanent in all kinds of ways. How is this page of text impermanent? Is it because sooner or later it will rot away, get torn or be spoiled by a bookworm or a greasy thumbprint? Or because the person looking at it is similarly going to fade away? Or because the visual sensation in question is extremely momentary? Or because the process of recognition is similarly short-lived? Or because all the myriad other physical and mental processes involved when 'I' 'look at' 'a page of text' are also transient? It is all these and more. You just have to dive in to the practice and get accustomed to its atmosphere. With practice comes the ability to see impermanence in all things quite naturally, even though you must still maintain your effort.

Any of the practices described so far can be used as a medium for developing insight once the essential method is grasped. For example, insight practice can be taken up as follows using mindfulness of breathing as a basis.

Method

Sit well, sit still, be in touch with the body and feeling; and when you are ready, let your attention settle finely on the sensation of in- and out-breaths. Let go into the simplicity of the practice until you are completely absorbed in the present moment of each breath, inducing access concentration or dhyāna.

You can start vipaśyanā just as you start noticing the detail of the constantly changing qualities and sensations in the spotlight of your awareness. The spotlight sometimes narrows to a pinpoint and sometimes illuminates a wider expanse. The sensations, along with various thoughts, impulses and feelings, arise and pass away like bubbles approaching a waterfall and then floating downstream. Notice these in as much detail as you can and see how they are all momentary, all impermanent, none

continues overleaf

ever-lasting. You will see that as soon as you manage to pinpoint something, it has gone or changes into something different. Don't be confused because this doesn't seem to make sense; know that that is how it is and be fascinated as you are drawn closer in to the actuality of it.

Relax: relaxation helps to maintain the shifting focus. Be so open that you lose all assumptions about what will happen and be so clear that you see precisely what is happening. Keep this up as well as you can, for as long as seems useful. Don't try to force perfection; just learn and practise again as soon as you can. As the approach becomes more familiar, extend the length of practice sessions to an hour or more.

Just Sitting is also a good medium for meditation on impermanence, as long as our mindfulness is undistracted. It works in the same way as with the breath: being open to what arises in experience and seeing its impermanent nature. The quality of the practice is much more open, with the spotlight opened right out to exclude nothing. This is an excellent way of deepening awareness of impermanence, and helps one to integrate the practice with general mindfulness and walking meditation. A number of related practices such as reflection on death focus on our emotional resistance to impermanence, drawing attention to the inherent dukkha, that is suffering, of unawakened existence. These will be explored in Chapter 9.

Because it is all impermanent, nothing is fixed or independent. Here the universal characteristic of non-selfhood arises out of impermanence. Things have no self – no substance or essence – because there is nothing in them that continues; they are completely impermanent. Every part of every material object is constantly changing, and therefore cannot have a fixed, consistent nature. Nowadays everyone is supposed to know that things aren't as solid and fixed as they appear. You're taught about atoms and molecules at school, and this, supposedly, has revolutionized humankind's conception of solid matter. However, you still tend to regard your car, bicycle or mobile as permanent, fixed entities rather than as a collection of components screwed or welded together. If any are damaged or lost, the immediate response may be highly emotional: you don't usually accept it calmly even though you know that it was inevitable at some point. You have come to rely on them for happiness, even security, as if they were permanent and substantial.

Emotional attachment creates an internal image of this 'thing' that is very different from the reality of coexisting, changing components. You look at all material objects with different forms of attachment, whether it's the food on your plate, a landscape, an electronic device, a journey or an article of clothing. You think of everything as though it existed independently and separately – almost as though it had a kind of 'self'. But actually, no thing is any more than an assemblage of its conditions. Nothing can exist independently of everything else.

A clear perception of this reality requires much reflection because the unconscious false assumption that physical things have a kind of essence, and our internalized image of that, isn't obvious. But if, using this kind of meditation, you closely examine the way you see yourself and other people, it will become clearer that this is what you do. It is one of the central insights of the Buddha. Your attitude, like mine, tends to be that 'I am what I am', that somewhere, beneath the facade of daily life, you never really change. Somewhere deep inside you have an image that you're eternal. This part of you, you unconsciously think, remains aloof and unchanged by the incidental phenomena of life. You may have the same unwitting attitude towards others, feeling that behind their everyday persona is 'the person themself', pure and incorruptible. 'Jerry hasn't changed a bit since I first knew him', you may think. And in a way, rather like those parents who treat their grown-up offspring as though they were still small children, perhaps your image of this essential Jerry comforts you. But it is delusional: though you may feel that people don't change, they do; and the process is continuous and unstoppable.

Your feeling of having some kind of permanent essence may be supported by a strong experience you had in the past that revealed a deeper aspect of existence. It may have been drug-induced, but that doesn't invalidate it; what counts is the view of existence you formed from it. It might have been a spontaneously arising visionary or mystical experience, and it would be natural in our culture if you felt yourself to be in the presence of God. There are big, ready-made labels for such deep experiences, and what else are you to use? The experience is far bigger than you, and there are no adequate words to explain it. Buddhism (which has plenty of its own concepts) points out that the ultimate nature of reality cannot be expressed in words, indeed cannot be understood at all – at least not by the ordinary mind. This is Perfect Wisdom, the 'wisdom beyond words'.

Although Buddhism sees the idea of a 'self' as delusional, it would be superdelusional to believe that you've got no self of any kind. The experience of self is important for human development, without implying narcissism or selfishness. Indeed, your sense of 'who I am' includes ethical standards that prioritize the welfare of others over your own. So whatever the ultimate truth about self may be, it isn't automatically something bad. You certainly experience a self; and in the first part of life, you needed it as you formed your individuality and became a relatively confident and integrated adult. In this sense, śamatha development is a stage during which you strengthen the very qualities with which you construct an illusory self, only to see through the illusion later with vipaśyanā. But there is no good way to bypass it.

What you strengthen through meditation and ethical Dharma practice are positive qualities such as effectiveness, feeling good about your life, discipline, a capacity for kindness and so on. As selfishness decreases, they naturally get stronger. Even so, there isn't any 'self' that possesses those qualities, no thing that corresponds to the feeling of 'me'. It's noticeable whenever your mind becomes tinged by certain emotions that you start to feel 'me' very strongly. You feel that 'he insulted ME' (angry) or that 'I want her' (intense craving) or you ask, 'Do you like ME?' (fear of rejection). In this kind of state 'me' definitely seems to mean something. You also have a very strong idea of the other person in such states of mind, though they maximize the likelihood of that particular idea, right then, being delusional. Vipaśyanā meditation eventually destroys the delusion that you actually are, or have, a permanent, unchanging self, and thereby removes the tendency to react in that kind of way.

This is progress! But expressing this in terms of 'destroying the ego', as people sometimes do, obscures the subtlety of what is involved. The practice of ethics and meditation can reduce the neediness that accompanies a wrong view of self. Ethics puts others' needs first, making your own less important even to you. As will be seen in the next chapter, the higher dhyānas can bring insight by thinning out the contrast between a sense of self and a sense of other. Generally everyone feels that there's a subject *here* in relationship with an object over *there*, a perception that parallels our strong identification with self. It highlights a sense of separateness, reinforcing the idea of 'me' and the accompanying tendency to strong emotional attachment. Insight dissolves this seeming division: it becomes clear through direct seeing that there is, in actuality, no real distinction between what is experienced and the one who experiences.

In another way, śamatha practice relaxes the same tension. As you get absorbed in the breath, for example, you start forgetting the artificial distinction between the body and 'you'. You transcend delusion to some extent, which is very satisfying: you're freed from some selfish needs and you become stronger, less driven by primary negative emotion. The urge to incorporate objects into yourself (craving) and to counter objects you find threatening (hatred) decreases. Progress through the dhyānas goes along with an increasing attenuation of the subject–object distinction. In the highest arūpadhyānas, where there is only the very subtlest distinction between perceptions of mind and matter, selfness and otherness almost merge. When this attenuation connects with insight, these are called vipaśyanā dhyānas.

In that way śamatha thins out the duality between you as a subject and the objects you experience as being separate from you. Vipaśyanā alone has the power to dissolve it finally and forever, but śamatha and vipaśyanā can be seen as intertwined rather than completely separate methods of making spiritual progress. Mettā Bhāvanā, not traditionally considered to be a vipaśyanā meditation, is a fine illustration of this. The commentarial tradition states that it can lead only to dhyāna, not to ultimate liberation. In the system of meditation practised in the Triratna Buddhist Community, it is generally seen also as a śamatha practice (generating 'positive emotion'). Yet it cannot be categorized exclusively as such, as in cultivating mettā you develop dispassionate well-wishing towards others; you have no selfish interest in wanting them to be happy. In developing this kind of unselfishness in your emotional life, Mettā Bhāvanā transforms attitudes to you as a subject and others as objects. It works, in other words, with the tension that always exists between subject and object. When developed to an advanced degree, especially in combination with the other three brahma vihāra practices, *no distinction* is experienced between you and others: you wish happiness equally for all quite unreservedly. Bodhicitta and Great Compassion come from the full, insightful development of this experience: the non-selfhood of others is perceived, with love, as keenly as your own. The whole field of compassion comes alive when others are seen not as fixed personalities but as 'empty', open-ended beings who can change and develop without limits. All are seen as the potential Buddhas they really are.

Chapter nine

....

Spiritual death and spiritual rebirth

The five basic methods of meditation

Our meditation system uses a set of five meditations that the Buddha taught. Later tradition correlated these as antidotes to the 'five poisons', the principal obstructions to Awakening[69]. As Table 13 shows, mindfulness of breathing counteracts doubt (initially in the sense of indecisiveness and hesitation); Mettā Bhāvanā counteracts hatred; the contemplation of impermanence counteracts craving; the six-element practice counteracts conceit; and the contemplation of conditionality counteracts ignorance. The last three of these practices will be introduced in this chapter. Just Sitting and sādhana meditation, the remaining core practices, are not directly mentioned in the early scriptures, but their precursors were taught by the Buddha in the form of mindfulness practice and the *Buddhānussati*, the 'recollection of the Buddha', which will be explored in Chapter 10.

This chapter will explain how to understand and to practise these five basic meditations, along with various other practices that stem from them, as ways to develop insight into reality. We shall start with the practices already explored as śamatha meditations: mindfulness of breathing and Mettā Bhāvanā.

Our focus shifts now to the final stages of the system of meditation: spiritual death and spiritual rebirth. The first is the collapse of delusion that comes about when you look deeply into reality with the concentrated, positive mind of the first two stages, Integration and Positive Emotion. That collapse triggers a transformational process so fundamentally different from what went before that it is in effect a new life. It is a renaissance or spiritual rebirth.

....

Spiritual death and spiritual rebirth

133

Table 13: The five basic methods of meditation

	Meditation method	Counteracted poison	Main correspondence in the Triratna system of meditation
Five basic methods	(1) Mindfulness of breathing	Doubt	Integration
	(2) Mettā Bhāvanā (Brahmavihāra)	Hatred	Positive emotion
	(3) Contemplation of impermanence	Craving	Spiritual death
	(4) Six-element practice	Conceit	
	(5) Contemplation of conditionality	Ignorance	
	Sādhana		Spiritual rebirth
	Just Sitting		

Spiritual death comes when you have a glimpse of nondual reality and see, even if just for a moment, the insubstantiality of everything and feel what that means. Yet it is not any kind of reasoned understanding: in that moment you know nothing at all about what is happening. You see only that all your ideas are empty, that even what you assumed was your actual experience is actually ideas, assumptions and concepts superimposed on indescribable reality. That knowledge, and that reality, is experienced intensely.

Every kind of insight meditation leads to this realization. All mundane, unrealized experience contains a subject, which you assume has some real substance but which, in reality, has no substance at all, and an object, which you assume to be some kind of thing but find, on closer examination, to have no stable existence. There is *no* actual thing! And every judgement, conclusion, feeling and emotion that takes place between this non-existent subject and object lacks reliable meaning when it is based on such a fundamental mistake. The real meaning lies deeper: when their emptiness is seen, the assumed subject and object naturally drop away, leaving peace, space and depth of understanding.

This really is like death, because it is the end of the world as the ordinary unawakened mind knows it. It can feel like death too, but then the idea of death affects people in different ways. It's understandable if spiritual death sounds like a frightening idea, but the actual experience may be blissful, beyond words, awe-inspiring or indeed anything. It can't be predicted. Descriptions sound abstract, and of course they are. The experience is overwhelming, yet it is subtle, so that, oddly, it may easily be missed or discounted. It's not as though something new has sprouted into existence: something has merely been revealed as *not being there* that you had unthinkingly assumed was there. It's become clear that your delusions were never reality, but suddenly to see without them is peculiar. In a strange way, there's nothing to change – and everything in the world carries on pretty much as normal. It's simply because you've seen, for a moment, that all of it is insubstantial and not really there in the way that you will continue, once the vision fades, to assume it to be. To others who have not had this experience it can only sound abstract. To avoid feeling misunderstood and creating confusion, you are strongly advised to be very careful about how and to whom you communicate about it.

Insight experience comes right into the centre of your life, and from that point you are subtly guided by it. Such experiences of spiritual death take us within the orbit of the dharma niyāma (discussed in Chapter 7), the special nature of conditionality connected with Awakening that is inherent in life. Shifting into that orbit is the start of spiritual rebirth. With the right preparation and conditions, the practices detailed in this chapter will stimulate and quicken the potential for both spiritual death and spiritual rebirth.

Mindfulness of breathing

Mindfulness of breathing (*ānāpānasati*) was introduced at a basic level at the start of this book, and further explanation is found in the *Ānāpānasati Sutta*.[70] The Buddha presents in it an extended method of doing the practice, in sixteen stages and based on the four fields of mindfulness described in Chapter 3.

The stages begin in a similar way to the two 'counting' stages in the basic practice and then take progressively deeper approaches to mindfulness of the breath, using, first, body awareness; second, feelings; third, one's current mind-state; and, fourth, the ultimate realities of impermanence and insubstantiality. Each of the four fields includes four substages, or tetrads, making sixteen stages in all.

Ānāpānasati in sixteen stages

Bhikkhus, when mindfulness of breathing is developed and cultivated, it is of great fruit and great benefit … And how? … here, a bhikkhu, gone to the forest or to the root of a tree or to an empty hut, sits down; having folded his legs crosswise, set his body erect, and established mindfulness in front of him, ever mindful he breathes in, mindful he breathes out.

1. *'Breathing in long, s/he understands, 'I breathe in long'; or breathing out long, s/he understands, 'I breathe out long.'*

2. *'Breathing in (or breathing out) short, s/he understands, 'I breathe in (or out) short.'*

In the first tetrad the experience of **body** (kāya), the basis for the meditation, is made increasingly familiar through repeated re-establishment of awareness in the breathing. These substages are equivalent to the initial counting stages of the practice as explained in Chapter 1: counting after the more 'relaxed' outgoing breath and counting before the more 'energizing' incoming breath. You can understand 'long' and 'short' in the text as referring literally to the length of the breath. The simple exercise of assessing the length of each breath will definitely help to keep awareness on it. This assessment is also aided by the counting.

You may also find that assessment useful for checking how aware you actually are of each individual breath. When you are paying full attention, you notice a breath's detail; and when appreciating the sensation in a detailed way, you observe that the breath feels 'long' because it has noticeable duration in time. The experience is also generally more relaxed, which enhances the sense of duration. On the other hand, when the practice deteriorates and you become somewhat insensitive and unaware, the breathing acquires an automatic in-out quality that feels 'short': there is no appreciation of detail; the experience makes little impact and is soon forgotten. This is also the 'short' breath, and noticing the distinction is an excellent way to stay focused.

To summarize: instructions 1) and 2) together make up the first stage as you check the quality of attention to each breath. Once you have become settled, this establishes the basis for the remaining stages of the practice, which are called 'trainings' from this point on in the sutta. In the first of these, the sensation of the volume of breath moving in the body is distinguished from the general body sensation:

3. *'I shall breathe in (and breathe out) experiencing the whole body [of the breath].'*

You now give attention to the whole breath body as in the third, no-counting stage of the basic mindfulness of breathing meditation. You also make sure that it is actually the touch sensation of the breathing you are experiencing, as distinct from a thought about the breath or a sensation that actually comes from somewhere else in the body.

4. *'I shall breathe in (and breathe out) tranquilising the bodily formation (kāyasaṅkhāra).'*

Here you allow the touch sensation of the breath at the nose-tip, upper lip, navel – or wherever you focus it – to relax the body at that location and then to relax the whole body. The effect of this is to further calm the breathing, which becomes very still and conveys a new depth of peace to the mind.

Note that the air cannot be experienced directly; throughout this section the emphasis is on the sensation of the breath as it touches the body.

Second comes a set of four trainings incorporating awareness of **feeling** (*vedāna*) into the meditation. Feeling is important as a connector in ānāpānasati meditation: it allows an intimacy that helps you to know and to direct the mind. Here the first two instructions are about connecting with the seeds of dhyanic rapture and bliss. These reflect the early awakenings of dhyāna as you move beyond the five hindrances into deeper integration.

5. *'I shall breathe in (and out) experiencing rapture' (prīti).'*

Contacting feeling helps you to enjoy the meditation. You become inspired and feel creative in doing it. This leads into, and can actively be directed towards, the beginnings of dhyanic rapture.

6. *'I shall breathe in (and out) experiencing bliss (sukha).'*

The concentration can deepen and becomes very peaceful if you can let go of attachment to the excitement of prīti. So here the training is in finding a new appreciation of the deep joy of sukha and diving into that while letting go of prīti. (We looked at the relationship between rapture and bliss in Chapter 6.)

Now come two instructions that quieten the mind further as you get even more deeply and intimately immersed.

7. *'I shall breathe in (and out) experiencing the mental formation.'*

Feeling does much to form your general state, your mood: the word is *citta*, a process the Buddha calls here 'the mental formation'.[71] With the arising of prīti and sukha, the experience of feeling has deepened. Now with each in- and out-breath you familiarize yourself with its continual effect on the mind's general state, with the continual responses of liking and disliking and the constant tendency for these responses to turn into craving and aversion.

8. *'I shall breathe in (and out) tranquilising the mental formation.'*

From this arises a new intimacy and trust in which liking and disliking lose their power and your mood becomes profoundly relaxed.

Third comes awareness of feeling having deepened the experience of *citta*, the heart/mind, and there follow four instructions relating to mindfulness of its various moods and states. Here the truthful experience of these mental states becomes crucial in the deepening of integration. This emphasis on truth sparks the beginnings of liberation.

First come two instructions: knowing the mind and gladdening it.

9. *'I shall breathe in (and out) experiencing the heart/mind.'*

Here you acknowledge the truth of your actual mental (heart) state, here and now. The content of each individual thought becomes clear. Though the effect is to deepen *śamatha*, the focus on the truth of experience sounds a preliminary note of insight (vipaśyanā). You are coming more and more into a position where you can enquire into what is really happening.

10. *'I shall breathe in (and out) gladdening the heart/mind.'*

Knowing and accepting the truth of your experience, especially its feeling aspect, brings some independence from its ups and downs. This strengthens the ability to exert a positive influence on the mind. You now train in gladdening the mind, encouraging its positive qualities, and align yourself with *pramodya*, the joy of engagement with ethical and spiritual practice. You rejoice in your amazing potential and present good qualities. (We shall look at prāmodya later in this chapter in the context of meditation on conditionality.)

11. *'I shall breathe in (and out) concentrating the heart/mind.'*

Feeling good about what is true enables a more wholehearted involvement and thus concentrates the whole being.

Then, as you bring the mind together, you are able to start freeing it.

12. *'I shall breathe in (and out) liberating the heart/mind.'*

Acknowledging the truth, you begin letting go of identification with moods and mental states as 'mine', as though they somehow belong to you. This is the beginning of the vipaśyanā process.

The fourth and final tetrad exclusively concerns vipaśyanā – in terms of both spiritual death and spiritual rebirth – as you progressively let go of clinging to fixed notions of self and world and align with the true nature of experience. Here each breath is accompanied by a contemplation that encourages direct seeing of an aspect of the unfolding Awakening experience.

13. *'I shall breathe in (and out) contemplating impermanence.'*

Things such as body and breath sensations come to an end in time, so reflecting on their impermanence may entail some questioning of the extent to which, as you experience each breath, you are holding on to an idea of its duration over the past, present and future. You might question whether your perceptions of them persist unchanged or whether new perceptions arise to replace them. If new ones arise, can you see that happening? When you reflect and see that experiences don't last – because they are impermanent – you may be forced to recognize that you don't actually know what it means for something to persist, let alone to pass from the present into the past. This may seem like riddle-making, but in meditation this kind of enquiry arises out of deep and honest wonderment at the primary, unquestioned facts of our experience. It has the power to amaze, humble, relax and give us confidence in the profound simplicity that unfolds from this enquiry.

14. *'I shall breathe in (and out) contemplating fading away.'*

15. *'I shall breathe in (and out) contemplating cessation.'*

16. *'I shall breathe in (and out) contemplating relinquishment.'*

In these final stages, the truth emerging from this engagement with impermanence enables you to contemplate the possibility of standing back from perpetuating all reactive tendencies whatsoever. From there it is possible to contemplate bringing involvement in that kind of activity to a complete standstill. Finally, it is possible to completely let go of all identification with saṃsāra, the state that perpetuates ignorance and the deluded emotionality springing from it. These contemplations are also inspired by the profound liberation that is simultaneous with the relinquishment of saṃsāra.

The Brahma Vihāras

The second of the five basic methods – Mettā Bhāvanā, which counteracts the mental poison of hatred and represents positive emotion in our system of meditation – is at the root of a family of practices all of which can be a basis for reflection on insight and for the direct seeing of reality. These are the four brahma vihāras, 'the dwelling-places of Brahma' or 'divine abodes'. They are also known as the Sublime or Limitless Abodes (*aparimāṇa*), so called because there is supposedly no limit to their intensity and scope. The four practices are Mettā Bhāvanā, Karuṇā Bhāvanā, Muditā Bhāvanā and Upekkhā Bhāvanā, *bhāvanā* meaning cultivation or development.

Mettā Bhāvanā

When introducing Mettā Bhāvanā meditation, I said that mettā is wishing for others' happiness independent from your personal interest. This emphasis is made deeper and broader by practising the three other methods: compassion (*karuṇā*), which is an active, loving response to others' suffering; sympathetic joy (*mudita*), which is that response in relation to others' happiness and good fortune (which only too often evokes jealousy or resentment); and equanimity (*upekkha*), which is a loving and insightful response based on applying *pratītyasamutpāda* so as to illuminate how others' joy and sorrow arise from conditioning factors that govern all beings.

Not everyone realizes that cultivating love (metta) begins a process that bestows real insight (*prajñā*). Maybe you think that emotion is so subjective and irrational that it's an unreliable basis for anything. However, metta and compassion (karuṇā) are ethical responses. This kind of training entails seeing your ego-based motives and responses for what they are. It means valuing others' needs as at least equal to your own. All this leads us into the existential territory of vipaśyanā meditation: who am I, what is the nature of existence, who suffers, who gains and who loses? And metta does it in a way that is embodied, that is not merely a thought or intention. Its basis in bodily experience effectively counters the alienation and abstraction that can sometimes result from purely awareness-based vipaśyanā methods rooted in ānāpānasati or satipaṭṭhāna. Acting with friendliness and kindness towards someone doesn't make them do what you'd like them to, but it definitely helps them. Eventually you come to wonder how valuable your own preferences really are. When self-interest is sacrificed, there's often a greater benefit and a sense of a deed well done that humbles you when you recall how rigidly you usually insist on your wants.

In engaging with these meditations it is helpful to watch out for the 'near enemy', the negative quality you easily assume is the real thing. The 'far enemy' is the simple opposite – hatred in the case of metta, cruelty in the case of karuṇā – which obviously isn't what you're trying to cultivate. Much more difficult to notice is the 'near enemy' *pema*, emotional attachment, which people often confuse with metta. Your practice is then coloured by a desire to get something back from the deal, such as recognition, love or friendship – or you make a connection that's soppy and sentimental. It is very likely that there's at least some pema in the mix, so these meditations are partly about refining that, growing out of need-based responses to others and moving towards a free, spontaneous desire to give and help. That is a long-term project, but meditation is a good way to make it happen.

Once you've established a stable focus in the meditation, you can include some reflection on the insubstantiality of the person generating the mettā (i.e. you, the self that is lacking in selfhood) together with the equally non-self person who is currently the object of your mettā. If you understand this, you'll find that the reflection works well to deepen and sustain the feeling of mettā – this is closer to how things actually are, so it makes the engagement more real. Having a mettā-filled mind is also just the right approach for vipaśyanā reflection: its 'immeasurable', unlimited quality works better than the usual critical, measuring attitude and its openness perceives more easily the absence of an inherent, permanent nature in things. It knows that real people are unfathomable and finds it natural to let go of the niggling wish that others should conform to our preferences.

Karuṇā Bhāvanā
Karuṇā is that same mettā-mind encountering suffering. It is a tangible shift into something a little more grave. The practice begins with developing mettā (by practising the first or the last stage of the Mettā Bhāvanā meditation). Once you have established a feeling of mettā, you call to mind someone who is suffering, whether through illness, bad luck, their own actions or for any other reason. If someone you know is suffering, you can meditate on them. However, when you are new to the practice, it is ill-advised to choose someone whose suffering is strong, especially if that is likely to evoke despondency or depression in you. The point, after all, is to develop the positive emotion of karuṇā, a quality that requires strength as well as sensitivity. The result of the practice should be positive emotion. Of course, it is painful when you encounter others suffering, but cultivating love helps you to be sensitive yet unafraid of their pain.

Don't try directly to develop compassion: that involves too much advance assumption of what having compassion will mean in this particular case. That understanding will come later. For now, you just develop mettā, and exposing yourself to their suffering will do the rest. For compassion must be a living response arising when you open in a friendly way to someone in the circumstances of their suffering. This is how it works. The response always shifts and goes deeper when friendliness encounters suffering. A special kind of response comes as it becomes clear that something needs to be done. You'll naturally want to do anything you can to relieve their suffering.

With that awareness of suffering, you develop friendliness in turn towards a good friend, a neutral person and an 'enemy'. You then finally 'break the barriers' (as tradition calls it) by imagining all five persons together – you, the suffering person, your good friend, a neutral person and an enemy – and cultivate it equally towards each one. You then radiate that equality of positive emotion to all beings throughout the universe.

Table 14: Stages of Karuṇā Bhāvanā meditation

1. Develop mettā towards yourself.
2. Develop mettā towards a suffering person.
3. Develop compassion towards a good friend, aware of their suffering.
4. Develop compassion towards a neutral person, aware of their suffering.
5. Develop compassion towards an 'enemy', aware of their suffering.
6. (i) Develop equal compassion towards all four people, aware of their suffering.   (ii) Extend compassion towards all beings throughout the universe, aware of their suffering.

Compassion is a more demanding emotion than mettā. Generally, people find the sufferings of others, even very slight degrees of suffering, difficult to handle, and acknowledging that can help you to gain insight and to transform your less skilful responses. It is likely that you sometimes find others' sufferings irritating, and even get angry. People frequently associate suffering with failure and feel reluctant to admit that failure can happen. Acknowledging that someone suffers can even feel as though you are letting him or her down. 'Oh, she's OK – there's nothing wrong with her. Leave her alone and let her get on with her own life," you might say. This can be an easy way to dismiss the matter from your mind, a way to justify your neglect of someone's needs. It is humiliating to see such patterns in yourself; but if you make them conscious, you'll want to change them.

Most people seem profoundly confused about suffering, but these meditations and their underlying outlook and values offer effective ways to clarify your views and to resolve the issues in your heart.

Looking into others' pain and developing love and compassion allows you to face with sensitivity and generosity the reality that people around you are all suffering in different ways. Avoiding it leads to indifference and eventually even to cruelty, the traditional 'far enemy' of compassion – when you see the suffering but do not care.

If you look into your day-to-day experience of others, you may recognize compassion's two 'near enemies': sentimental pity and horrified anxiety. It is possible to mistake these emotions for compassion, or at least to regard them as something vaguely beneficial, even though they have very negative effects. Both stem, again, from the pain and confusion of seeing others suffer. And this time you are unable to respond warmly and open-heartedly because you are immediately preoccupied by your *own* discomfort. Sentimental pity is a strategy for covering up your own discomfort at seeing someone suffer. Typically you produce a stock, socially acceptable response, some expression of feeling sorry for them. However, their suffering is actually confusing you. You are feeling inadequate and unable to face up to their situation. This pseudo-pity may be subtly combined with (unconscious) contempt and condescension, expressed in responses such as 'Oh, I'm *so* sorry to hear that' but without any real care. You might even think you are genuinely being compassionate. (And maybe you are, but here I am challenging some common unconscious strategies.) Communication will feel false to another person when you clearly aren't interested in helping yet continue to make assurances that you are. And once this sentimental kind of reaction becomes settled, it gradually slides into coldness and neglect. A characteristic of true compassion, and an encouraging result of the practice, is that you feel like taking the trouble to actually get involved.

Horrified anxiety is another counterfeit form of compassion. It originates somewhat differently. There is no avoidance and you fully allow yourself to experience the discomfort aroused by someone else's suffering. But you become so strongly affected that you lose perspective and then cannot bear to meet the energy rising up in you. You stiffen in horror and are unable to be of any actual help, even if you busy yourself in all kinds of 'helpful' ways. Since you are feeling *something* apparently for them, you may tell yourself that this is a kind of compassion; but this again is missing the reality of their suffering. So it's important as you practise and relate to others in life generally to look out for these distorted responses and to use them as opportunities to change deep-seated tendencies. In the case of pity, you should recognize the need to acknowledge and engage with your actual feelings. In the case of horror, you must recognize the anxiety in your mind and see the way it prevents you from really sympathizing or being of any use. Of course, in the protected space of meditation, the response can be simpler and more direct: you can more easily recognize emotions and work to transform them.

> Even if for the moment you cannot actually help anyone in an external way, you should meditate on love and compassion constantly over the months and years until compassion is knit inseparably into the very fabric of your mind.
>
> Dilgo Khyentse Rimpoche [72]

Mudità Bhàvanà

Sympathetic joy (mudità) poses a very different kind of test. When you encounter someone who is happy and whose life is going well, how do you feel? Does it depend on your mood? The natural, healthy response is just to feel glad, and this is mudità: rejoicing in others' happiness and well-being. It is connected to the Buddhist practice of rejoicing in merits, in which you outwardly celebrate the good qualities of another person. Just try telling someone how much you appreciate them and you'll be surprised at the effect.

Start the practice as before by developing loving-kindness. Then direct it towards someone who is particularly happy and joyful at the moment. Inwardly congratulate them on their good fortune. Wish that their happiness continues for a long time. As you continue, the initial feeling of mettà will eventually transform into a sympathetic, appreciative joy.

Then, develop this feeling towards a good friend, a neutral person and an enemy in turn, dwelling particularly upon their good qualities and their happiness.

Next, 'break the barriers': equalize the feeling of sympathetic joy between you, a happy person, a good friend, a neutral person and an enemy. This of course means that you rejoice in your own merits and appreciate your *own* good qualities in just the same way that you appreciate those of others.

Finally, as with the other brahma vihāras, radiate the emotion outwards towards the whole universe of sentient beings.

Table 15: Stages of Mudita Bhāvanā meditation

1. Develop mettā towards yourself.

2. Develop mettā towards a happy person, creating sympathetic joy.

3. Develop sympathetic joy towards a good friend, aware of their potential for happiness.

4. Develop sympathetic joy towards a neutral person, aware of their potential for happiness.

5. Develop sympathetic joy towards an 'enemy', aware of their potential for happiness.

6. (i) Develop equal sympathetic joy towards all four persons.
(ii) Extend sympathetic joy towards all beings throughout the universe.

The opposite or 'far enemy' of mudita is resentment or envy, which for most of us is, unfortunately, not really that far away. We'll quickly agree that someone's good fortune is a matter for rejoicing but somewhere inside we'll still feel resentful about it. Sometimes it's our own habitual lack of self-esteem that prompts this. If this pattern is strong in us, then Mudita Bhāvanā is a good way to strengthen our appreciation of our own merits.

The 'near enemy' of mudita often seems like genuine appreciation, but it actually takes a sentimental kind of pleasure in someone's happiness. There's a vicarious satisfaction in which you are, in a way, avoiding really connecting with them. You may express great admiration while having no awareness of, or even interest in, them and their lives. Your satisfaction comes from your *idea* of their happiness; it's a kind of complacency. This needs looking into honestly, as it's easy to fool yourself that you are appreciative and their great friend and supporter. As with the other obstacles, the key is to pay closer attention to the person themself, to appreciate what *their* experience is like.

Upekkhā Bhāvanā

Equanimity (upekkhā) is the fourth and final brahma vihāra practice. It combines all the others, and your work with mettā, karuṇā and mudita provides its foundation. Upekkhā as a brahma vihāra is more transformative than the dhyāna factor of the same name. The upekkhā dhyāna factor arises from deep integration in meditation; it is the equanimity that comes from a tranquil mind. Upekkhā brahma vihāra comes from a powerful combination of other-regarding love and insight into conditionality.

The practice starts, once again, by developing mettā. Choose a neutral person. Consider, and try to engage emotionally with their suffering *and* their joy. At the same time, bear in mind that they themselves have at least partially created their own life. Reflect on conditionality and the nature of existence generally; respond with mettā to this person's conditionedness. As you engage with them in this way, you may develop a quality of patient understanding that is the beginning of equanimity. Then choose a good friend, then an enemy, and work with them in the same way, deepening the sense of equanimity.

Break the barriers by applying equanimity equally to each person, including yourself, and then take that out to all beings everywhere regardless of what sort of person they are or how they may see you. This raises the sense of equanimity to a universal level: developing upekkhā can unite and synthesize the experience of the three other brahma vihāras to the highest possible degree. It can become all of them interacting without any bias or partiality – with equal love, equal compassion, equal joy in the joy of others.

Table 16: Stages of Upekkhā Bhāvanā meditation

1. Develop mettā towards yourself.

2. Reflecting upon their suffering, their joy and their conditionality, develop mettā towards a neutral person, creating equanimity.

3. Develop equanimity towards a good friend, aware of their conditionedness.

4. Develop equanimity towards an 'enemy', aware of their conditionedness.

5. (i) Develop equal equanimity towards each person, including yourself.
   (ii) Develop equanimity towards all beings throughout the universe.

Upekkhā is subtle as well as universal, a quality that is illustrated by its traditional 'near' and 'far' enemies, which superficially may appear similar. The 'near enemy' easily mistaken for upekkhā is neutrality and the 'far enemy' is cold indifference; the distinction is between passive and active indifference. Cold indifference is opposed to the universal insightful love that is upekkhā. With neutrality, however, the feelings are so weak that it seems pointless to take any interest – which could seem like a kind of equanimity if one were emotionally disconnected. The neutral person is chosen in the second stage *because* you have little or no feeling for them. This does not imply dislike; it means that the relationship is subtle for some reason. In the case of the 'near enemy', neutrality or pseudo-equanimity, you are again avoiding really experiencing this person. Maybe your conditioning leads you to find them boring or uninteresting.

By providing a medium through which you can work with these responses to people experienced as neutral, the brahma vihāras allow you to extend yourself beyond the current limitations of your imagination. Upekkhā teaches you about empathizing with others and makes you better able to imagine how people you normally find uninteresting might feel. It's helpful to work with the other brahma vihāras beforehand in order to gain more experience of appreciating others' suffering and joy. It is extremely useful to be aware of the enemy within of indifference, whether active or passive. After all, most of the thousands of people you encounter are more or less neutral, just as most of the thousands of feelings you have each day are neither pleasant nor painful. Seeing the subtlety of indifferent responses helps you to engage more with feeling, to work with subtler shades of pleasure and pain and to appreciate subtler emotional responses in all your dealings with people.

Upekkhā is the development of equality of positive emotion towards all living beings. This doesn't just mean 'equal' positivity, which sounds lukewarm, but a love that is equally strongly felt for all. True equanimity arises in its fullness when mettā, karuṇā and muditā have already been cultivated: Karuṇā Bhāvanā and Muditā Bhāvanā help to free us from attachments and aversions, which keep us preoccupied with self-serving interests and dilute our interest in others. True equanimity requires us to be emotionally independent of whatever pleasures and pain others create for us. Karuṇā and muditā arise from the 'no-strings' desire for the happiness of others that is mettā – karuṇā is mettā's response to pain and muditā is its response to pleasure. Upekkhā does not see others in terms of pleasure or pain, even though it embraces both compassion and gladness. Its response is rooted in a deep realization that our sufferings and joys arise from a vast complex of conditioning factors. Everyone inherits the effects of past actions, our own and those of countless others, on our present mental states. Upekkhā combines the most positive of emotions with insightful clarity, and emerges from seeing the universality of action and consequence. Accepting the way things actually are, you realize a new kind of connectedness between yourself and others and a new kind of kindness.

> At the moment, when we are happy ourselves we feel that that
> is enough, and if other people are unhappy it is not our problem.
> When we are unhappy, we just want to get rid of whatever we find
> unpleasant as soon as possible – we neither remember nor care that
> others might be unhappy too.

> This is all delusion. Instead, put others in your place, and put yourself
> in their place. This is called *'exchanging yourself with others'*.

> Dilgo Khyentse Rimpoche[73]

Bodhicitta meditation

Imaginatively exchanging ourselves with others, or putting ourselves in another's place, is an important Mahāyāna Buddhist practice and is especially associated with the teacher Śāntideva. Śāntideva felt that the Buddha's motivation had not been to end his own suffering but to help all beings to end their suffering. From the viewpoint he made famous, the Dharma practice is really about cultivating bodhicitta, the attitude of an awakened being. [74] Insight practice cultivates seeing the real nature of self and world; the real nature of the self is that it is completely unfixed. This means that you can change and that the main obstacle is your own selfishness. So can you reverse that tendency in your relations with others and go beyond valuing yourself over them? That would accord with the approach to insight found in the brahma vihāra practices.

The Pali and Sanskrit word *Bodhi* means Awakening; *citta* means heart, mood, mind-state or attitude. Thus Bodhi-citta is the essence of the awakened or enlightened mind. At a more ordinary level, it is the love that arises for others when you know, out of deep experience of suffering and joy, that what everyone really needs is Spiritual Awakening. Though it is a response to the unsatisfactoriness of life, bodhicitta is not pity; nor does it involve a sense of superiority. It sees, through insight, that others are more important than you are; it is the very essence of friendship and love.

In practice, bodhicitta begins with a mature and responsible attitude towards others and deepens from there as you come truly to understand what moves others and are able to give more. It is not just a meditation method; bodhicitta can be generated effectively only in the context of actual relationships. However, meditation is a helpful part of its development because its method generates an intense awareness of the quality of all our relationships. It draws to your attention the fact that you are in a constant relationship with the whole of nature with all its diverse life forms. So what you do, say and think eventually affects them all, just as their lives also indirectly affect you. Through this meditation you therefore immerse yourself in your connection with the reality of others' existence and generate true compassion for them.

The method is to make contact, with a loving mind, with the billions of other unenlightened beings around you and to cultivate empathy with them. This is done by recollecting that insofar as they do not know how to overcome their own negative emotions, people's lives are relatively, if not extremely, unsatisfying. Realize this by looking with mindfulness and love into your own behaviour and acknowledging the influence on you of all these beings and by taking responsibility for your influence on them now and in the future. Take this step not in some theoretical way but by generating a deeply felt love for them. Every part of the practice – making contact, reflecting on their situation, cultivating empathy, acknowledging their influence and taking responsibility for your own – is done by generating loving-kindness, or mettā. Take courage too from the inspiring individuals who make up the age-old Dharma practice tradition. Recollect that countless practitioners have cultivated bodhicitta to completion and gained full Enlightenment. This particular bodhicitta practice comes from Indo-Tibetan Buddhism and is often referred to as *tonglen*.

Reflect that the aim of bodhicitta is to transform all activity and bring it into the path of Enlightenment. You develop a completely new vision of existence by reflecting with strong compassion on the lives of other beings with their vast range of fortunate and unfortunate existences. However fortunate or privileged they are, all are vulnerable, just as you and your all-too-human parents are. All of us do all kinds of regrettable things and thereby get mired in all kinds of stresses and difficulties. As you reflect in this way with mettā and compassion, there will arise a hopeless desire to do something for them (which includes you). With this sense of longing, repeat the following prayer internally to yourself many times (traditionally, one practises regularly over weeks and months until 100,000 repetitions have been made).

> Beings who are one's own mothers and fathers wander in the Saṃsāra and with unbearable longing we all produce the unbearable longing to become a Buddha.

The words themselves do not particularly matter; this is a translation of a traditional verse. You need to get to the point with the repetition at which you become fully immersed in the meaning and the vastness of its implications. See that it's true that entanglement in saṃsāra makes for our ruin, that the only effective solution is for all beings to practise the path to Awakening and therefore that this has always been our most heartfelt desire. When you connect to this fully, the feeling becomes so unbearably strong that it may burst out in new, unexpected ways.

Once you have connected with the desire, which is bodhicitta, you are ready to go on to the next phase: linking it with the breathing. It will probably help to keep the connection with the feeling of bodhicitta if you continue to repeat the verse, for now at least.

You need to connect with what in traditional Buddhism are called 'roots of goodness'. People are basically good. Trust in their basic goodness despite possible mixed feelings about that and imagine that your own goodness, such as it is (there is no need for pretence – this is just how it is), mixes with the outgoing breath and like moonlight penetrates the whole world, conferring happiness on all beings.

This imaginatively represents the prayer; it is a dramatization of what you'd really like to happen. Just let go into the outward breath, ignoring any doubting voices that say this is peculiar and irrational. It is because this meditation method is non-rational – is beyond mere good reasons – that it can have such powerfully positive effects. Simply go along with the feeling and give the practice your all, all the while refining the overwhelming desire for the well-being of others.

Then, on the incoming breath, imagine all beings' obstacles to Awakening, their negative emotions and views, assuming a dark, shadowy appearance and coming right into your own body, where they are purified by your good qualities. You shouldn't take any of this literally – no one can literally assume the results of others' actions – but the imagery offers a powerful way to engage with the reality of others and the many terrible problems that exist. It should feel like facing the real world.

> One should reflect [and say]: 'May all beings enjoy happiness and the cause of happiness! Whatever freedom from suffering they enjoy may it never come to an end! May their minds dwell in the immeasurable equanimity which has neither near nor far, attraction nor repulsion!'

> This one should say and reflect upon many times.[75]

Once the bodhicitta method is familiar, it can become a vehicle for all kinds of reflection, insights and transformations of attitude. Table 17 shows a number of ways that our breathing can channel awareness of ourselves and others together with love and compassion, giving and receiving.

Table 17: Stages of bodhicitta meditation

	Receive (breathe in) →	← Give (breathe out)
1	My experience of the incoming breath →	← My experience of the outgoing breath
	I, as experienced in the present moment, taken in with the in-breath →	← My response to my present experience, let out with the out-breath
2	The presence of all others and their influence on me, with the in-breath →	← My influence on others, with the out-breath
	The fact of others' suffering, with the in-breath →	← My response to others' suffering, with the out-breath
3	The fact of others' good influence, with the in-breath →	

Contemplation of impermanence

In a general way we looked at the third of the five basic methods, the contemplation of impermanence, an antidote to the mental poison of craving, in Chapter 8. Now we shall consider some applications of this practice.

In this practice, you are presented with an opportunity to look clearly into impermanent reality, which you continually keep at arm's length, and to use the wisdom sword to cut through your craving and realize your potential for freedom. The first method for looking our existence straight in the eye is contemplation of death. This is the aspect of impermanence that probably produces the most anxiety. The approach a practitioner chooses depends on his or her temperament. As will soon be apparent, it can be important to get the method right, so get advice from a spiritual friend before proceeding. These methods are only for those who are reasonably happy and mentally stable.

The first and the most radical method is to contemplate the changes in a dead body as it decomposes. For this, one should employ an actually present corpse, as tradition recommends, and not rely on one's imagination, photographs or movies. Especially the latter two play on negative aspects of the imagination as warped by the largely commercial obsessions of horror and thriller films. You need to get away from such associations with death, for they will ruin the positive potential of the contemplation. A real dead person has a very different atmosphere around them: it's sobering but not intrinsically frightening or panic-inducing. If you do experience fear or panic, it is important that you have the calm and mindfulness to see how those emotions derive from your own mind, to see their connection with various kinds of craving and to let them go. You really need a calm, open atmosphere to do this. You need to be able to believe that what is before you is real, so that you can take the experience in properly and reflect on its truth. In the end, the best conditions will usually be found in the natural opportunities you get. Dearly loved friends, family and all of us do of course die, and then it is natural and appropriate to spend time with the body, whether in hospital, at their home or at the undertaker's.

I can recommend this, having spent time with my parents, other close relatives and personal friends after their death. The *idea* of seeing a corpse may well arouse fear or loathing, but the actual experience of simply being with someone you have known who has died cannot be anticipated. If you can settle and concentrate, it can evoke a deep sense of clarity that is the antithesis of craving. You can really learn something. I recommend focusing on impermanence, reminding yourself that this person was recently animated and alive and that although that's how you are yourself right now, after a while you too will die. Your body will appear similar to this. Moreover, this will happen to everyone without exception.

Some Buddhist (and pre-Buddhist) cultures simply left human remains to decompose naturally or to be eaten by wild beasts. This is how it was in the Buddha's day. Meditators would go to the charnel ground and just observe the bodies scattered around in various states of decomposition. Recollecting that their own body would go through similar processes after death, they would continually acknowledge their experience and come to terms with whatever emotions might arise. The effect would be a conquest of craving and anxiety through a deep sense of inspiration.

To benefit from this method you'll need to be an emotionally positive and well-balanced individual not prone to moroseness or gloom. This proviso is particularly necessary in the modern West, where many people are disconnected from their experience. The 'recollection of impurity', as this meditation is sometimes called, really does require a firm basis in mettā and mindfulness in order to avoid the danger of sustained depression and mental instability. If that basis is there, you'll be able to engage with the intuitively incredible fact of death with a real interest and inspiration. Difficult emotion is sometimes to be expected, but if reflection is developed gradually within a balanced and happy frame of mind, the effect will be to loosen our small-minded clingings to security and create a sense of confidence and freedom.

The second way of meditating on death is simply to recollect, on the basis of a concentrated state of mind, that one day you are going to die. Everyone knows this, of course, but that knowledge is more or less theoretical; it's extremely difficult for us actually to realize and fully accept the fact. Start the practice with a good session of Mettā Bhāvanā, taking the practice towards at least access concentration. Then simply reflect on the fact of death over and over again. You can repeat inwardly the word 'death' or a phrase such as 'death will come', which will keep the fact of death in mind. The main thing is to keep a receptive and peaceful attention to this idea until the fact of death really does sink in.

A third meditation in this group, an extended variant of the 'phrase' approach outlined above, is to repeat slowly to oneself these 'Root Verses' from the Bardo Thodol (*The Tibetan Book of the Dead*):[76]

1

Oh now, when the Bardo of Life upon me is dawning!
Abandoning idleness – there being no idleness in a devotee's life –
Entering into the Reality undistractedly, listening, reflecting, and
    meditating,
Carrying on to the Path knowledge of the true nature of
    appearances and of mind, may the Trikāya[77] be realised:
Once that the human form has been attained,
May there be no time or opportunity in which to idle it away.

2

Oh now, when the Dream Bardo upon me is dawning!
Abandoning the inordinate corpse-like sleeping of the sleep of
    stupidity,
May the consciousness undistractedly be kept in its natural state;
Grasping the true nature of dreams, may I train myself in the
    Clear Light of Miraculous Transformation:
Acting not like the brutes in slothfulness,
May the blending of the practising of the sleep state and actual
    waking experience be highly valued by me.

3

Oh now, when the Dhyāna Bardo upon me is dawning!
Abandoning the whole mass of distractions and illusions,
May the mind be kept in the mood of endless undistracted
    samādhi,
May firmness both in the visualising and in the perfected stages
    be obtained:
At this time, when meditating one-pointedly, with all other
    actions put aside,
May I not fall under the power of misleading, stupefying
    passions.

4

*Oh now, when the Bardo of the Moment of Death upon me is
  dawning!*
*Abandoning attraction and craving, and weakness for all worldly
  things,*
*May I be undistracted in the space of the bright enlightening
  teachings,*
*May I be able to transfuse myself into the heavenly space of the
  Unborn:*
The hour has come to part with this body, composed of flesh and blood;
May I know the body to be impermanent and illusory.

5

Oh now, when the Bardo of Reality upon me is dawning!
Abandoning all awe, fear, and terror of all phenomena,
*May I recognise whatever appears as being my own thought-
  forms,*
May I know them to be apparitions in the intermediate state;
*It has been said, 'There arrives a time when the chief turning-
  point is reached;*
*Fear not the bands of the Peaceful and the Wrathful, who are your
  own thought-forms'.*

6

Oh now, when the Bardo of taking Rebirth upon me is dawning!
One-pointedly holding fast to a single wish,
*May I be able to continue the course of good deeds through
  repeated efforts;*
May the womb-door be closed, and the revulsion recollected:
The hour has come when energy and pure love are needed;
*May I cast off jealousy and meditate upon the guru, the Father-
  Mother.*

7

Oh procrastinating one, who thinks not of the coming of death,
Devoting yourself to the useless doings of this life,
Improvident are you in dissipating your great opportunity;
*Mistaken, indeed, will your purpose be now if you return empty-
  handed from this life:*
Since the Holy Dharma is known to be your true need,
Will you not devote yourself to the Holy Dharma, even now?

The Bardo Thodol, or Liberation through Hearing in the Intermediate State, is so entitled because its content is for reading aloud as an aid to someone who has recently died and is now undergoing the after-death state. According to the Bardo Thodol tradition, the inner dying process can take some days to complete in the case of long-term practitioners of meditation, and this enables them to benefit from direct instruction relating to the states of consciousness they may be experiencing.

More generally, the notion of an intermediate state (*bardo*) refers to the way in which our experience is continually transforming from one state into another. In the Bardo Thodol six main transitions are highlighted: the waking state, dreaming, the state of higher meditative consciousness, the moment of dying, the visionary period after death when the freed imagination displays itself fully and the phase of rebirth. Each of these transitions is very significant from a spiritual point of view, affording special opportunities for insight and personal transformation. This becomes clear as you do this practice, as well as in the times after meditation, as the mind gradually becomes accustomed to the vision that it evokes. The vision itself is profoundly transformative. Through it you connect deeply with the fact that you will die, will continue to undergo experiences stemming from your actions in life and will be reborn accordingly. You also see that you are vividly alive and acting right now. It is a call to awaken in this life as part of a far bigger picture.

Here is a brief explanation of some important points in the verses.

Verse 1 is exhorting you not to be distracted, because life's opportunity is short and of great importance. Focus instead on the path of reflection and insight, especially recalling that you currently perceive appearance, not reality. So give up laziness and practise wholeheartedly until Awakening.

Verse 2 draws attention to the extraordinary fact that consciousness continues after you fall asleep, often without any acknowledgement or even memory on the part of the mind when it wakes up. This is an important and much neglected transition: you spend a third of your life asleep, and the text is urging you to use this time for spiritual growth by training in dream yoga. The aim of this training is to become self-aware in dreams, gaining access to a mental space that is more efficacious for personal transformation than the ordinary waking mind. Becoming aware that one is dreaming while still maintaining the dream state is hard to achieve: most people gain patchy results at best unless they practise intensively over a long period of retreat. However, everyone gets some result, and the simple benefit of extending mindfulness to the sleep state, whether it produces lucid dreams or not, is profound and highly recommended. What usually happens is that as you attempt to become self-aware in dreams and start asking the question 'Am I awake or not?' fairly often, you start to notice that it is unclear what it means to be awake. The 'I' sense continues into the altered consciousness of sleep; and there seem to be different gradations of sleeping and waking.

This raises fascinating, insight-provoking questions of identity. As you're reading now, no doubt the answer is clear enough if you ask, 'Is this a dream?', yet it is still a challenging question. Now try this. Look at your watch and ask, 'Is this a dream?', and over the next few days consciously ask the same question whenever you glance at your watch. Actions like this have a galvanizing effect on the mind, so a few nights later you may have the experience of looking at your watch *in a dream*. When in the dream you ask the question, you may suddenly realize that you are indeed dreaming. If the shock does not immediately catapult you into the waking state (tell yourself to relax – this happens every night), you could meditate, reflect on the Dharma or take (as my teacher once suggested) the best use of such an opportunity: go and find the Buddha and receive teachings from him. All this is possible in a dream because there is no hard, physical reality and no physical limitations. The physical world as experienced in a dream is completely mind-made, and you can change it into anything you want and go anywhere in it. This is very interesting; it raises questions about the nature of the waking reality that you feel contains inflexible limitations.

Verse 3 is urging you not to fall into distraction when you're meditating: this is such a fine opportunity, so don't waste it. Dhyāna is another altered state of consciousness in which great leaps of spiritual progress can be made. The 'visualising and the perfected stages' line refers to the traditional division between the stages of 'generation' – practice up to and including spiritual death – and 'completion' – the whole realm of spiritual rebirth.

Verse 4 takes us to the moment of death itself, that intense crisis in which one can be overwhelmed by fear and confusion about what is happening. Don't you have conflicting expectations of death – that it will be a blank, the complete end or that it will involve some kind of extraordinary transitional experience? Yet there is no way to know beforehand, and it will certainly be a time when you can panic or be overcome with dread. The verse is saying do not panic; do not faint, however intense this feels; stay awake and do not be distracted. Instead, pay attention to what is actually happening. This certainly implies that death is not the end. But you are being told clearly that it is time to let go of the connection with the impermanent body, which is at the end of its natural span. It is very difficult to let go, yet it must be done; otherwise you will pass unwillingly through the portal of death in a panic of grasping. You need to let go of that tight instinctive response and open up to the positive potential of this crucial moment, for you are now entering a space of 'bright enlightening teachings'. The quality of your experience at this juncture gives it the power to teach you profoundly, and even allows you to let go of saṃsāra altogether and achieve full Awakening, if only you are able to listen.

Verse 5 is about the state that arises after the swoon that often follows the crisis of death. It is analogous to the arising of the colour and liveliness of the dream state that manifests every night when waking consciousness 'dies' and you fall asleep. Indeed, another benefit of extending mindfulness into dream life is that you become familiar (in this close, experiential analogy) with the experience of dying and emerging into the bardo of reality. The experience of the bardo after death is said to be extremely intense in an unimaginably vast, expansive way. The archetypal visions of peaceful and wrathful Buddhas are awe-inspiring and terrifying by turns. The particular forms described in the Bardo Thodol are presumably not exactly what those from non-Tibetan cultures would experience, but you get a sense from their depiction in the Book of the Dead of how this experience could be for you. The message is again do not fear, stay awake and mindful – and know that, in a way that's beyond your current comprehension, *what you are seeing is your own mind*. The spiritual principle here is accepting the nature of reality as oneself, however difficult that may seem ('oneself' means here not in any egotistic sense but assuming from the start that self is merely an experience, empty and conditionally arisen like every other thing).

Verse 6 is concerned with the pressure to escape the unbearable intensity of the bardo and settle somewhere – anywhere. There is an intense desire for a home port, a body: it becomes too much being constantly adrift. You yearn for the anchor-point of a physical body. The verse counsels you to take care here and seek a situation in which you will be able repeatedly 'to continue the course of good deeds' – in other words, to practise and to continue on the path. The attraction to rebirth is overwhelmingly strong now, but you should resist being drawn into the open door of the nearest womb. Ideally you should, even at this point, decide not to be reborn but to continue practising here and now. But if you must enter the confusing currents of the ordinary world, exercise great discrimination about the situation you steer towards. Remember your spiritual goals and recall the example of your teacher, who has been both father and mother in the spiritual life.

Finally, verse 7 is exhorting you to stop dissipating the great opportunity that life affords and get on with deepening the practice.

A good way to start practising this meditation is to learn the verses by heart. The process of doing this is itself a way of doing the practice, for it instils the words deeply into the mind. The import of the verses reveals itself increasingly as you enter into a deepening dialogue with existential reality. It is good to be well prepared with Mettā Bhāvanā, and one way of doing this is to reflect on the verses within the final radiation stage of that practice, since all beings are constantly changing from one bardo to the next. However, more of an anchor may be needed if you are to stay with the moment-by-moment experience. So keep aware of the touch of the breath as you listen internally to the verses, perhaps combining this with developing mettā. Recite a verse to yourself three times so as to get absorbed in the meaning and then sit quietly for some minutes before going on to the next verse. Reciting the verses is an excellent way to begin any meditation.

Perhaps the most essential form of meditation on impermanence is the practice we explored earlier: reflecting upon the actuality of change. Established in a concentrated state of mind, heedfully observe your mental and physical state as the details change from moment to moment, always flowing on and on like a river. Observe objects in the outer world as, little by little, they age and begin to break up, always turning into something slightly different. Reflect upon the fact that things are never as solid and fixed as they appear to be. In this way, you move back and forth from reflection on impermanence to directly seeing it in experience.

> *The lovely flowers of turquoise-blue,*
> *Are destroyed in time by frost –*
> *This shows the illusory nature of all beings,*
> *This proves the transient nature of all things.*
> *Think, then, you will practice Dharma.*
> *The precious jewel that you cherish*
> *Soon will belong to others –*
> *This shows the illusory nature of all beings,*
> *This proves the transient nature of all things.*
> *Think, then, you will practice Dharma.*
> *A precious son is born;*
> *Soon he is lost and gone –*
> *This shows the illusory nature of all beings,*
> *This proves the transient nature of all things.*
> *Think, then, you will practice Dharma.*

Milarepa[78]

The six-element practice

The fourth of the five basic methods, **the six-element practice**, is an antidote to the mental poison of conceit (*māna*). This is a strongly held self-identification. Conceit is not so much a deluded conviction that you're wonderful as it is the universal assumption that 'I am me', that you know what you are and really believe that is you. This (completely normal) attitude is narrow and proud. There is no humility in relation to the vastness of being and time.

The six-element practice meditation is an investigation of what really makes up this self in terms of the elements of existence. Traditional societies throughout the world have viewed human experience in terms of earth, water, fire and air, to which some ancient Indian traditions added space and consciousness. These six elements describe the psychophysical reality of living, with all its variations of solidity, wetness, heat, movement, space and awareness. Here is everything you could possibly identify with as a self. The practice is to dwell on each element, seeing the way each manifests naturally in the world. Next, turning to its manifestation within your own body and mind, you reflect that you cannot regard this as your own. Then you let go of that deeply held conviction. In reality, you consciously created neither your body nor your mind, and have no control over their continual changes. So what aspect of your experience can you call 'me'? By wondering about this, you begin experiencing yourself more as a continually changing flux of processes. The practice ideally begins in the first dhyāna or access concentration, and you need to make sure that you are in a state of clear concentration and positive emotion. Then you reflect upon each element as follows, allowing (say) ten minutes for each.

The earth element represents everything that is perceived as solid and resistant. So first get a sense of that quality by recalling houses, cars, roads, trees and rocks outside in the world. Then come back to yourself and feel that same quality of relative hardness in bones, sinews, muscles, hairs, skin etc. Spend whatever time it takes to settle into a sustained mindfulness of the body's earth quality. This is also an image, or felt sense, that is not really describable in words. Now look into the real nature of this quality. Notice how you identify with bones, hair etc. as 'me' and think of them as your own. Connect with the feelings this arouses. If your hair fell out or went grey or if you lost a limb in an accident, wouldn't it somehow feel as though *you* had lost something? But though conventionally everyone regards these relatively solid parts of the body as 'mine' and feels strongly about that too, you cannot say that you actually possess them. Who possesses what? You have certainly played no conscious part in their creation. The earth element in your body naturally formed itself; your body grew automatically as you put food into it. You can't truly regard it as your own. As you will have to give it up one day, it is more as though you have borrowed it for a while. You cannot predict when or how you will die; but when that happens, the earth element in your body will once again become part of the earth element in the universe outside. It is the earth element now and it will be earth in the future too. The process doesn't involve a self at all, and doesn't need to – life works fine without one.

In many ways this is quite straightforward. It is just that normally you don't look into such things. It is easy to see that both the inside and the outside aspects of solid physical experience – you and the world you live in – have always had the same nature of earth. So conclude the stage of earth by sitting in acceptance of this basic reality and absorbing its lessons. This same pattern is followed in each of the six stages: get a sense of the elemental quality by recalling its form in the outside world; then feel that in your body; next feel how you identify with it as a self; then reflect that actually it cannot be a self – it is simply the element; and, finally, let go of the clinging to it as 'me'.

The water element refers to everything that flows downwards, that drops, that dribbles and splashes, that oozes, drips or forms into puddles. In the outer world, for example, there are seas, oceans and great lakes, rivers and streams, clouds and raindrops. In your body too there are many varieties of fluid, such as tears, joint-lubricant, sweat, urine, blood, mucus, saliva and digestive juices. Again, these have been 'borrowed' from outside. And again in the meditation practice you reflect that all will inevitably have to be 'returned' when the body breaks up and becomes part of the universe at large. Though you may feel a sense of identification and possessiveness about it, you nevertheless cannot claim any ownership of the water element.

The fire element comprises everything to do with *relative* heat and cold. In the outside world there is, above all, the sun. There is hot and cold weather; there are volcanoes, hot springs, frozen seas, glaciers and icebergs. Nearer home, there are man-made fires and heating systems. In you there is the heat caused by physical exertion and the digestive processes. Heat is involved in the body's processing of food as its fuel and in the need for clothing to keep your body warm or cool. But when death comes, your body will gradually lose all its heat. That was not your own warmth in any real sense, for it is entirely dependent upon the natural processes involved in maintaining a body. In accepting this fact, in coming to terms with it, let the fire element go back, in imagination, to its source. Without clinging on to it, without thinking that it is yours, let the borrowed fire element in the body return to the fire element in the universe.

The air or wind element is movement – every kind of vibration within or streaming through space – just as the wind blows everywhere and air flows in and out of countless bodies giving life and breath. Imagine the all-pervasiveness of air and its vast movements through space, along streets and round city buildings, across immense land masses – mountains, oceans, deserts – sometimes hot, sometimes cold, sometimes moving, sometimes still, carrying with it fumes and fragrances of every kind, coloured by every kind of light and shade. You can also notice the movements of the various 'winds', the vital energies, breath and inner motions within your body. Reflect too that you cannot possess the air or the process of breathing or any other body process in any way. You cannot reasonably identify yourself with the air element any more than you can with earth, water or fire. It is not yours. It is not you. It is not part of you. You are not part of it. Even though you *feel* it is yours – and feel, above all, that you would be losing something if its movement in your lungs were to stop – you try to realize the illusion and to accept that these are impersonal processes that go on regardless of any feelings of ownership. It is just the air element.

The space element is that in which all the other elements exist, and it is infinite: you are surrounded by this inconceivable vastness containing all beings and all worlds and within which your body occupies a minute portion. You also enclose space, forming a 'me'-shaped space that you identify with. But consider: how can this space actually be yours except in a very temporary sense? Like the other elements, it is 'borrowed' just for the time that the body exists. At death the earth, water, fire and air elements dissolve and the space that was 'me' will simply join the space which was 'not-me'. At this point in the meditation you reflect on this, accepting that you cannot identify yourself with the space your body occupies. It is just space.

The consciousness element refers to your experience of perceiving things, whether they are thoughts, memories perceived in the mind or objects perceived through the senses. That is, you see, hear, smell, taste and touch things – and also think, feel, remember and imagine things. All these are ways in which you are conscious of things. So first get a feeling for this element; get an image. Notice all the perceptions coming and going. Attend, for example, to sensations in the body, listen to sounds, notice ideas and notice the quality of perception itself – the feeling of it, the way it happens. Recall that other people, animals and the great diversity of other beings around you are also conscious in various ways. Ask 'Is this me or mine?' It would be unusual if you didn't think of the mind as somehow 'me'; but look closely into it and see how that can actually be, what that claim really means.

As with the body, this experience of consciousness has arisen naturally without having been wished for; and it changes in every instant in the same way. You can sometimes control its direction, just as you can more or less control your arms and legs – but you can't control its nature or the way it arises. As this consciousness too is beyond our control, then even it cannot be yours. Once again, you need to accept the fact that consciousness is 'borrowed' and one day will return to the consciousness element as similarly 'owned' by other beings throughout the universe. What exists is just consciousness: it is neither your consciousness nor something other than consciousness. What exists is ownerless consciousness, and that is fine: owners are unnecessary, just abstractions. The interaction of ownerless elements, including consciousness, is simply how everything works, how it actually is.

Thus in the six-element practice you dissolve attachment to every aspect of experience and abandon the limiting idea of a self. If no self is found in earth, water, fire, wind or consciousness, where else can it possibly be? Sit in meditation experiencing the constantly changing phenomena of the mind, seeing that it is all perfectly ownerless. Even the perceiving mind is an impersonal process, and the whole phenomenon of personal existence, though thoroughly real as an experience, is conditioned by that partial view of reality.

There is no doer of a deed
Or one who reaps the deed's result;
Phenomena alone flow on –
No other view than this is right ...

The kamma [i.e. action] of its fruit is void;
No fruit exists yet in the kamma;
And still the fruit is born from it,
Wholly depending on the kamma.

For here there is no Brahma god,
Creator of the round of births,
Phenomena alone flow on –
Cause and component their condition.

Buddhaghosa[79]

This meditation is deeply stimulating and very effective. The way in which I have described it emphasizes *anattā*, non-self. But the practice is often done as a kind of reflection on impermanence – especially in terms of the dissolution of the body, the emphasis being on the fact that death will come. The physical elements are not yours because at death earth will decompose, water will flow away or dry up, your body will lose its heat and become cold, the breathing will stop and you will no longer occupy this you-shaped space.

A poem by Sangharakshita demonstrates the spirit of this approach and gives an inspiring positive emphasis on the unlimited nature of space, the indefinable nature of mind and the mystery of being.

The Six Elements Speak

I am Earth.
I am rock, metal, and soil.
I am that which exists in you
As bone, muscle, and flesh,
But now I must go,
Leaving you light.
Now we must part.
Goodbye.

I am Water.
I am ocean, lake, rivers and streams,
The rain that falls from clouds
And the dew on the petals of flowers.
I am that which exists in you
As blood, urine, sweat, saliva and tears,
But now I must go,
Leaving you dry.
Now we must part.
Goodbye.

I am Fire.
I come from the Sun, travelling through space
To sleep in wood, flint, and steel.
I am that which exists in you
As bodily heat, the warmth of an embrace,
But now I must go,
Leaving you cold.
Now we must part.
Goodbye.

I am Air.
I am wind, breeze, and hurricane.
I am that which exists in you
As the breath in your nostrils, in your lungs,
The breath that gently comes, that gently goes,
But now I must go,
For the last time,
Leaving you empty.
Now we must part.
Goodbye.

I am Space.
I contain all,
From a grain of dust to a galaxy.
I am that which exists in you
As the space limited by the earth, water, fire, and air
That make up your physical being,
But now they have all gone
And I must go too,
Leaving you unlimited.
Now we must part.
Goodbye.

I am Consciousness.
Indefinable and indescribable.
I am that which exists in you
As sight, hearing, smell, taste, touch and thought,
But now I must go
From the space no longer limited by your physical being
Leaving nothing of 'you'.

Table 18: Stages of the six-element practice

Earth (paṭhavī-dhātu)	Water (āpo-dhātu)	Fire (tejo-dhātu)	Wind (vāyo-dhātu)	Space (ākāsa-dhātu)	Consciousness (viññāṇa-dhātu)
Recall the earth element's solid quality in the world outside, in rocks, trees, houses.	Recall the water element's cohesive quality in the world outside, in dew, tap water, rivers, oceans.	Recall the fire element's quality of hot and cold in the world outside, in sunshine, icicles, kitchen stoves, hot drinks.	Recall the wind element's quality of movement in the world outside, in wind, traffic, crowds, bird flight.	Recall the space element's quality of location and containment in the world outside, in place, space, containment, dimension.	Recall the conscious element's quality of awareness in the world outside, in the senses and the mind, in perceptions of others.
Experience the same quality in you, in bones, sinews, skin.	Experience the same quality in you, in tears, saliva, perspiration, blood.	Experience the same quality in you, in heat, cold, warmth, coolness.	Experience the same quality in you, in breath, blood circulation, subtle energies, the movement of limbs and thoughts.	Experience the same quality in you, in the sense of having a personal space that contains the body's parts and organs, of particular places in the body.	Experience the same quality in you, in experiences of seeing, hearing, smelling, touching, tasting and mentally perceiving (feeling, knowing, noticing, recognizing etc.).
Notice that the real nature of solidity is not you, not yours, is not in you and does not contain you.	Notice that the real nature of liquid is not you, not yours, not in you and does not contain you.	Notice that the real nature of fire is not you, not yours, not in you and does not contain you.	Notice that the real nature of wind is not you, not yours, not in you and does not contain you.	Notice that the real nature of space is not you, not yours, not in you and does not contain you.	Notice that the real nature of awareness is not you, not yours, not in you and does not contain you.
Reflect that at death the basic experience of solidity, which cannot be owned, will have to be relinquished anyway.	Reflect that at death the basic experience of liquidity, which cannot be owned, will have to be relinquished anyway.	Reflect that at death the basic experience of hot and cold, which cannot be owned, will have to be relinquished anyway.	Reflect that at death the basic experience of movement, which cannot be owned, will have to be relinquished anyway.	Reflect that at death the basic experience of location and containment, which cannot be owned, will have to be relinquished anyway.	Reflect that at death the basic experience of awareness, which cannot be owned, will have to be relinquished anyway.
Accept this basic reality and learn its lessons.	Accept this basic reality and learn its lessons.	Accept this basic reality and learn its lessons.	Accept this basic reality and learn its lessons.	Accept this basic reality and learn its lessons.	Accept this basic reality and learn its lessons.

There is no one from whom to part,
So no goodbye.

Earth dissolves into Water,
Water dissolves into Fire,
Fire dissolves into Air,
Air dissolves into Space,
Space dissolves into Consciousness,
Consciousness dissolves into – ?

HUM

Sangharakshita, Summer 2002

Whichever of these slightly different approaches is taken, the six-element practice will almost certainly throw you back on the lack of clarity in your views. When your view is unclear, you sit to do the meditation but waste your energy wrestling with intellectual doubts. You need to feel confident that – to give just one example –when your body no longer exists, your present mode of consciousness will no longer exist. If that is clear, you'll be happy simply to dwell on that idea and let it soak in, transforming your whole being. If not, you are likely to lose your concentration and be tossed this way and that, thinking 'Well, does consciousness *end* at death then? How can I be sure that it does? Am I expected to know that from experience?' and so on. You'll be thrown back into the stage of reflection, which of course is valuable too. Pursuing prajñā, you encounter truth-concepts that are like that irritating speck of grit in an oyster that is supposed to cause the formation of a pearl. You need to be able to trust these somewhat indigestible nuggets of wisdom, at least provisionally. The questions that arise and the need for clarification are very necessary and not to be suppressed, even though they are not meditation. As I have said, some intellectual preparation and study is necessary for a practice like this, as well as some contact with an experienced teacher.

Stūpa visualization
There are several practices connected with the six elements in Buddhist tradition. For instance, there is a section on the four elements in the body awareness portion of the *Satipaṭṭhāna Sutta*, the primary teaching

on mindfulness. One that I have found to be very effective is the visualization of the six-element stūpa. This employs simple images similarly to the kasiṇa meditations. Various forms of the Buddhist stūpa are well known from Nepal to Japan. They were originally monuments for holding remains of Buddhas or other saints, and are often honoured by circumambulation as though they themselves are actually Buddhas.

The stūpa represents the six elements because they are what you were produced from at birth and what are given up at death. The classic stūpa consists of six symbols representing the elements assembled vertically from ground level, with the symbol for earth and the other elements arranged above one another in order of subtlety. Occasionally only four, or even just two, elements are represented. The Buddha is said to have designed the first stūpa in the simplest possible form. Asked what kind of burial mound would be appropriate after his death, he silently folded a yellow robe into a cube shape, placed it on the ground and laid upon it his upturned begging bowl. So the yellow cube symbolizes **earth**. Square shapes express some of the qualities of earth: solidity, strength, support and so on. As you visualize this, you are not required to get a clear, stable picture; you need only get a sense of the symbol's earthy quality – some feeling, sensation or other impression that enables you to dwell easily on the earth element. Use direct sense experience as well, noticing, for example, the solid floor supporting you or the hardness of your teeth and nails.

Then, above the cube, imagine the **water** element, represented by a white dome or a globe like the full moon. The water element certainly expresses the quality of flowing, but then fire and air also flow. The distinctive elemental character of water is its cohesion. So the white sphere is like a bubble or a drop of water that in nature holds together as though by magic. To engage more with the water element, notice the wetness of your eyes and tongue – and also swallow, triggering an experience of the liquid nature throughout the body. Getting more deeply involved with the elements can be unusually satisfying, and there is perhaps some relief in being able to acknowledge a level of experience that is present in everyone before they are even born. You were intimate with the elements well before you were self-aware. The energy of earth is stable and unmoving; the holding energy of water moves only inwards and downwards. With the fire element, the energy radiates only outwards and upwards. Fire is symbolized by a bright red cone, rather like a flame. As you allow this new form and its colour to influence you, the qualities of temperature and light in your present experience become clearer. Notice, for example, that your eyes are actually receiving light and that your body is warm.

Above that, the symbolic element of **wind** or air is a pale green dish shape, delicate like porcelain. At least that is how I imagine it. You are free to play around with these forms. They can be lively and even comical. I see wind like a sensitive satellite dish, picking up sensations and vibrating with them, or like a pale green frisbee juddering as it skims through space.

The air element is not about air as a gas; here 'air' is a symbol for movement. Thus the alternative term is 'wind' (Sanskrit: *vāyu*), which expresses that essential moving characteristic as found in the pulsing of the blood, the tidal flow of breathing and the progressive relaxation of the muscles as the body stills in meditation posture. In deep meditation, the movements within the body's subtle energy channels become apparent. These are known as winds (*lung*); and if you watch very closely and gently, the play of thoughts and emotions is sometimes observable in particular parts of the body, riding as though upon flowing breezes. Everything that exists, inside and outside, not only has movement but also often moves in different ways at the same time. Even if something could be completely solid and stable, which is impossible, it would still be moving, for the planet itself is moving in several ways. Thus the element air spreads out simultaneously in all directions.

No movement, temperature, coherency or stable matter can exist without **space** to contain it. The element of space is symbolized by a single point, a 'drop' that is gently flaming, showing its vibrant living quality. Elemental space is not a vacuum. The single point symbolizes the fact that space is everywhere all at once: it is infinitely out there and is also infinitely 'in here', in the endless microspaces in the body. Notice how distinctly (and also how emotionally) you are sometimes aware of the particular location of various parts of your body. Everything has to take place somewhere. So this 'flaming jewel

Buddhist Meditation: Tranquillity, Imagination and Insight

drop', as it is sometimes called, stands for the fact that this space *here* is one of an infinite number of possible points.

Finally, the element of consciousness or **awareness** is the 'space' within which space itself happens. This is not to imply the solipsism that 'it's all in the mind' but to offer the simple reminder that whatever the ultimate truth may be, earth, water, fire, movement and space are all experienced by the mind. So you can call this the element of 'experience'. Philosophical questions about whether or not the elements take place outside experience and exactly how they might are interesting to contemplate but they are not relevant here. This creates a rare and precious opportunity to dwell on the experience of experiencing itself. Is this sensation 'me' or is it 'mine' – or what is its nature otherwise? This most basic of all the elements is symbolized by an open sky, which is clear, blue and boundless.

In fact, the practice begins here. Start with the blue sky and let it contain, in order one by one, the symbols for earth, water, fire, wind and space. The stūpa of the elements, surrounded by clear blue sky, symbolizes your entire experience and response to a world filled with many sensations of resistance, cohesiveness, temperature and movement in space. As you connect with each element through its symbol, experience its special qualities directly in the body as much as you can; appreciate its particular life-energy, its role in your existence. Once the connection is there, you reflect that, despite your habitual attitudes, this characteristic of your body experience is not something that you can possibly own in any literal way. Its nature is completely free, and you can let go fully into that quality of freedom. For that letting go to be meaningful, you need to acknowledge and to feel the particular ways you grasp experiences and sensations as 'me' or 'mine'. These may not be obvious at first. In the end, the practice requires a commitment to the deepest reflection and a genuine desire to enquire into what really happens in the thoughts and feelings you have about yourself and the world. This will come in time if you want it to – depth and skill come from applying these reflections in a sustained way.

Ending the practice is done in a special way, to reflect that profound process of letting go. Just as they were conjured up in the blue sky of awareness, now the elemental symbols all dissolve back into it.

In turn from the top, each symbolic form melts and dissolves into the element beneath: the space element melts down and is absorbed into the wind element, then wind melts into fire, fire into water and water into earth. The earth element melts into the sky. The sky itself dissolves like mist, and gradually you return once more to the direct experience of the six elements as again and again they emerge, solidify and dissolve in the course of daily life.

If pursued, this meditation will develop real, living connections to the elements and with nature generally, helping you to live more ethically and in harmony with the earth. If you want, it can become a special eco-Dharma practice. All Buddhist meditation methods can have this kind of effect, since all of them include mindfulness of the physical body. The same feeling of harmony arises as you engage with other Buddhist methods such as ethics, wisdom, right livelihood, study and community. It is not surprising that the stūpa is held in such high honour in the East, representing as it does both the wonders of the natural world and the amazing nature of the Buddha which can be awakened in all of us.

Table 19: Stages of stūpa visualization

1	Building up elements one by one into stūpa image	Blue sky symbolizing…	Consciousness
2		Yellow square or cube symbolizing…	Earth
3		White disk or sphere symbolizing…	Water
4		Red triangle or cone symbolizing…	Fire
5		Pale green crescent or dish symbolizing…	Wind
6		Rainbow dot or drop symbolizing…	Space
7	Dissolving elements one by one	Space element (drop) dissolves into	Wind
8		Wind element (crescent) dissolves into	Fire
9		Fire element (triangle) dissolves into	Water
10		Water element (disk) dissolves into	Earth
11		Earth element (square) dissolves into	Consciousness
12		Consciousness element (sky) dissolves	

Fig. 1: The stūpa

The contemplation of conditionality

Fifth in the list of five basic meditations is contemplation of conditionality, through which one examines, and tries imaginatively to experience, how our world of the 'ten-thousand things' comes into being. *Paṭicca Samuppāda*, or dependent arising, the Buddha's central teaching, is often misunderstood as being about causation (or mistranslated thus, as in the quotation below) but is really about conditionality. Four walls (or at least three) are a condition of having a roof; a roof would be impossible without them. Walls are a condition for the existence of roofs but do not cause them; roofs depend on walls but are not caused by them.

Contemplating this principle as universal eventually reveals a view of existence that eradicates the mental poison of spiritual ignorance (*avidyā*). This ignorance is far more than simply not knowing: it is our deep-seated tendency not to want to know about the real nature of things.

[Ānanda:] How deep is this causal law, and how deep it seems! And yet do I regard it as quite plain to understand!

[The Buddha:] Say not so, Ānanda, say not so. Deep is this causal law, and deep it appears to be. It is by not knowing, by not understanding, by not penetrating this doctrine, that this world of men has become entangled like a ball of twine, become covered with mildew, become like muñja grass and rushes, and unable to pass beyond the doom of the Waste, the Way of Woe, the Fall, and the Ceaseless Round (of rebirth).[80]

As Ānanda observes, the Buddhist teaching of conditionality is in a way very simple. Yet, as the Buddha insists in reply, its implications are vast beyond imagination. Events and objects arise when the appropriate conditions are present; if certain conditions are present, then particular events have the potential to arise, not others. The Buddha summarized the teaching as 'this being, that becomes' – in other words, if *this* phenomenon arises, then *that one* can arise on the basis of the first. You tend to think that a thing has just one cause, but every object and event you experience is the product of innumerable conditions, some immediate to the event's arising, others far away in its historical background. This applies especially to the ideas in your mind at this moment.

The factors that have conditioned your ideas are innumerable. You have them not only as a result of reading them but also because of other ideas you have had and other books you have read – in fact all the ideas that have ever arisen in your mind have played some part in the evolution of your present set of ideas. Yet all that is just one aspect of the situation. A seemingly infinite number of factors have conditioned this book itself. It has come about partly because I wanted to write it – so there's a lifetime's worth of factors particular to me – and partly because people are interested in its content. That interest comes from movements in our culture springing from the actions, thoughts and emotions of many generations. Moreover, each one of these has conditions that also go infinitely back in time. Meditate on the universality of conditionality. See the conditions that you experience in your own life going further and further back, wider and wider out. Reflect how all of them have affected your particular experience of the present moment. Consider how the present moment also carries all that richness with it and even now conditions the infinite future.

According to the Buddha, there are two modes of conditionality, two ways that events can arise. These are represented by the wheel of dependent origination and the spiral of liberation and describe sequences of change that inevitably occur in our being and consciousness – in the first case when you do not try to develop towards Enlightenment and in the second case when you do. The concepts of the wheel and the spiral give an overview of the whole process of conditioned existence and its relation to the realm of the Unconditioned.

The wheel of dependent origination is the closed circle of conditioning factors within which you normally live unless you become aware of your situation and attempt to break out of it. To summarize the main conditioning factors: you see that your ignorance of the true nature of things has necessarily led to a particular kind of birth, and it has inevitably led, as you have a body with senses and feelings, to the predicament of craving. This tends to produce an addiction to particular ways of behaving; and over a lifetime, these habits usually become so entrenched that you never break out of the patterns. The entrenched patterns condition the next life, in which you of course tend to repeat them. The spiral of liberation moves upwards, representing the fact that this predicament can be transcended. Just because you have feelings does not mean that you must react with the craving, hatred and other unskilful emotions that are binding you to the wheel. You can break out by developing a positive series of conditions – faith in yourself, śamatha, vipaśyanā, Enlightenment – that support one another to produce more and more happy and insightful states of mind. The circular, repetitive nature of the wheel and the unrealized creative potential of the spiral express the human situation in a nutshell.

The method of meditation upon conditionality is to dwell upon each of these principal links (*nidānas*) on the wheel and the spiral, having established a good basis of śamatha. You need to understand at least roughly what you are doing before you can attempt any

Table 20: Stages of contemplation of the twenty-four nidānas

Mundane 'spiral' nidānas (Integration towards dhyāna)	In dependence upon dissatisfaction (*dukkha*) arises faith (*śraddhā*).
	In dependence upon faith arises joy (*prāmodya*).
	In dependence upon joy arises rapture (*prīti*).
	In dependence upon rapture arises calm (*praśrabdhi*).
	In dependence upon calm arises bliss (*sukha*).
	In dependence upon bliss arises concentration (*samādhi*).
First transcendental 'spiral' nidāna	In dependence upon concentration arise knowledge and vision of things as they really are (*yathābhūtajñānadarśana*).
Cyclic nidānas (arising)	In dependence upon ignorance (*avidyā*) arise karma-formations (*saṃskāras*).
	In dependence upon karma-formations arises consciousness (*vijñāna*).
	In dependence upon consciousness arises the psychophysical organism (*nāmarūpa*).
	In dependence upon the psychophysical organism arise the six sense organs (*ṣaḍāyatana*).
	In dependence upon the six sense organs arises contact (*sparśa*).
	In dependence upon contact arises feeling (*vedāna*).
	In dependence upon feeling arises craving (*tṛṣṇā*).
	In dependence upon craving arises attachment (*upādāna*).
	In dependence upon attachment arises becoming (*bhava*).
	In dependence upon becoming arises birth (*jāti*).
	In dependence upon birth arise old age and death (*jarā-maraṇa*).
Cyclic nidānas (dissolving)	Upon the cessation of birth, old age and death cease.
	Upon the cessation of becoming, birth ceases.
	Upon the cessation of attachment, becoming ceases.
	Upon the cessation of craving, attachment ceases.
	Upon the cessation of feeling, craving ceases.
	Upon the cessation of contact, feeling ceases.
	Upon the cessation of the six sense organs, contact ceases,
	Upon the cessation of the psychophysical organism, the six sense organs cease.
	Upon the cessation of consciousness, the psychophysical organism ceases.
	Upon the cessation of karma-formations, consciousness ceases.
	Upon the cessation of ignorance, karma-formations cease.
Remaining transcendental 'spiral' nidānas	In dependence upon knowledge and vision of things as they really are arises disenchantment (*nirveda*).
	In dependence upon disenchantment arises disentanglement (*vairāgya*).
	In dependence upon disentanglement arises freedom (*vimukti*).
	In dependence upon freedom arises knowledge of the destruction of the biases (*āsravakṣayajñāna*).

useful practice. Ideally, you need to understand the exact meaning of each nidāna as well as the relationship between the various nidānas. So it's likely that much thought, further reading[81] and preferably access to people who can help you to clarify questions are necessary. This doesn't mean that you cannot engage in the practice until you completely understand, because you could never start if that were so. Provided there is some basis of prior reflection, the meditation itself will feed back and nourish your intellectual understanding. But for the Dharma seed to grow, you'll need to acknowledge the incompleteness of your understanding.

As usual with vipaśyanā, begin in a good state of concentration and positive emotion. Ideally, be in the first dhyāna. Then turn the concentrated attention upon the opening nidānas of the spiral, dwelling on each one for a while before moving on to the next. See Table 20 for the complete sequence of stages of the meditation, which is followed by a brief commentary to aid contemplation at each stage.

The practice has three phases. In the first, you contemplate the seven 'spiral' nidānas, which describe the whole path of spiritual progress from the point where you make the decision to work with your experience, difficult though that might be, right through to the point where the mind is sufficiently inspired, concentrated and open for insight to arise. In the second phase, contemplation switches to considering the details of how our repetitive and unawakened experience depends on a cycle of conditions. The third phase is a contemplation of the process of disenchantment and progressive freedom from that cyclic conditioning process.

1)– 2) **In dependence upon dissatisfaction (*dukkha*) arises faith (*śraddhā*).** Dukkha is dissatisfaction with cyclic existence. It is not simply 'suffering' as often translated because it may well include pleasures. It is the unsatisfactoriness of so much of our experience, even when it's pleasant; it's the I-just-can't-let-go-of-this feeling that gets us looking for a better way of living. In a Buddhist context faith, or śraddhā, is confidence in the possibilities of spiritual development and trust in the spiritual path. Even if there is little actual experience so far of the path unfolding, it is not blind: śraddhā draws on intuition, experience and reason. The two nidānas dukkha and śraddhā encapsulate a reflection on the fact that inspired confidence can arise only when someone really wants to abandon their old ways. It is not that suffering inevitably leads to faith in the path of spiritual progress, otherwise everyone would have become enlightened long ago – faith can arise only when dukkha of some kind is present. If there is no sense of spiritual disquiet, faith is unlikely to arise.

So the practice is to reflect on how this pair of nidānas works and then to work through the rest of the nidāna series. Feel each one too – connect with your personal experience and feel each one directly, right now. Some study of the Pali terms and traditional understandings of each nidāna will be needed. The following explanations are intended as a recapitulation for those who have done this. Don't just take it as read that one nidāna gives rise to another; understand why and how it tends to happen like that. The phrase 'in dependence on x arises y' can unintentionally suggest that the succeeding link arises automatically from the preceding one. However, each nidāna just represents a condition with various potentials: the nidāna succeeding it *could* now arise on that basis, but that won't necessarily happen. In the case of the current set of 'spiral' nidānas, it must be deliberately developed.

At each link of the nidāna chain you can either reflect upon and explore the current connection or directly see it and rest in its felt image. A good approach is to rest in direct seeing as long as that feels stable and true, returning to reflection when direct seeing is not stable.

3) **In dependence upon faith arises joy (*pramodya*).** Prāmodya is that joyful feeling of self-respect and good conscience you get when you know you are acting appropriately: you're doing the right thing. You know you are on the right track because you're getting results from the practice. If faith is present, there's a possibility that joy will also arise; but without faith, it won't. Ask yourself if that is really true and what implications that would have for the nature of faith. When you can, rest beyond

thinking in the felt image of the causal link 'in dependence upon faith arises joy'.

4) **In dependence upon joy arises rapture (*prīti*).** You are becoming more deeply integrated through the Dharma practice. This and the next three nidānas describe entry into dhyāna. The current nidāna of prīti is the dhyāna factor of physical rapture; it arises at a certain point in concentrated meditation. Reflect on the link: these dhyāna factors, starting with *prīti*, become possibilities only where there is an experience of joy – 'in dependence upon joy arises rapture'.

5) **In dependence upon rapture arises calm (*praśrabdhi*).** This is the 'containment' of physical rapture through calm and bliss, the next nidāna. Rapture is a condition of deeper calming. The integrative calming-down process of praśrabdhi can begin once the bubbly feeling of rapture has leapt into your concentration meditation.

6) **In dependence upon calm arises bliss (*sukha*).** The deep happiness called sukha comes out of this calm; the deep, contained calming process is a condition for sukha.

7) **In dependence upon bliss arises concentration (*samādhi*).** The full dhyāna experience is dependent on all the previous stages, bliss being its immediate condition. So once there is deep happiness, full concentration can arise; sukha is a condition for full concentration.

8) **In dependence upon concentration arises knowledge and vision of things as they really are (*yathābhūtajñānadarśana*).** At this point, when full concentration has been established, the possibility arises that in the right conditions transcendental insight may arise. The reflection on the twelve cyclic nidānas that follows represents those necessary conditions for the arising of knowledge and vision. The fully concentrated mind now turns to reflect upon the details of cyclic, repetitive and unawakened life; it recollects the various ways in which all cyclic existence is impermanent, unsatisfactory and insubstantial.

The twelve nidānas of the wheel of cyclic existence appear in symbol form round the rim of the wheel of life. It's well worth looking back to the earlier image and using it as a basis for reflection, taking in the symbolism and letting it suffuse your imagination. The pictures convey meanings that probably won't come across in what I write here. There is a huge variety of ways in which one set of events can condition another, and many of the nidānas in the sequence exert a different kind of influence from others. This is the kind of thing you need to explore and to get a good conceptual understanding of. Then real understanding, i.e. direct seeing, will eventually come out of the meditation.

The symbolic nidāna pictures, however, are less conceptual and offer some good clues to their experiential meanings, though some will speak more to us than others. I feel that the blind man is a very appropriate symbol, for the nature of ignorance is that one simply cannot see; one has no idea of what is there. Then the potter making pots symbolizes to me something about us acting and thereby fashioning our own fragile conditioning. The monkey is the spontaneous wild functioning of consciousness jumping here and there, chattering and grabbing fruit. The boat is your body with consciousness at its helm, its passengers your mind functions. The house is your life with five windows and a door – the five senses plus the mind sense. The contact of the senses is like a kiss, that climactic moment of contact with so much happening within the kisser. Feeling is an even more powerful juncture, like being struck in the eye by an arrow – once it's hit, something has to be done, something that's not easy.

Engaging in life's pleasures is a symbol for easy acts based on craving. Plucking fruit from a tree shows that all actions have consequences. A pregnant woman shows our constant growth in a particular direction as the consequence of action, and her giving birth shows the decisive outcome of that activity. Then comes the corpse being carried to the burning ground, the inevitable consequence of having been born. The qualities of the cyclic nidānas are emotionally far more dark and complex than the ascent into the simplicity, joy and concentration of the transcendental nidānas. They are also very familiar to you, if you look closely, as *you* are what they are describing. And as already noted, this is another important clue to understanding the nidāna chain: look for everything in your experience because that is all it's about – nothing else.

i) – ii) **In dependence upon ignorance (*avidyā*) arise karma-formations (*saṃskāra*).** These two nidānas represent the crux of the whole reactive, cyclic process, and it is worth stopping here and spending extra time on reflecting about what they are getting at. The darkness and confusion of spiritual ignorance is one's inevitable state when not knowing how things really are. Not knowing has a profound effect; it creates strong predispositions – deep-seated likes and dislikes, tendencies to go this way or that – that wield a decisive influence upon your general consciousness. This is the core of saṃsāra, the cyclic tendency, like a snake unknowingly biting its own tail. The bite hurts, the snake becomes enraged and bites back harder in an attempt to destroy the pain. Reflect here on how, in your own experience, your lack of understanding has conditioned particular assumptions, from which have arisen activities that have become habitual. See how that with condition i) in place, condition ii) is inevitable. Or is it?

iii) **In dependence upon karma-formations arises consciousness (*vijñāna*).** Consciousness refers here to the initial spark of consciousness arising at conception. Note the word 'vi-jñāna', which refers to awareness that is divided into a knowing subject and known objects (rather than 'jñāna', which means the timeless wisdom that transcends subjects and objects). It is thus a deluded consciousness, as is to be expected in view of the conditions it springs from. Reflect here on ways that particular emotional habits – towards irritation, craving, fear etc. – affect the way you see things in the world now. Think also about how this particular dependence may affect the way that you and others arrive in the world in the first place.

iv) **In dependence upon consciousness arises the psychophysical organism (*nāmarūpa*).** The psychophysical organism is your mind (psyche) and body. The basic meaning is that mind and body start to develop in the womb because a consciousness has arrived ready to participate in the process of foetal growth, a process whose details are still not understood though the physical facts are well known. The current theory is that consciousness arises once 'the circuit elements necessary for consciousness are in place' by the third trimester of pregnancy. The foetus is thought to be in a dream state. But its dreaming is assumed to be contentless because any content would have to be informed by memories[82] and, the assumption continues, 'there could not be anything to remember'. Buddhist teaching does not speculate about any of this, stating merely that the nāma and rūpa components of the organism (its 'name' or mental part and its 'form' respectively) are codependent, both essential to each other. Yet it is clear from this series of nidānas that consciousness conditioned by a previous existence, and thereby coloured with particular emotional and volitional energy, exerts a conditioning effect prior to the arising of the foetus in the womb. This controversy aside, what you can usefully do in the practice is to focus on the fact that we have all been foetuses in a womb. From there, if you wish, you can wonder at the fact that many babies seem to emerge with certain traits already in place.

v) **In dependence upon the psychophysical organism arise the six sense organs (ṣaḍāyatana).** Without a body and mind, there would be no senses, no means of contact with the outside world. This is a simple dependency of conditions. It is perhaps interesting to consider that in Buddhism, whatever the state of mind, and whatever kind of being (whether visible or invisible, born or unborn, in life or after death) is possessed by that state of mind, it always experiences a body of some kind. In other words, there are no disembodied entities in Buddhism. In a dream, for example, where temporarily you have another life, you experience a different kind of body; and even in the after-death state, there is an experience of body, according to Mahāyāna tradition. That body has some kind of sensory apparatus that creates an internal image of an external world.

Consider also that the physical sense organs depend on the existence of a body and a mind. Remember: the practice is not about understanding this in an intellectual way; just be mindful of the fact without trying to understand it. Something happens as one simply calls this dependency to mind, and that is enough for the purpose of the practice.

vi) **In dependence upon the six sense organs arises contact** (*sparśa*). This is an important juncture, so let us summarize the sequence described so far: owing to unenlightened predispositions, an unenlightened mentality has come into being, complete with body and senses. Now that those sense organs exist, the possibility arises for the first time for them to make a connection with an outside world and to receive various impressions – sights, sounds, smells, tastes, touches and mental perceptions. This is not the five senses but the six senses, as the organ of the mind sense is included. Reflect that because the organs are there, sensations can arise. That is what is happening now; it is happening all the time. It is happening because of the pre-existence of eyes, ears, nose, tongue, body and the various physical bases for the mind sense.

vii) **In dependence upon contact arises feeling (*vedāna*)**. With contact with the external world via the senses, there always arises some kind of feeling. Feeling arises because of the contact, because of the sensation arising from the contact. A sight, sound, smell and so on always induces some kind of feeling, whether pleasant, painful or neutral. We explored this subject in Chapter 9 in some detail. Ponder here that one depends on the other, that feeling always depends on contact and can arise only when there is some kind of sensation that comes with contact.

viii) **In dependence upon feeling arises craving (*tṛṣṇā*)**. When you experience pleasure, there's a tendency to want to repeat it; the desire to repeat it is craving – a kind of wanting that you cling on to and that won't easily go away. Craving is an example of the kind of negatively charged emotion that can arise in response to a feeling. Hatred, say, or anxiety would need to be substituted if the conditioning feeling were painful. This is the crux of the whole wheel of becoming. If you allow craving or hatred (frustrated craving) to take hold, you bind yourself to the links of the Wheel that follow. This is the last point at which you retain some degree of choice about whether you continue ignorantly round the wheel – becoming now this, now that on the basis of more or less mindless responses to the pleasant and painful feelings that life deals out to you – or cultivate the spiral path towards full Awakening, nirvana. Reflect on the particular way that craving comes up for you as a response to pleasant feeling and notice that the dependence comes only here, not elsewhere. Contact does not give rise to craving or hatred; nor does merely having sense organs: these emotions are always responses to particular feelings. The nature of a response is that there is an element of choice: you needn't identify with it so strongly or even have that response at all. Perhaps you can learn to have different responses. This is the turning point at the core of the Buddhist path.

ix) **In dependence upon craving arises attachment (*upādāna*).** If you do not cultivate the spiral path at this point, you will start becoming 'hooked' on the experience that gave rise to the feeling concerned. You will repeat the pleasant experience whenever opportunities arise or, in the case of responses to painful experiences, usually generate habitual angry responses, resentment and bitterness. You can't let it go: you somehow identify with it. A type of monkey trap is cunningly designed so that when the bait is grasped, the monkey's hand is trapped. Escape is easy – the monkey just needs to let go of the banana – but it can't do that![83] You may think that this is funny, and it is. But it's your problem too and in ways that often, unfortunately, are serious, just as for the monkey and for all sentient beings similarly trapped by their attachments. So think here on the nature of attachment and its relationship with the emotion it depends on. The difference between a desire to repeat a pleasure and the confirmed desire to definitely repeat it is subtle, but very important, in personal transformation. You need to get right in there and see how it works in your own experience.

x) **In dependence upon attachment arises becoming (*bhava*).** The habit of repeating the pleasant experience (or continuing to avoid the painful one) becomes so entrenched that you become that habit. It becomes a confirmed part of you and will have many effects as all your activities and responsibilities become configured around this and other attachments. In your life there are likely to be many of these strands of becoming, which may even cause you to become ill, thin or obese and to adopt mannerisms or ways of holding the body. Ponder how becoming sets in on the basis of attachment and how, where attachment has set in, becoming has already started, the one being an intensification of the other.

xi) **In dependence upon becoming arises birth (*jāti*).** According to the teaching of rebirth, the character of the next life is determined by those entrenched habits. You may not be able literally to check the connection for yourself but you'll be able to see the underlying logic. The strands of becoming continue to accumulate; and even where the continuity of the body is interrupted, the process itself moves into another mode, that of the after-death transitional state (bardo), and later re-emerges in a new existence.

Here you are recapitulating the earlier nidānas of ignorance → karma-formations → consciousness → psychophysical organism → sense etc. The process of craving → attachment → becoming is essentially the same process as ignorance → karma-formations. The process of birth is essentially the same as consciousness → the psychophysical organism → the six sense organs. The latter nidānas pertain to experience as it affects each individual, whereas the ignorance-karma link pertains to the universal situation, to something all beings are subject to.

Reflect here on how beings arrive in the world and where their faculties and dispositions come from, on the fact that becoming has to have an outcome somewhere and on the dependence of birth upon previous conditioning and in particular upon previous becoming.

xii) In dependence upon birth arise old age and death (*jarā-maraṇa*). Here you get back to the universal perspective, the big picture of cyclic conditioning affecting all beings. We have all been born into an impermanent body, and it is the nature of all physical bodies gradually to lose their fine bloom, to deteriorate and eventually to die. So muse here on the dependence of decay and death on birth. If you had not been born, there would have been no ageing and there would be no death. But of course you have been born.

This kind of reflection – if y hadn't been there, there wouldn't be x – now characterizes a different phase of reflection as you contemplate the dissolution phases of conditionality. You now go back through the nidānas already covered and contemplate how, if the previous conditions were not present, each stage would dissolve.

Upon the cessation of **birth**, old age and death cease. Reflect here on the dependence of ageing upon birth by thinking that if birth hadn't happened, there would be no ageing. Resist impatiently thinking that it's obvious. It is obvious in a way, but there is more to it. Don't let its obviousness cut short the reflection. Rest, relax, concentrate, be receptive to the significance of the dependence of death on birth and let that simple fact speak to you. Just continue observing these backward dependences in the same way for the nidāna pairs that follow.

Upon the cessation of **becoming**, birth ceases. Were it not for the process of becoming, there would be no birth. Reflect here on that particular relationship and see how it affects your experience of the particular qualities of becoming and birth.

Upon the cessation of **attachment**, becoming ceases. Becoming depends on attachment; if there were no attachment, becoming would cease, which would be a good thing. Reflect here on the dependence of becoming on attachment.

Upon the cessation of **craving**, attachment ceases. Reflect here on the fact that attachment depends on craving and on how, without it, there can be no attachment, which would be a good thing. Explore again from this perspective the particular way in which attachment arises or simply rest in the fact of it without analysis.

Upon the cessation of **feeling**, craving ceases. Craving depends on feeling; in the absence of feeling, there would be no craving. There's a simple, factual dependency. However, experience without feeling actually does not exist for you, since you are an embodied being with senses making continual contact with the world. So for you, there is always the possibility of craving, and that situation will continue throughout your life. Reflect here that the only situations in which there would be no danger of craving or hatred arising would be those in which you had managed to avoid certain conditions giving rise to pleasant and painful feelings.

Upon the cessation of **contact**, feeling ceases. Reflect here, in the same line of enquiry as above, that contact is the condition for feeling and that without it, there is no feeling.

Upon the cessation of **the six sense organs**, contact ceases. Reflect here in the same way that any particular sense contact depends on the relevant organ existing in the first place. Without it, no contact could happen.

Upon the cessation of **the psychophysical organism**, the six sense organs cease. Reflect here in the same way that these sense faculties depend directly upon the existence of a physical body and that without it, there would be no sense organs.

Upon the cessation of **consciousness**, the psychophysical organism ceases. Reflect here in the same way that without that initial spark of consciousness, no physical body or basis for mind would evolve in the womb.

Upon the cessation of **karma-formations**, consciousness ceases. Reflect here in the same way that were it not for the existence of deeply ingrained emotional predispositions, that is karmic tendencies, no consciousness would arise.

Upon the cessation of **ignorance**, karma formations cease. Reflect here in the same way that were it not for the pre-existence of spiritual ignorance, there would be no karmic tendencies.

This completes the contemplation of the cyclic nidānas. Having reflected on the nature of the arising and passing away of your life and that of all unawakened beings, which is a basis for the arising of insight, you return to the spiral path and contemplate the stages leading from that initial insight towards full Enlightenment.

9) **In dependence upon knowledge and vision of things as they really are arises disenchantment (*nirveda*).** Reflecting again and again on the endless frustration that is the wheel of becoming, you eventually come to see it truly and clearly as it really is. Seeing the big picture that you exist in brings about an experience of illumination – seeing things as they really are. Having this experience starts a process of disenchantment with saṃsāra, the beginning of the end of the craving attachment that up to now has fuelled your endless becoming. You see clearly that there isn't really anything there worth clinging on to, that you have been under a spell and that it is possible to step out of it. You realize that basically you are free. Reflect here on the nature of disenchantment, *nirveda* or *nibbidā*, and how it depends upon that moment of clear seeing, upon 'knowledge and vision of things as they really are'.

10) **In dependence upon disenchantment arises disentanglement (*vairāgya*).** The word 'virāga' literally means the absence of *rāga*, passionate craving not only for sense enjoyments but also for a particular kind of existence. The translation 'disentanglement' communicates its experiential aspect: you are now able completely to let go of entanglements. Reflect here that this (actual) disentanglement rests upon the previous disenchantment with samsaric attachments.

11) **In dependence upon disentanglement arises freedom (*vimukti*).** Once the process of disentanglement is complete, you get to a point at which you are free, released from saṃsāra.

Reflect here on the nature of that freedom and its dependence upon disentanglement.

12) **In dependence upon freedom arises knowledge of the destruction of the biases (*āsravakṣayajñāna*).** On the basis of your actual freedom, you know directly and immediately that the *asavas*, the poisonous tendencies towards sense indulgence, becoming, wrong views and ignorance, are no longer there. Not that you necessarily think in these technical terms – asavakāyajñāna refers to the confidence of knowing that you are completely free and have gained full Awakening or Buddhahood. Reflect here on the dependence of this on the freedom of having disentangled from identification with saṃsāra and on its special quality.

These reflections may lead to insight experiences during the actual practice, depending of course on many factors. But the effect of reflecting regularly on these core aspects of your existence is likely to lay a very firm foundation for insight practice in general. Somewhere, you will be thinking and reflecting on these matters all the time if you regularly practice. This is the kind of involvement most likely to bring you to a point of real seeing.

Chapter ten

···

Imagination and the influence of the Buddha

Iti'pi so bhagava araham sammā-sambuddho
vijjā-caraṇa sampanno sugato
loka-vidū, anuttaro purisa-damma-sārati
satthā deva-manussānaṃ buddho bhagavā-ti.

Such indeed is He, the richly endowed: the free, the fully and perfectly
    awake
Equipped with knowledge and practice, the happily attained,
Knower of the worlds – guide unsurpassed of men to be tamed,
The Teacher of gods and men, The Awakened One richly endowed.[84]

The Buddha's qualities praised in the Buddha Vandāna

The historical Buddha Gautama, also known as Śākyamuni, is the originator of all Buddhist teachings. He is the basic reference point; it is through him that you know about Enlightenment. Moreover, you can check your understanding of his teachings, and your practice of them, by studying the records of the Buddha's original teaching as recorded in the Pali canon and the contemporary Chinese Āgamas. An important aspect of Buddhist practice is referring to the Buddha and his teachings as a touchstone.

Making that connection opens up a further possibility: you can receive teachings directly from the Buddha. This direct link is a characteristic of all practices at the stage of spiritual rebirth. 'Receiving teachings' can be regarded as a metaphor, indicating that after the point of genuine insight, your experience is aligned with the Awakening that Buddha Śākyamuni experienced. So it is as though the Buddha begins to be perceived inside you, as the teacher within. But there is also a sense in which you can receive teachings from the Buddha as though from outside you. That will emerge as this chapter unfolds and you start to wonder, who or what actually is the Buddha? To address this, we need to look at the way in which Buddhist meditation methods evolved in the early tradition.

According to Buddhaghosa, the Buddha over his lifetime presented forty methods of meditation, known as the *Kammaṭṭhānas*, or 'work-places'.[85] If you look closely at the following list, you'll see that most of them are touched upon elsewhere in this book, sometimes in detail.

The Ten Kasiṇas: varieties of the kasiṇa practice using concentration upon discs of various colours: earth kasiṇa, water kasiṇa, air or wind kasiṇa, fire kasiṇa, blue kasiṇa, green kasiṇa, yellow kasiṇa, red kasiṇa, white kasiṇa, limited space kasiṇa and light kasiṇa.

The Ten Asubhas, the 'impure' or unbeautiful meditations:[86] contemplations of a swollen corpse, a discoloured corpse, a festering corpse, a fissured corpse, a mangled corpse, a dismembered corpse, a cut and dismembered corpse, a bleeding corpse, a worm-infested corpse and a skeleton.

The Ten Anussatis (Recollections): the Buddha, the Dharma, the Sangha, ethics, generosity, the gods, death, the body (mindfulness of the body), breathing (mindfulness of breathing) and Enlightenment.

The four brahma vihāras: Mettā Bhāvanā, Karuṇā Bhāvanā, Muditā Bhāvanā and Upekkhā Bhāvanā.

The Four Formless Spheres, i.e. the arūpadhyānas: the sphere of space, the sphere of consciousness, the sphere of no-thingness and the sphere of neither perception nor non-perception.

The Perception of Loathsomeness in Food, an antidote to craving, and

The Analysis of the Four Elements, which is similar to the six-element practice.

The first of the ten recollections (the anussatis listed in Chapter 9) is Buddhānussati, recollection of the Buddha. The traditional form of Buddhānussati involves calling the Buddha's qualities to mind using the Buddha Vandāna verse, quoted above. These qualities recollect his intelligence, wisdom and compassion, his freedom and full wakefulness of mind, his amazing stock of knowledge and experience, his extraordinary happiness, his familiarity with all realms of experience and his unsurpassed ability as a teacher not only of human beings but also of gods.

To think strongly about a quality, good or bad, is to evoke it in the mind. To dwell for a long time on someone's kindness, or their nastiness, correspondingly softens or hardens your attitudes. So at least to some degree, recollecting the Buddha's qualities can gradually bring them about in you. This principle is employed in an important range of meditation practices called sādhana. Imagining the Buddha's qualities through traditional verses, reading biographies of him and studying his teachings, the meditator naturally forms some kind of impression. This impression of the Buddha acts like the 'Dharma seed' of insight mentioned in Chapter 8, which eventually takes on a life of its own and is a channel for the Dharma niyāma, the awakened influence of the Buddhas.

Sādhana as an evolutionary process

The process of recollection probably explains how visualization practices developed in the later, Mahāyāna Buddhist tradition, though the trend began much earlier.[87] Buddhānussati meditation itself is mentioned in the Pali commentarial tradition. In the account of his last days in the older scriptures (the *Mahāparinibbāna Sutta*[88]), the Buddha recommends that his disciples set up stūpa monuments as a reminder of him.

The clearest connection of all is the earliest account of Buddhānussati, found in the final verses of the *Sutta Nipāta*.[89] An elderly disciple, Piṅgiya, is too sick and frail to travel to meet the Buddha, but he practises imagining him vividly:

With constant and careful vigilance it is possible for me to see him with my mind as clearly as with my eyes, in night as well as day ... there is not, to my mind, a single moment spent away from him. I cannot now move away from the teaching of Gotama: the powers of confidence and joy, of intellect and awareness, hold me there. Whichever way this universe of wisdom goes, it draws me with it.

At this point in the sutta, the Buddha seems to appear through the power of Piṅgiya's visualization, speaking to encourage him in his practice. 'Piṅgiya ... other people have freed themselves by the power of confidence ... you too should let that strength release you; you too will go to the further shore, beyond the draw of death.'
In this spirit of dialogue with the image of the Buddha, new meditation practices arose among practitioners of his teaching, calling up over time countless images of his wisdom, compassion, energy, charisma, kindness, directness and so on. This method of meditation is symbolically connected with spiritual rebirth, the spontaneously arising spiritual progress that unfolds out of genuine Realization. This unfolding is easily attributed to the influence of the Buddhas because in experience, some kind of transformation is felt to be coming from 'beyond' the practitioner. At the point of Realization (spiritual death), the practitioner's meditation and conduct shatters the normal assumption of an unchanging, definite self, and a new kind of transformation is activated by a power felt as 'other'. This transformation happens according to the ultimate nature of things (*dhammaniyāma*) and again is how, literally, one may receive teachings from the Buddha.

Sādhana: Connection to the Buddha and his way of practice

Sādhana is a practice for confident, committed practitioners, so its principles are best illustrated by real-life examples. All authentic Buddhist traditions connect somehow with the Buddha and practise to realize their connection in a variety of ways. Sādhana is a symbol of one's deepening 'going for refuge to the Buddha', of having made a strong commitment to practise his teaching in this life as a means of gaining Enlightenment for the sake of all beings. It is also a way of making contact with the Buddha more personally, by discovering him and deepening your appreciation of him through his image. For many practitioners, this act of opening to the Buddha's influence may become central to all other Buddhist practices.

Even though a sādhana practice often takes the form of a written text, the form of that text is always secondary to its enabling the practitioner to make personal contact with the Buddha's presence through an image. The sādhana texts used by the Triratna Buddhist Community existed originally within the context of (Indo-)Tibetan Buddhism: this was the culture of the various teachers who initiated its founder Sangharakshita. Towards the end of his twenty-year stay in India, these teachers encouraged him to practise the sādhanas and to pass them on. [90] Although he drew important lessons from Tibetan Buddhism, his teachers were happy for him to remain a Theravādin monk, as he was at that time, rather than to formally become part of their tradition. All taught in the spirit of a contemporary Tibetan non-sectarian Buddhist movement known as Rimé, which values the teachings of all the Tibetan schools. Continuing something of the spirit of the Rimé tradition in the West, we in the Triratna Buddhist Community seek to connect with the essentials of all forms of Buddhist practice. And we do this, as I have mentioned, by taking the Buddha, who originated them, as our touchstone.

Forms of sādhana practice

The most fundamental form of sādhana practice is simply to sit in meditation, with a good foundation of concentration, mindfulness and trust. You then connect with the image of the Buddha, however you find yourself perceiving it, and open yourself to his teachings. There is no need for the image to be visual. The way in which what I've called 'teachings' are transmitted to you may well be quite other than what you conventionally expect – as words or clear images – though they may also appear in that way. Essentially you are receiving the blessing of the Buddha, his *adhiṣṭhāna*. As long as when you sit to meditate you have established śamatha and right view, in the sense of awareness of śūnyatā and conditionality (*pratītyasamutpāda*), there will be some kind of experience of increased clarity or inspiration if you open yourself to the Buddha's influence. The experience may be subtle, and you'll need to learn how to read it. But if you give enough time and trust to absorbing it, it will be of real spiritual value. In this way you receive directly from the Buddha experiences of inspiration whose significance you can explore, if you wish, using traditional texts and in discussion with your teachers.

This simple, intuitive form of practice is the essence of sādhana meditation. It is akin to Just Sitting inasmuch as after you have contacted the image, you simply make yourself open. It cultivates a mood of freshness and originality in relation to the Buddha that is essential for authentically exploring the more developed aspects of sādhana that will be outlined shortly.

An actual sādhana text may give you a more concrete idea of what is involved. Such a text should be used as a jumping-off point rather than as a set of fixed instructions. In some ways the quasi-ritual form of this kind of sādhana is best experienced as a mythic drama that unfolds the authentic message of the Buddha.

A sādhana meditation on Śākyamuni Buddha

1) First, generate śamatha.
2) Standing, pay respects to the shrine:
   Namo Buddhāya
   Namo Dharmāya
   Namo Saṅghāya
   Namo Namaḥ
   OṂ
   ĀḤ
   HŪṂ
   [Bow]
   [Homage to the Buddha, Homage to the Dharma, Homage to the Sangha, Salutations, Oṃ Āḥ Hūṃ]

Seated, recite the three refuges and the ethical precepts:
   Namo Tassa Bhagavato Arahato Sammāsambuddhassa
   Namo Tassa Bhagavato Arahato Sammāsambuddhassa
   Namo Tassa Bhagavato Arahato Sammāsambuddhassa
   [Homage to the Buddha, the Dharma and the Sangha]

Buddhaṃ saraṇaṃ gacchāmi
Dhammaṃ saraṇaṃ gacchāmi
Saṅghaṃ saraṇaṃ gacchāmi
[I go for refuge to the Buddha, the Dharma and the Sangha]

Dutiyampi Buddhaṃ saraṇaṃ gacchāmi
Dutiyampi Dhammaṃ saraṇaṃ gacchāmi
Dutiyampi Saṅghaṃ saraṇaṃ gacchāmi
Tatiyampi Buddhaṃ saraṇaṃ gacchāmi
Tatiyampi Dhammaṃ saraṇaṃ gacchāmi
Tatiyampi Saṅghaṃ saraṇaṃ gacchāmi
[For the second/third time I go for refuge to the Buddha, the Dharma and
    the Sangha]

Pāṇātipātā veramaṇī sikkhāpadaṃ samādiyāmi
Adinnādānā veramaṇī sikkhāpadaṃ samādiyāmi
Kāmesu micchācārā veramaṇī sikkhāpadaṃ samādiyāmi
Musāvādā veramaṇī sikkhāpadaṃ samādiyāmi
Surāmeraya majja pamādaṭṭhānā veramaṇī sikkhāpadaṃ samādiyāmi

[I undertake the training principle of not harming living beings.
I undertake the training principle of not taking the not-given.
I undertake the training principle of refraining from sexual misconduct.
I undertake the training principle of refraining from false speech.
I undertake to abstain from drink and drugs that cloud the mind.]

The precepts can be rendered positively:
With deeds of loving kindness, I purify my body.
With open-handed generosity, I purify my body.
With stillness, simplicity and contentment, I purify my body.
With truthful communication, I purify my speech.
With mindfulness clear and radiant, I purify my mind.

3) Affected by these verses of commitment and connection to the purpose of
   Dharma practice, now imagine clear blue sky.

4) Imagine among green grass and spring flowers the great trunk and spreading branches of a magnificent tree filled with masses of heart shaped-leaves. It is the bodhi tree under which the Buddha gained full Enlightenment. Under it is a heap of soft kuśa grass where Śākyamuni Buddha silently sits cross-legged in meditation. He is wearing the saffron robes of a religious wanderer and holding a black begging bowl. His eyes are half-closed and he smiles with compassion.

5) From his heart, a ray of brilliant golden light streams into your heart carrying the golden letters of the mantra OṂ MUNI MUNI MAHĀ MUNI ŚĀKYA MUNI SVĀHĀ. Slowly and mindfully recite the mantra, at first out loud and then internally, feeling that the Buddha's wisdom, compassion and purity are entering you and transforming you from the unenlightened to the enlightened state.

   Recite the mantra many times and eventually sit for a while in samādhi before

6) dissolving the visualization back into the blue sky and

7) dedicating the benefits gained from doing the practice to the well-being of all: *May the merit gained in my acting thus go to the alleviation of the suffering of all beings. My personality throughout my existences, my possessions and my merit in all three ways I give up without regard for myself for the benefit of all beings. Just as the earth and other elements are serviceable in many ways to the infinite number of beings inhabiting limitless space, so may I become that which maintains all beings throughout space, as long as all have not attained peace.*

It is clear from the way the practice begins with an open, clear blue sky that the perspective here is one of spiritual death and rebirth. This image symbolizes the beauty and potential in the insubstantial nature of all experience. Experience never really consists of things, even though a thousand things appear: each one is conditioned and thus empty, in its own unique way, of any actual substance. The blue sky represents spiritual death, the collapse of what once appeared as a solid and substantial 'me' and my solid and substantial world. As a none-too-solid wall is actually a helpful condition if you want to demolish a dangerous old building, insight into insubstantiality is the condition that allows spiritual rebirth to flourish as open, transparent and unimpeded as the sky. Thus in the succeeding stage of the practice, the form of Śākyamuni

Buddha (or a Bodhisattva such as Tārā or Mañjuśrī) is imagined as an expression of the wisdom and compassion that can flow when the delusion of substantiality collapses.

Stages of sādhana practice

Sādhana practice generally consists of several stages. These may be adapted as the practitioner deepens his or her personal connection, but learning them helps to direct your imagination and to connect with the Buddha.

1) First, cultivate basic śamatha through Mettā Bhāvanā, mindfulness of breathing.

2) Next recollect the purpose of the practice and generate inspiration. This may be done in many ways, such as by chanting the verses above or by doing *pūjā*, ritual celebration of the spiritual life – in other words by focusing on a particular form of the Buddha and worshipping it, making offerings, going for refuge to the Buddha's teaching, confessing shortcomings, rejoicing in your own good qualities and asking for the teaching. Another way of generating inspiration and recalling the purpose of practice is to imagine the lineage of enlightened teachers and their influence coming down to your own teacher, from whom you receive blessings and encouragement. This stage of a sādhana meditation may include generating mettā or bodhicitta, recollecting the impermanence of things or reflecting on the six elements. These are preliminaries for what follows.

3) The main practice begins with reflection on the insubstantial and conditioned nature of all appearances and with imagination of the blue sky of emptiness.

4) Then, out of that blue sky, imagine the Buddha, glorious in colour and form, appearing as though made out of light (though subjectively the form may seem less visual, depending on the way your imagination works). The text will prescribe particular colours and forms as a general

indication of the Buddha's qualities, but this is a template for making a start. What is important is a sense of an actual connection, enhanced by the conviction that can come from the reflection on insubstantiality. It is as though you are actually meeting the Buddha and being witnessed by him as a practitioner of his teaching.

5) From this comes a sense of an open communication, strengthened by you repeating the Buddha's name in the form of a mantra. Imagine the Buddha witnessing your sincere desire to practise and bestowing blessings in the form of coloured light rays entering your heart from his. This central moment of the drama is known as the transmission of *adhiṣṭhāna* (blessing), also referred to in tradition as empowerment, as it gives great confidence to connect with the living influence of the Buddha, your great spiritual ancestor.

What does this influence consist of and how is it alive? The ancestral metaphor is helpful. We have all been subject since birth to innumerable influences, some of which have stamped their mark on us more than others. The main ones have been people – parents, teachers and friends – but you are also influenced by cultural movements of all kinds – music, media, language – as well as by the ideas you take in through education and reading. You have walked into the ambit of some of these influences seemingly by accident. As a Dharma practitioner, you have somehow come into the range of the Buddha's influence; it may well have become your greatest influence. This is what adhiṣṭhāna represents: an intense transmission of the Dharma culture that originated from the Buddha's Realization and has since been kept alive in the practice, personal development and dialogue of countless teachers and their disciples right down to your time. And now it includes you and others like you.

6) Finally, when the adhiṣṭhāna has been received from the Buddha, the sādhana comes slowly to an end. The image may dissolve back into the blue sky it emerged from or straight into your heart. The dissolution may also be

accompanied by reflection on the inseparability of form and emptiness. The sky is then itself dissolved and you then

7) Dedicate the merit of doing the practice to the welfare of all beings.

Sādhana, imagination and insight

Sādhana is very rich as a practice. It is not just concerned with discovering the Buddha in one's own illumined imaginative experience. There are, at least in the more complex forms of sādhana, meditations within its meditations, such as the reflection on image and reality, rūpa (form) and śūnyatā (insubstantiality or emptiness). These meditations explore the beauty of the image of an ideal human being, on the one hand, and the truth of that image's real nature, on the other hand. The truth of things is that they are impermanent and have no substantial existence. The manner of their existence is deeply mysterious and cannot be described or understood with the ordinary mind, though with spiritual death come the beginnings of that understanding.

So when you imagine the boundless space of the blue sky, you meditate on the fact that the Buddha image and the blue sky of śūnyatā are inseparable, even in a sense identical. The image was never a substantial thing – its nature is śūnyatā – and śūnyatā is never a thing either – it is the insubstantial nature of things. The Buddha-form is empty, and its emptiness is no different from the form. As the image of the Buddha manifests out of the insubstantial nature of all things, you take that as the ideal object for reflection on rūpa and śūnyatā.

Formally, you do this reflection on the nature of form and the nature of śūnyatā both at the beginning and at the end of imagining the Buddha. At the point when you start to imagine the Buddha appearing out of the blue sky, you have a special opportunity to reflect on how form arises out of emptiness. And then, when the Buddha dissolves back into the blue sky, you have a special opportunity to reflect on how emptiness is not different from form. Often the śūnyatā mantra is recited at this point, to mark the transition: OM SVABHĀVAŚUDDHĀḤ SARVADHARMĀḤ SVABHĀVASUDDHO 'HAM. Mantras usually don't translate well but this one has a clear meaning: 'Oṃ – all dharmas are pure in their nature and in the same way I too am pure', in other words all dharmas (i.e. things), including me, are pure because they are all śūnyatā, all perfectly empty of substance yet vividly real as forms.

You know you have created the image yourself from your relatively impoverished imagination. Certainly your ability to find and to focus on this image is imperfect, and maybe sometimes you hardly perceive anything at all during the sādhana. Yet you are imagining *something* when you sincerely make the attempt, and that something, whatever it is and however imperfect it may be, is the image that connects you to the Buddha. What is relevant is that it emerges from śūnyatā and that it stands in your mind for the Buddha. When you visualize the Buddha as an image of form, colour and light, it is a very crude approximation of how you would experience the Buddha if he were actually present. Each person you know has a distinct and recognizable atmosphere with certain characteristics that can be recognized but not adequately described. Visualizing or imagining involves working not only with shapes in imaginal space but also with indescribable images in the mind, impressions and vibrations that don't translate into the usual visual terms.

It is interesting to reflect on the nature of form. What is form? You can say that there are visual forms you see, audible forms you hear and tangible forms you touch. Ideas and feelings also have a form, though not a visual one. These images, which engage your attention all the time, are in some way beyond verbal description. For example, you can say that a perfume has a form, and I can very clearly imagine the perfume of a rose. I can also very easily imagine the smell of frying onions, yet I can't *describe* the images of these odours. Or I may be able to find words that evoke those sensations but the words will never be the same as the experience itself and cannot encompass it fully. It is similar with the image of the Buddha: you can only make rough attempts to paint a mental picture of the Buddha's form. That is not so much because your imagination is limited as because you're not awakened, so your imagination doesn't have much to go on when trying to imagine an awakened being. Nonetheless, dwelling on the Buddha and his Awakening can place the mind in a much bigger space, that of the awakened mind, and it offers the imaginative possibility of opening up to it.

Imagination uses stored memories of previous sense impressions – memories of all the sights you've seen, the sounds you've heard and the ideas you've had – as a kind of clip art, ready-made images for the imaginative process. You can see these images playing freely in your dreams and daydreams, but they also come sharply into focus when you think and imagine. The key to sādhana is to realize that your imagination is at play everywhere and all the time. Imagination does not take place on an exalted plane; it is a faculty that everyone uses in every moment. It is continually at work in all the various worlds you inhabit, not only in waking life but also in dreams, in meditation and in distractions from it – and also in the transitional states after death, according to the Bardo Thodol teachings of Tibetan Buddhism. Awareness always changes, but like matter and energy, it never stops forever. Doing sādhana helps to show you the extent to which your world consists of self-created images. This deepens your realization of the Buddha's teachings of conditionality and insubstantiality and opens your heart to the transforming influence of the Dharma. By working with the imaginal faculty of the mind, sādhana introduces a new level of mindfulness practice in which you explore how you continually create your own world.

While you are awake, you see, you hear, you smell, you taste, you touch and you perceive mental objects – you experience the six sense consciousnesses. The six sense consciousnesses are what make up waking life. However, sense consciousness is not unique to waking life, for in dreams you also see, hear, touch, remember and sometimes plan in detail, driven by strong feelings and emotions. In fact, when you see the richness of your consciousness in dreams, it is disconcertingly difficult to pin down what is special about the waking state. You naturally view waking life as the most real and significant part of your existence; yet while it happens, a dream is as real to you as waking life. Your world is always an interpretation of whatever data your senses present. You might object that experiences in the dream state are not real sense impressions but memories of sense experiences mediated by the mind sense. This is true, but sense experience is mediated by the mind sense in waking life as well. The retina and tympanic membranes don't see or hear – the raw data is processed by the brain and the various mental faculties in ways that make it meaningful to you. So waking and dreaming are indeed very different, but you can learn a good deal from being mindful of both experiences.

Because in the stages of integration and positive emotion you approach meditation through sense-withdrawal, you may come to view sense experience as pertaining to a lower form of consciousness. Actually, moving into dhyāna is not a matter of escaping sense experience as much as transcending your habitual attachment to it. It's the attachment that keeps you in a distracted state. Withdrawal from the senses in meditation, as when you close your eyes and focus your attention away from sounds and ideas, is a method of temporarily transcending sense attachment. In terms of the traditional layering of integrating consciousness, in dhyāna you temporarily go beyond kāmaloka. However, kāmaloka is not the realm of the senses but the realm of *sense desire* in which your relationship to the senses has been distorted by unhelpful emotions. The emotions that you habitually generate towards the objects in your world tend to fix the way in which you experience those objects, until the whole process congeals and sets your world in particular, narrow forms. This ingrained habit is what prevents your imagination from taking wing. Within the dhyanic realm of rūpaloka, the internal sense bases, freed from contact with coarse external objects, operate in a more visionary way. Even when you're not meditating, sense experience in itself is perfectly pure and undistorted. You cover it over with your emotional habits and expectations.

This purity is explored through a deeper application of mindfulness that occurs in sādhana meditation as you start to notice how you continually create the world you inhabit. It is a story you tell yourself using sense memories; and as you discover yourself doing that, you recognize the faculty of imagination used in sādhana. Actually, in normal life, you are imagining everything – from what you might have for dinner, to what it might be like to meet someone, to how that person themself might feel. You imagine your spiritual teacher, imagine the Buddha, imagine other people generally. And you don't only imagine others when, for example, practising Metta Bhāvanā; you even imagine them when meeting face to face. It takes an act of imagination to see who someone else is and to empathize with them. You even imagine yourself – indeed, you do that more than anything else. This endless imaginative play is the way your mind works. To see it happening allows you to free up its prodigious energies and enables a far more effective imagination of the state of Enlightenment and its embodiment in Buddhas, Bodhisattvas and enlightened teachers. This brings you closer to them and to your potential to be like them.

Imagining a Buddha, however, is more demanding than imagining an ordinary person. Being enlightened, the Buddha lies outside your normal range of experience. Sādhana practice establishes a bridge by creating an image rich enough to carry the power of your inspiration and eventually to 'possess' you with the essence of Awakening. In using the traditional iconographies (such as a tawny light, a sword and a book of wisdom for Mañjughoṣa, white snowy radiance for Vajrasattva and red sunset glory for Amitābha), the sādhana texts help you to make a relatively crude connection with the actual Buddha that is potential in you. The potential is in the expanded, self-transcended, insightful mind that is so much beyond you that it makes just as much sense to speak of the Buddha as existing outside you, which is how you usually envisage the Buddha in these visualizations. You do all you can to imagine the Buddha externally, but what eventually happens transcends your concepts of internal and external. The sincerity of your attempt to make this bridge allows the awakened consciousness to come and 'inhabit' the experience of sādhana you're creating.

This process through which the real Buddha inhabits your constructed, inaccurate image is traditionally described as follows. The image you create is known as the *samayasattva*; the actual awakened consciousness is the *jñānasattva*. *Jñāna* means the wisdom of Awakening and *sattva* means 'being'. *Samaya* refers to the bond or commitment that you make (at ordination, for example) to become awakened through practising this particular sādhana and that the Buddha has made through his vow to liberate all beings, including you. You evoke the Buddha through ritually worshipping him or her, recollecting śūnyatā, creating an image and imagining yourself connecting with it. So far, all this is something you do yourself, but you are also creating the conditions for something that you cannot imagine to come from the 'other side'. Until that bridge becomes actual you simply pray, have faith and make yourself receptive; and provided you fulfil your side of the commitment, there will definitely be a response from the Buddha's 'side'.

The notion of the Buddha's influence reaching out to you in the stage of spiritual rebirth may sound pretty much like God, which Buddhism is supposed to reject. Buddhism certainly finds the idea of an omnipotent creator deity incoherent; indeed the notion is satirized by the Buddha in the Pali canon.[91] But then practitioners who believe in God have spiritual experiences just like those we are discussing, so it is only natural that they attribute them to the deity they believe in. Buddhism would deny the attribution but not their experience. All spiritual traditions must use language in their attempts to point towards what ultimately cannot be expressed in words but can be experienced in practice. The Buddha believed that his radical way of putting things – especially in terms of universal conditionality and insubstantiality – was a more helpful guide to practice than the substantialist language of God.

Sādhana: practice in the round

Though the term 'sādhana' generally refers to the imagination of a particular Buddha-form as encapsulated in a specific ritual text, it can also be used in a broader sense to mean your entire practice in all its aspects centring on the Buddha. Sādhana is the complete body of all your Dharma practices (for example, mindfulness of breathing, Mettā Bhāvanā, the Six-Element Practice, walking meditation, study, mindfulness, ethical practice and Just Sitting), which form a mandala with the Buddha in the middle. Each aspect of the mandala contributes in some way to the experience of the Buddha and keeps his image alive. Practising any of these methods enriches the mandala and maintains a connection with the central image. So your imagination of a Buddha and recitation of his mantra also develops and enriches the whole collection of spiritual practices, drawing out the specific spiritual qualities that you wish to emulate. The Buddha's compassion is developed through the imagined form and Mettā Bhāvanā, his wisdom through Dharma study and insight practice and his skilful means through your practice of the precepts.

The Ch'an teacher Huangbo Xiyun (d.850) said:

> All the Buddhas and all sentient beings are nothing but (the mind), beside which nothing exists. This mind, which is without beginning, is unborn and indestructible. It is not green nor yellow, and has neither form nor appearance. It does not belong to the categories of things which exist or do not exist, nor can it be thought of in terms of new or old. It is neither long nor short, big nor small, for it transcends all limits, measures, names, traces, and comparisons. It is that which you see before you.[92]

'It is that which you see before you.' This is the key.

A Tārā sādhana

What follows is another typical sādhana practice, a meditation to invoke the presence of **the female Bodhisattva Green Tārā,** whose enlightened quality is fast-responding compassion. Like the previous example of Śākyamuni Buddha, the Tārā sādhana is a template, a ritual portal to be used as a way to imagine the real Buddha, who is none other than Tārā, who is none other than the Buddha.

Begin with these verses of evocation:

> *From your sublime abode at the Potala*
> *O Tārā – born from the green letter TAṂ,*
> *Whose light rescues all beings –*
> *Come with your retinue, I beg you.*
> *The gods and demigods bow their crowns*
> *To your lotus feet, O Tārā.*
> *Oh you who rescue all who are destitute,*
> *To you, Mother Tārā, I pay homage.[93]*

Now imagine that in every direction to infinity you see nothing but the deepest and most transparent blue sky. You also experience yourself as insubstantial and empty, of exactly the same nature as that infinite blue. Its open and infinite quality invests you with a sense of wonder and profound inspiration. You are experiencing your mind in its greatest clarity and calmness; at the same time you are contemplating the ultimate insubstantiality that is its essential nature. After a while, you become aware of something that expresses this in an image. It is a single letter made of the softest green light that glows and vibrates in your heart. It is the Sanskrit letter 'tam' standing upon a horizontal disc of silvery light like the full moon. You imagine the taṃ visually while also hearing its timeless sound. The moon disc is in the calyx of a tiny flower, a lotus blossom of pure light, and the lotus is in the heart of a goddess, the beautiful and gently smiling Bodhisattva Tārā. She is the quintessence of compassion – and she is also you. *You* are Tārā.

Seated cross-legged as though in meditation, but with her right foot outstretched as though ready to rise and aid a troubled being, Tārā is dressed in the silks and ornaments of a princess. Her right palm is opened outwards upon her knee in a gesture of giving. Her left hand is at her heart, its fingers expressing a quintessential point of the Dharma. Her radiance is a delightful green, like that of a spring leaf.

As you sit, and as the vision unfolds out of the openness of the sky, you feel as though you are formed of light, transparent and empty. Around the taṃ at your heart, the letters of Tārā's mantra, which contain her entire energy of wise, quickly-responding compassion, begin to revolve anti-clockwise. Peacefully listening, you hearken to their sound, *oṃ tāre tuttāre ture svāhā – oṃ tāre tuttāre ture svāhā – oṃ tāre tuttāre ture svāhā*, over and over again. From the letters, which stand erect and dance gracefully around the seed-syllable, emerges a diaphanous rainbow radiance. Rainbows curl upwards and downwards like incense smoke, and slowly your whole body, outwardly Tārā, inwardly fills with rainbow light.

After a while, your/her body is so permeated with this light that it overflows and eight rainbows emerge from the crown of your head. At the tip of each rainbow is the tiny figure of a goddess bearing an offering: water, flowers, lights, incense, perfume, delicious fruit, refreshing drinks and music. The eight goddesses rise upwards, presenting their offerings to Buddha Śākyamuni at the zenith, far above your head. As the rainbow light continues to rise, the purest snow-white light begins to pour down from above in a stream of blessing that descends onto the crown of your head and enters your body. It flows into your heart, into the taṃ; and from your responding heart the rays of light flow outwards towards all beings. All beings, you now notice, are all round you. You are sitting in the midst of a great multitude of beings of all kinds that stretches to infinity, all quietly reciting the Tārā mantra, *oṃ tāre tuttāre ture svāhā*. Over and over again the mantra sounds as the rays of light rise up from Tārā's heart and the rays of blessing pour down upon her heart and then out to help and heal the sufferings of all beings.

Sādhana is a complex form of Dharma practice, yet it still involves concentration, positive emotion and reflection on the Dharma. It incorporates both śamatha and vipaśyanā. Śamatha is accumulated through concentration on the image and repetition of the mantra, which is beautiful and naturally brings forth helpful emotions.

Many sādhanas include the development of mettā and the brahma vihāras as a preliminary stage, and a vipaśyanā reflection is often included in the sequence of the ritual. The main vipaśyanā aspect, however, comes through the image itself: an experienced *sādhaka* is able to create an extremely vivid image while understanding it to be a mental creation, fashioned from the insubstantial reality from which everything arises. As mentioned, a sādhana may incorporate for reflection Dharma verses that encapsulate insights. The various elements of the practice also contain insights in symbolic 'seed' form: the clear blue sky, the mantra, the body expression, hand gestures, form, clothing and so on. These have a symbolic significance that grows within the mind over years of daily practice. Even without reflections such as these, sādhana is an excellent śamatha practice: the beauty of the mantra's sound, together with the form and colour, integrate the mind and induce the rich calm of dhyāna. Vipaśyanā is brought into play when the imagination is 'embroidered' with discursive reflection and the direct seeing of its various insight-related components.

To some in the West traditional images such as Green Tārā can be obscure and difficult to relate to, especially as the relationship with our own native mythologies and local gods has been suppressed by the sustained antipathies of religion, rationalism and materialism. We all need to find our own way into Buddhist imagery, and perhaps one obvious way to do this is by imagining the discoverer of the Dharma, Śākyamuni. I respond easily to purely archetypal images such as Tārā, but it seems important to connect her qualities with those of the founder of Buddhism. Śākyamuni Buddha is also in some ways an archetypal figure, yet he was also a living human being whose life has been well documented.[94] By reading the various biographies, you can get a clear sense of his character and come to see him more in the round. And by studying his teachings in depth and following his activities in the extensive Pali scriptures, you can get a very full picture of what he, and any awakened being, is like. This will inform your image of other Buddha and Bodhisattva figures such as Tārā too, as they express the same awakened qualities.

'Tell me, Gotama, what kind of vision and virtuous conduct would justify calling someone "calmed"?'

'… Someone not dependent upon the past, not to be reckoned in the present, and without preference in the future,' said the Buddha. 'A real sage, of restrained speech, who speaks in moderation without anger, trembling, boasting, remorse or arrogance … Without desire for pleasant things, not given to pride, gentle and quick-witted, someone beyond over-conviction & dispassion.

'It's not for material gain that he trains, nor is he upset at the lack of it. He's not obstructed by craving or greedy for flavours. He's equanimous, always mindful, and has no haughtiness: he doesn't consider himself equal, superior or inferior to anyone in the world.

'Knowing the Dharma, he's independent, without craving for becoming or otherwise. He is at peace, indifferent to sensual pleasures. Nothing ties him; he's crossed beyond attachment.

'He possesses no sons, cattle, fields, or land. Nothing is taken up or laid down; and since he doesn't incline towards the kind of offences people might accuse him of, he's never agitated by their words. Greed and avarice are gone …

'So someone who can call nothing his own, who doesn't grieve over non-existent problems or get lost amidst mental phenomena – he's rightly called "calmed".'[95]

Conclusion

The methods laid out in this book, and the system of practice that underlies them, can bring all these qualities to life in you. The Buddha himself devised most of them. His story gives us an image, a picture of his total freedom from craving, hatred and delusion. 'Gentle, quick-witted … not given to pride' – yes, he's a human being like you and me but with a gentle strength and disconcerting lack of compromise that allows him to see into the nature of things. It enables him to be a human resource and a friend like no other.

It is a challenge to imagine the Buddha because his qualities are so rarely found combined in one person. Maybe you could imagine them combining in you? In any case, these are the qualities you need for true happiness and spiritual freedom. They can be drawn out by the practices of ethics, meditation and wisdom that this book has explored in terms of the developing imagination – the heart-mind that can be trained to open, be still and see the truth. By applying the core principles of meditation, systematized in the five phases of integration, positive emotion, spiritual death, spiritual rebirth and mindfulness, everyone can learn to become fully aware, tranquil and filled with deep insight.

Appendix one

....

Deepen the practice

Regular meditation lies at the heart of Buddhist training. It provides a unique working ground for integrating current experiences, cultivates the seeds of calm and compassion, shines the clear light of insight and refocuses energy on the path. It offers an extraordinary opportunity, and it shouldn't be taken for granted. When you start making progress, you can easily get complacent and lazy and lose what you have gained. You need to sustain your Buddhist practice by clarifying your views, concentrating your attention, relaxing deeply held attitudes and connecting with profound spiritual qualities. In meditation, activity and receptivity need to join together in a stream of mindful action – receptively aware of experiences as they arise and actively responding by cultivating higher consciousness. In this way you create the depth and space to see into the nature of things.

You need balance in your engagement and the perspective that allows you to see what needs balancing. You may sometimes go into your meditation in a driving, ambitious manner when the basis for your concentration is weak. The heat immediately disperses, like that of a red-hot stone dropped in water. To develop a stronger basis for sustaining concentration, you must proceed from a *general* awareness of all aspects of yourself before investing energy in the *particular* intense awareness of the meditation object. You can call the ground – the broader, generalized awareness – the breadth of the meditation practice and the narrowing of attention onto the object, its focus.

Your ability to focus is supported by the breadth of the practice, just as the summit of a mountain stands upon a huge mass of rock. Perhaps this is where the idea of 'sitting like a mountain' in meditation comes from. It all starts at the base, with body awareness. You may focus, say, on the breathing process or on the development of mettā; but if it's to lead to full concentration, a broad base of experience has to support it. When you don't have such a balance, concentration (and any insight reflection you're engaging with) tumbles over. While it's ungrounded, it feels as though you are gritting your teeth to hold it all together. That is weak concentration; strong concentration feels relaxed, flexible and stable.

Your 'breadth' is how you are as a whole. So you sit mindful of the body and its vitality, feelings and emotions, its mental states and moment-to-moment perception. If these elements are given a place in the practice, your focus will be relaxed and, most important, there will be energy available for concentration. When contacting breadth, the idea is not to get involved with the content of the experience but simply to acknowledge the existence of its elements. If you are overinvolved with breadth, you'll become distracted. So the breadth needs to be balanced with focus.

People tend to work inappropriately when concerned with results. That's because this concern can arise from greed or a kind of escapism that is running away from the difficult messages coming from the breadth of your experience. When the dominating idea is to get results, there seems little time to stop and consider what you are actually experiencing. It is right to want success but unhelpful to have too precise an expectation of what that will be. Actually, expectations are always abstractions based on memory – fantasies that don't exist and never will in the form you imagine. It's the same story when you try to recapture a previous meditation experience. You should remember that whatever happens in future will be different; and when it happens, it will be happening now.

It is best to cultivate a resolve always to start afresh and to maintain that attitude in the session, allowing new experiences to arise. It is easy to become rigid and create habits, so that you end up just going through the motions. Some meditators sit religiously every morning, doing it in exactly the same way year in, year out. They put themselves through a set sequence of mental actions with no regard for their actual mental state. This is not effective meditation, or mindfulness. It is what the Buddha called the fetter of clinging to rites and rituals. The typical result of inappropriate or wilful effort is pain and mental confusion. Forcing concentration may bring headaches, digestion problems and stiff shoulder muscles, along with mental agitation, anxiety, dullness or a spacey, disconnected condition. Since you are a sensitive creature, phenomena such as these obviously affect your feelings about meditation. They may put you off forever or get you gritting your teeth in an even more rigid attempt to 'get on with the practice'.

Whenever you realize that you are doing some of these things, just stop for a moment. The mindfulness bell has been struck. Stop and take the time to tune in to what is actually happening and the thoughts and feelings that are involved. Recover a genuine experience of yourself. Stopping the momentum of habit and establishing real mindfulness takes time and patience; but whether such a readjustment in your practice takes hours, days or weeks, it will be worth it. It could teach you a new kind of relaxation in your approach both to practice and to daily life.

You need to look at what these issues are pointing to more broadly. In this case, they seem to be saying that you could do with more richness and colour in your life. All of us need inspiration, a more imaginative ingredient, in our practice and our life. You can find it in thoughtful and well-written literature, making or enjoying art, playing or listening to music, meeting people, spending time alone, walking in nature or whatever keeps the wellsprings flowing.

Journals

At times when you're practising meditation more intensively, or when you want to look at your daily practice more closely, some form of meditation diary can be a useful aid. It can be a simple log, a systematic analysis or an informal journal. An analytical diary might track the factors of dhyāna, meditation conditions etc. over a retreat. I like to keep a journal from time to time, writing down reflections about each meditation session as well as other current thoughts, sometimes describing what happened or speculating upon the significance of the experience. Making a record of your inner life can connect you with meditation in a new way and even become a focus for your life generally.

I have also found a journal to be very helpful when alone as a way to hold a dialogue with myself, ask questions and formulate more clearly what is happening. By recording what happens in meditation, you'll find yourself reflecting more about it, and that's the best support for practice. The records you make can sometimes be an important reminder of where you've been because, like dreams, meditation experiences are often subtle and easily forgotten. But for me the greatest use of a journal is not in reading it but in expressing and clarifying thoughts that might otherwise remain unexamined.

Working in more subtle states of concentration

You may already have discovered that when you break through to a new level of concentration, a period of *less* concentrated meditation frequently follows. This can be confusing and disappointing, but it is fairly normal and not a bad sign at all. It seems that getting to a new level of integration is a shock to the system and that you need a certain amount of meditation time simply to absorb its impact. You should not be discouraged but recognize the significance of what is happening and persevere through the slump. If you continue sitting regularly, you will eventually find your way back to access concentration and become able to sustain it for longer periods.

In your practice of śamatha you should aim to get beyond this threshold of access or 'neighbourhood' concentration, as it is not very stable: the first dhyāna is a better basis for vipaśyanā. If you are regularly getting into access but no further, you can check for certain subtle obstacles that commonly prevent entry into dhyāna. A typical example is excitement: it's common for meditators to experience a few moments of access concentration and then to become excited and fall back into the hindrances. This is partly due to unfamiliarity with the process itself. So when access does start cropping up more regularly, it's worth doing some extra sitting in order to gain experience of it.

Once established in access concentration, you have entered a more subtle, balanced state in which there is no pull from the hindrances. Yet the balance remains relatively weak and you need to make it firmer by counteracting the subtle hindrances, those tendencies of the mind to lose even a well-established balance. You lose that through either a subtle form of dullness (called sinking) or a subtle form of restlessness (called drifting). Access concentration is such a vast improvement upon your usual state of mind that it's tempting to rest on your laurels, whereupon these hindrances creep in unawares and topple your stability. Sinking and drifting are tendencies that occur all the time; and if they aren't counteracted, they will become stronger and eventually turn into the gross hindrances of either sloth and torpor or restlessness and anxiety.

Body, breathing and mind

A good method of working in these more subtle states of concentration is to use the three basic elements of **body, breathing and mind** in order to maintain access concentration and to develop it further. You need 1) to maintain your body in the best possible posture, so that the vital energy is flowing; 2) to maintain smooth and calm breathing; and 3) to maintain balanced absorption by adjusting your mental state whenever you notice it becoming slightly dull (sinking) or slightly excited (drifting).

Body: Structure and energy

You can attend to the **body** in terms of both its physical **structure** of bones, muscles and sinews and the **energy** and vitality that pervade it.

Maintaining a clear sense of physical **structure** and position will lend stability and continuity to the concentration. You'll probably find that in access concentration you are already in a reasonably good meditation posture, as an enhanced sense of your body shape and form is a natural part of this mental state. From the position of the sitting bones on your cushion, you can feel the natural curve of the spine extending through the centre of the shoulders and up to the head. The legs and hips feel stable and 'triangular', and you feel the shoulders and arms encircling the vertical line of the trunk. There is an equivalent to this enhanced awareness while sitting on a chair too.

Awareness of structure will also help you to contact the vitality and sense of physical aliveness that is the **energy** aspect of body awareness. Simply being aware of your physical vitality will bring energy, enthusiasm and inspiration into the meditation. And because the experience of pleasure is concerned with body energies, this awareness is an indispensible basis for developing the pleasurable dhyāna factors prīti, sukha and, eventually, even upekkhā.

But you are not always in touch with your energy. Your awareness of it can sometimes be dull and obscure, usually either because of tiredness or physical tension. Simply resting can cure tiredness, but tension is more complex. Physical tension can be due to physical causes – the result of imbalances in the sitting position – but more often the causes are emotional. A tense face, neck or shoulder or tight stomach muscles is often triggered by emotions that have not been acknowledged. In principle, if you can ease the tension, however it has been caused, then blocked energy is freed. This new energy enriches consciousness, enabling you to take more interest in the meditation and to achieve deeper concentration. However, if tension is emotionally based, then physical relaxation alone cannot resolve it. It's necessary to tackle the underlying emotional cause.

For example, if you are tense because of being angry about something, you need to acknowledge that emotion before it will be possible to ease the tension. Without that acknowledgement, any attempted relaxation will be superficial and even forced – in fact at first, rather than relaxing, you may need to allow yourself to experience the tension and to feel the emotion behind it. If you do not allow for the presence of underlying emotions, you will experience a feeling of dullness, not the enhanced vitality you are looking for. Attending to the physical 'echo' of an emotional state can be a way of working with that state without getting caught up in the thoughts that go along with it.

A good way of tuning into and working with both structural and energy aspects of the body is to sit very still and receptively, making a decision not to move whatever resistance you may feel. That decision can create a deep stillness in both body and mind: the less you move, the more concentrated you tend to become. This will also reveal subtle imbalances in your posture and energy. Of course, you will need to move a little so as to adjust for these, but you should preserve the stillness of the posture as much as possible by being economical with the adjustments. Take whatever time is needed and move only when you are sure exactly what you need to change. Such economical use of energy will deepen your focus on the meditation object still further.

Breathing: In harmony with mind

Zhiyi says:

> By audible breathing is meant that when sitting we can hear a faint
> sound of the breath as it passes through the nose. If we were standing
> or working we would not notice it, but in our practice it is enough to
> distract the mind.

> By silent breathing is meant that there is no sound, no compression, no
> force, simply the slightest feeling of the tranquillity of our breathing,
> which does not disturb the mind but rather gives to the mind a pleasant
> feeling of security and peace.

> Blowing disturbs concentration, panting gives it heaviness and
> audible breathing wearies it. We can attain samādhi only with silent
> breathing.[96]

When the mind is calm, the breath is silent and has a smooth,
subtle feeling; when the mind is disturbed or excited, the breathing is
audible and rough. There is also a relation between the breathing and
the body: physical stimulation has a large effect upon the breathing;
and after you exert yourself physically, the breathing may sometimes
remain coarse for an hour or more. You may notice, on the other hand,
that when doing some very detailed physical task such as painting
a picture or threading a needle, you breathe very lightly, sometimes
even holding your breath in order to concentrate. Since breathing is
so intimately involved with both body and mind, it is an important
key to meditation. By noting the quality of your breathing, you can
maintain a sensitive awareness of both body and mind and can focus
even more sensitively upon the meditation object. As the quality of
your breathing is such an influence upon your mental states, it is
not surprising to learn that full dhyāna is attainable only with fine
breathing. But although fine breathing is an ideal to aim for, you
shouldn't force the breathing to calm down. That effort would be a
strain and could even be damaging. With patience, you can let the
breathing gently quieten naturally.

Access concentration is quite responsive to any attitude you bring
to it, and simply maintaining awareness of the quality of the breathing

may suffice to remain balanced in meditation. But awareness of the breath is also the basis for a number of active methods of counteracting the subtle hindrances. For a dull state of mind (e.g. sinking), you can stimulate energy by imagining the breathing coming into the body from the toes up through the body to the head. Or you can simply focus on the breathing high in the body, perhaps at the nose. For excitement (e.g. drifting), you can imagine the breath flowing down the body from the head to the toes, which has a calming, quietening effect, or you can focus upon it low in the body. It is possible to imagine that the breathing is coming into the body at almost any point.

Generally, if you feel you are too much 'in your head' (full of thoughts, perhaps dreamy, without much awareness of the body), it may help to use the breathing gradually to transfer awareness away from the head and down into the body. You can do this by concentrating on the breathing lower down, at the point where it touches the abdomen, for example, or perhaps by paying attention to the external sensation of the abdomen rising and falling with the breathing. Alternatively, take awareness of the breathing into the heart area. Or take it down the body in stages: from the head to the throat, then to the heart and lungs, then to the diaphragm and abdomen etc. You may need to spend as much as twenty minutes doing that, but it's time well spent when you cannot otherwise engage with the practice.

Mind: in constant need of harmonizing

Attending to the mind means here engaging with the subtle hindrances of sinking and drifting as well as with a third, less problematic, subtle hindrance known as stray thought. From the viewpoint of mind, working in access concentration involves maintaining constant awareness of the possibility of one of these subtle hindrances arising and adjusting as soon as you notice it happening. All three are characterized by the lightness of feeling and emotion typical of more concentrated states – in contrast to the five gross hindrances, which are all charged with greed, hatred and confusion.

To recognize these in experience, you need to understand how the body-mind complex operates in deeply integrated states. Dhyāna is a 'middle way' that brings into harmony the positive aspects of the receptive and the dynamic sides of your nature, which are often in tension. In fact, each needs the other's support to prevent it going to an extreme. Your capacity for receptivity, when left alone, can become dull and turned inwards; your dynamic energies tend to rush off on their own and to get rigid or overexcited. So at the receptive pole of experience you may be calmly, openly aware, patient and still, in a state that can normally be maintained only for a limited time – unless another element, say inspiration, is also present. If your mind was merely calm and still, without dynamic energy, you'd gradually become dull, lazy or gloomy and fall, sooner or later, into sloth and torpor. Only when you unite the receptive aspect of your mind with its dynamic aspect can you maintain balanced concentration. Bringing both energy poles together in meditation, you move towards the harmonious state of dhyāna.

Various aspects of the polarity are shown in Table 21, with the extremes at the sides and the balanced qualities of dhyāna in the middle. In life you probably tend towards one of these poles, though you also oscillate between one and the other. Some people tend to be dull and unemotional in the morning and then get excited in the evening, sleep poorly overnight and awake dull once more. The aim in meditation, mindfulness and ethics, as all these influence behaviour, is to cultivate a balanced state that contains both heightened vigour and heightened calm. You can learn to generate this by developing the positive qualities of the pole opposite to the one you are sliding towards. When you are feeling energetic but are moving towards distraction, allow an element of receptivity to enter the practice; and when calm but tending to dullness, cultivate more inspired, active energy.

Table 21: Sinking and drifting

Extreme receptive pole	Dhyāna: positive aspects in harmony	Extreme dynamic pole
SINKING		DRIFTING
Sloth and torpor	Calm and energy	Restlessness and anxiety
Dullness	Receptive and active	Distraction
Laziness	Grounded and inspired	Overexertion
Depressed, gloomy		Enthusiastic, hysterical

Going into this much detail in the abstract can sound technical, but it does relate to actual lived experience. Apply it – its usefulness will become clear. With this overview in mind, let us now look at the subtle hindrances themselves.

Sinking describes that state of mind which, though concentrated, is becoming dull. In terms of your subjective state, you are just beginning to lose your intensity of focus. There is less vibrancy and aliveness in the way you experience the object of meditation – perhaps the breath is a little less interesting, your mettā is a shade uninspired or your imagination is losing its immediacy. Sinking is caused by a slight neglect or lack of awareness. At some point, you don't register the need for a change in the quality of your effort, and the character of your concentration changes without you knowing it. Since you are in access concentration at least, you are still stably concentrated upon the meditation object. The object is quite clear and the concentration is quite pleasant, but you have unconsciously begun to lose a little of the dynamic, energizing and inspiring quality of concentration. The focus has become a little too stable and the mind is gradually becoming more fixed and wooden. The longer you delay, the more the sinking will increase. There are two stages to sinking: first, the intensity of the concentration fades while the object remains clear; next, the object's clarity also starts to fade. This is usually reversible when you notice it, but you need to learn how to notice the sinking process earlier.

Table 22: Aspects of sinking

Stages of sinking		Subjective experience	Experience of object
Subtle hindrance	1. Subtle sinking	The intensity of concentration fades.	Object remains clear
	2. Gross sinking	The intensity of concentration fades further.	Clarity of object fades
Gross hindrance	3. Sloth and torpor	Dull concentration Heavy feeling Very little interest in object	Little or no awareness of object

Drifting starts to cast its veil over your concentration by invisibly introducing subtle thoughts and sensations. It often has an emotional tone of slight dissatisfaction and is stirred up by you making slightly too much effort. Perhaps a few minutes ago you were sinking and worked to counteract it, but that effort was a little too stimulating. Or perhaps your mindfulness wasn't quite clear enough and you maintained effort beyond what was appropriate, with the same result. When you drift, the meditation object is in the forefront of your attention, remaining clear and stable; yet the attention has started, very subtly, to blur and to include things other than the meditation object. For the time being, concentration may remain strong enough to include both the meditation object and this slight distraction. But if the tendency remains unchecked, the mind will drift further and further away from the receptive mental pole, which so far has been anchoring your attention. Eventually, the gross hindrance of restlessness and anxiety will interpose itself and you'll fall away from absorption.

Table 23: Aspects of drifting

Stages of drifting		Subjective experience	Experience of object
Subtle hindrance	1. Subtle drifting	The intense edge of concentration blurs.	Object remains clear
	2. Gross drifting	The concentration scatters outwards. Slight sense of dissatisfaction	Clarity of object fades
Gross hindrance	3. Restlessness and anxiety	Very scattered concentration Restless feeling Strong interest in other objects	Little or no awareness of, or interest in, object

Sinking and drifting are the main obstacles to look out for as you work to maintain balanced concentration. But a third factor, **stray thoughts**, may also arise in access concentration and dhyāna. Stray thoughts are the flotsam and jetsam of the mind: fragments of thoughts, images or feelings you're not especially attracted towards – but there they are. These are not distractions in the usual sense but are simply present in consciousness in parallel with the meditation practice. It's a bit like being engaged in conversation while hearing music playing in the background. It's easy to ignore the music, but there's still a temptation to give it your attention. The content of this stray thinking can be any old disconnected idea: a memory, an image, a conversation, a remembered sound. Because you are so absorbed, these insignificant phenomena lurk harmlessly at the edge of awareness. Nonetheless, they represent a potential danger to concentration and may be worth counteracting, especially if they start to hook you into drifting.

The most effective antidote to stray thoughts is recognizing them merely as stray thoughts on the edge of the mind and not actual distractions. Once you put them in perspective, you'll feel confident enough to ignore them and focus more strongly on the object. Another effective method is vipaśyanā reflection: reminding yourself that the stray thoughts are conditioned phenomena, which, having arisen, are eventually going to disappear. If this is a familiar reflection in other contexts, then shifting into this bigger perspective will dissolve their power by giving you the confidence to let them go.

Knowing about the subtle hindrances – in experience, not in the abstract – enables you to retain balanced concentration. In access concentration or dhyāna, it should become second nature to notice these signs, so that as soon as you recognize that sinking or drifting has started, you'll spontaneously adjust and quite naturally maintain smooth, continuous concentration. The practice is in learning to recognize what is happening and in providing what is missing: dynamic vigour in the case of sinking, calm receptivity in the case of drifting.

Spotting the loss of edge that indicates sinking eventually becomes clear enough to draw forth an effort, and that intensifies the experience of the object without overintensifying it. Breathing a little more fully or experiencing the breath higher in the body could do this in, for example, the mindfulness of breathing meditation. Or the clarity of your Mettā Bhāvanā could be intensified by creating a clear image of a good friend. These efforts need to be intelligent and gentle, and they should happen relatively spontaneously, almost effortlessly. Too strong an effort will push you back into drifting and even restlessness; if the effort is too weak, you'll fade and sink. It's likely that you will oscillate between sinking and drifting for some time, applying now a stimulating antidote, now a calming antidote at subtler and subtler levels until the meditation becomes effortless.

When merely read about, this work may seem bloodless and technical, but in practice it is suffused by the bright, subtle tone of access concentration and dhyāna. Also, part of the emotional content will be a strong positive desire for Realization: you deeply desire the clarity and the transparent openness that is coming from the practice and also the insight that is in the longer view. Without them, no progress can be made. Ultimately this desire is bodhicitta, the wish that all beings should become awakened.

As we have seen, the general antidote to **sinking** is to introduce a more dynamic quality: concentrate more strongly, grasp it more tightly, perceive it more intensely. However, there are times when the necessary intensity is there but you already feel tight and withdrawn, so more of this quality cannot help you to avert sinking. In such a situation, it is possible to enlarge the scope of the object in a number of ways and to widen out the feeling of the practice in a way that links to the bright, dynamic quality in a gentler way. If doing the mindfulness of breathing, you can imagine the breath entering through all the pores of the body in a precise way. If doing Mettā Bhāvanā, you can concentrate on sending mettā out to all sentient beings. If it's a sādhana practice, you can concentrate on perceiving the colours or other details of the image and brightening it.

As we saw earlier, the chief antidote to **drifting** is receptivity. You slacken the intensity of concentration very slightly, being careful not to go too slack and to start sinking. The usual cause of drifting is too much effort, so at this point you can relax a little and be more receptive to the experience. Enjoyment, emotion generally and joyful enthusiasm are important in gaining balanced concentration, and you should always check for the presence of feeling: if that's absent, you're likely to sink. So you will need to recover the feeling. That isn't the issue with drifting, which always has a recognizable feeling tone such as greedy excitement. Drifting will diminish once that excited feeling is met and acknowledged.

After prolonged experience with this stage of meditation, you will alternate between sinking and drifting only very subtly. Eventually the simple recognition of whether sinking or drifting is arising will suffice to maintain the equilibrium of the practice.

This gives another approach in working from access concentration towards full absorption. And moving from the first dhyāna towards the second dhyāna and from the second to the third and beyond involves the same technique of balancing. Sinking and drifting keep occurring at subtler levels and with differing time spans. You saw earlier how the mind can ascend from the first dhyāna to the second dhyāna as you leave behind the absorption factors of initial and applied thought. With a little experience, it is possible to encourage this to happen. It is done by recognizing the unsatisfying quality in the present situation, intuiting how much more enjoyable it is at the next level and letting go of the coarser aspects of your mental state. Of course, once you know from experience how much more calm, clear and enjoyable the second dhyāna is, you acquire a route beyond the gentle directed-thinking quality that characterizes the first dhyāna. You can move from the second dhyāna to the third dhyāna in a similar way, recollecting that bliss is a far calmer and more deeply concentrating experience than rapture and so on.

> On emerging from the now familiar first dhyāna, he can regard the flaws in it in this way: 'this attainment is threatened by the nearness of the hindrances, and its factors are weakened by the grossness of the applied and sustained thought'. He can bring the second dhyāna to mind as quieter, and so end his attachment to the first dhyāna and set about doing what is needed for attaining the second.
>
> When he has emerged from the first dhyāna, applied and sustained thought appear gross to him as he reviews the dhyāna factors with mindfulness and full awareness, while happiness and bliss and unification of mind appear peaceful. Then, as he brings [the meditation object] to mind ... again and again, with the purpose of abandoning the gross factors and obtaining the peaceful factors, [knowing] 'now the second dhyāna will arise ...'
>
> With the stilling of initial and applied thought he enters upon and dwells in the second dhyāna, which has internal confidence and singleness of mind without applied thought, without sustained thought, with rapture and bliss born of concentration.
>
> Buddhaghosa[97]

As so much depends on confidence born from experience, it may take some time to penetrate the higher dhyāna levels. Much depends also on the conditions under which you meditate and the time you're able to devote to the practice. It's important as well for you to understand that proficiency in dhyāna is not just a matter of manipulating your mind by the techniques described in this chapter. Dhyāna is best regarded not as something you get into but as something you become, something that reflects your whole life with all its thoughts, feelings and actions. Dhyāna is the outcome of the integration of a multitude of unresolved emotions and ideas in a process that never follows a smooth, logical course. It often comes to a head in a temporary resolution, a dhyāna experience the clarity of which may immediately reveal the presence of new unresolved material. There is so much to engage with, so many challenges to meet, so much potential for change! Dhyāna is never a permanent attainment, but its presence indicates important inner changes. Many of the factors governing the arising of higher states of consciousness are happening in the unconscious mind outside your direct control. You can only provide the best possible conditions by living a life as conducive to meditation as possible and by working systematically in meditation to the best of your ability.

Dhyāna is the best basis for meditation upon ultimate reality, and vipaśyanā is the only method that brings permanent progress. To practise vipaśyanā regularly you need to maintain a good general level of śamatha. Having had experience of dhyāna, you may sustain it if you meditate very regularly – at the very least twice a day but preferably more. I suggest at least two, and ideally four, hours daily. With that level of regular practice, a sufficient level of both dhyāna and vipaśyanā reflection may be sustained, even in a city environment.

Appendix two

....

Sitting posture

At least sometimes, most meditators have to deal with physical aches and pains during meditation. Pain recedes into the background once you're deep in concentration, but often the back muscles or the knees nag at you long before you get to that point, and pain can scupper the whole enterprise unless you counteract it. A good deal of pain derives from unhelpful habits resulting from a lifetime's use of poorly designed chairs. Unfortunately, people normally adopt slumped sitting positions that support their back temporarily but in the longer term are harmful and difficult to correct. What you need is a practical understanding of the principles of good posture. This appendix aims to give enough advice for you to avoid serious problems and to offer general guidance on the principles of meditation posture.

The core principle is this: the best meditation posture is one in which you can become completely still, completely relaxed and completely alert. Sitting in any posture which minimizes strain and in which you can also be awake and alert creates a sense of free vitality that makes it much easier to concentrate. Relaxing from strain supports awareness, and that awareness enables further relaxation. This is revitalizing and refreshing, and frees new energy that helps you to direct the mind in concentration. This progression is similar to that taught by the Buddha in the *Satipaṭṭhāna Sutta*, in which he shows how mindfulness of the body supports awareness of feeling. Once awakened, these aspects of awareness enhance your sense of presence and purpose, helping you to give attention more wholeheartedly. Maintaining mindfulness of the body is the way to learn, experientially, the principles of meditation posture because it enables you to understand the body–mind relationship.

Postural work has little to do with holding a particular pose, as meditation can be practised in almost any position if that is necessary.

....

An invalid, for example, may have no choice but to lie in bed, but that need not present any problems once he or she is accustomed to it. In walking meditation, you are standing up and moving; and there's no reason why you can't learn to meditate while standing still. But most people find that some form of sitting position gives the easiest access to still, deep concentration. You are seeking a way to sit with a minimum expenditure of energy, with the heart at its quietest and the lungs unrestricted so that the air intake and outflow is gentle and natural.

Have awareness in the upright spine, enabling balance in the weight of the trunk above the seat – to left, right, front and back – with a minimum of muscular effort. Then, once every part of the body (especially the legs and arms) is positioned so that it feels symmetrically balanced, the whole structure will feel unified. A good posture keeps the skeletal structure balanced and aligned: you manage the force of gravity running through the body by aligning the bones rather than by holding the muscles in a rigid pose. From there, you will need occasionally to make fine adjustments.

It is noticeable that when sitting, the main support for the body structure is the pelvis. To enable the pelvis to take the full weight of the upper body without imbalance, the lower back should neither slump nor overarch – these are the two most typical sitting errors. The entire weight of the upper body bears down on the pelvic sitting bones, two bony projections that press against the cushion or seat. The weight should be distributed equally between these so that the muscles on both sides of the spine and neck work evenly. The sitting bones themselves need to roll evenly front to back; in other words, the tailbone should neither protrude outwards nor turn inwards.

The problems that usually arise from long sitting in one position are that the knees, back or neck start aching. Initially, these may have to do with lack of practice, but the likely cause is muscular tension that has been caused by your poor posture. Sometimes tension develops because of an unconscious habit of using more muscular effort than necessary or because muscles remain contracted even when they're not in use. Sometimes the strain is emotionally conditioned, as we'll see in a moment. Whatever the reason, tension habits frequently become chronic. The result is muscular pain, restricted movement and fatigue. Chronic levels of muscular tension and neck, shoulder and back discomfort are often an outcome of poor posture. It stresses the body to sit for hours each day in an uncomfortable chair; and if your occupation involves much sitting, your sitting posture will be a big influence on your health.

Some postural defects come from the body itself. A weakness on one side of the body will strain things on the other side, which will weaken the affected part or cause the body to develop new muscles compensating for the difference. Patterns of tension and compensatory reaction can alter the way you hold yourself in several parts of the body. A person with one leg shorter than the other, which is not uncommon, has to work the back muscles on one side more than on the other. To compensate, one shoulder is held higher than the other and the neck and head tilt to one side as a result. This slight irregularity may remain unnoticed until they start sitting still for forty minutes every day.

Another cause of physical tension is emotional strain. Someone who is round-shouldered and closed-chested, for example, may have a poor self-image and lack confidence. The habit of holding the body in this constricting way may also have strengthened that negative emotion, dulling your energy and making you oversubjective. So posture can cause negative emotion as well as be caused by it. Physical awareness can help in generating positive emotion. If you notice how you are carrying yourself, you can learn to stand more upright, hunching less in the shoulders and relaxing in the head and neck. Your mental state will almost certainly improve.

Just as a joyful emotional state is reflected in the way you sit, stand and move, a happy state in meditation naturally enables an improved sitting posture. As you meditate, relatively chaotic mental states gradually clarify as the body feels lighter and more relaxed; the distracting, niggling physical discomforts gradually lessen. The back can straighten, the chest can open and the shoulders and arms can relax. At the very least, you can notice how restricted the present posture is, and sooner or later a straighter back and an open chest will begin to feel more natural. In this way, you start acquiring an intuitive understanding of how to work with physical posture.

Physical awareness, on its own, is a very effective way in which to work constructively in meditation. Sometimes just a subtle movement of the angle of the pelvis, or of the alignment of the head on the neck, suddenly makes energy available and concentration easier. It is worthwhile experimenting with slightly different alignments sometimes. When your mind, body or both are dull and sleepy, it can seem painful to try to practise at all. You can feel so reluctant to engage in meditation practice that it seems inevitable that you will drift into daydreams. This kind of condition can have so much power that it seems impossible to work with.

However, there's a good antidote: spend the whole session working to maintain a good posture. Though your mind is unable to grasp a more subtle meditation object, it's possible to make the effort to remain awake and to sit correctly. If you persist in bringing attention back to the body, checking for overarching in the back, slumping and misalignment of other posture points, the hindrance is likely to disperse before the end of the session, allowing you to move on to a definite meditation technique. But even if sloth and torpor is overpoweringly strong, as it sometimes can be, and you cannot concentrate at all, even after half an hour or forty minutes, nevertheless you will have weakened its power over you just by being active and holding it at bay. And you will probably notice an improvement in subsequent meditation sessions.

It's easier to work with the body in the case of the opposite mental extreme, the hindrance of restlessness and anxiety; you just determine to sit absolutely still. The stillness needs to be relaxed and calm, not forced. By taking that resolution as the main factor in the meditation, the restless mind will eventually calm down and be at peace. If agitation is very strong, though, there will be resistance; patience will be very necessary and the process will take some time. But if, without forcing, you persist patiently in stilling the body, you'll eventually succeed.

Fig. 2: *Full lotus*

Cross-legged postures are not the only positions you can meditate in: it's fine to use an upright chair or to kneel on a meditation stool. But if your hips are supple enough to allow you to sit cross-legged, you should try that method first because it will probably suit you better. Most people are too restricted in the hips and thighs to place their legs in the classic 'full lotus', but many will be able to do an approximation of the 'half lotus', which differs only in having a simpler leg cross. Instructions for the spine, hands, shoulders, head, eyes and mouth are the same.

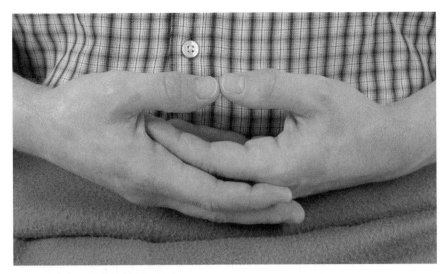

Fig. 3: Hand position (dhyāna mudrā)

The full lotus posture consists of seven aspects:

1. The legs are crossed, with each foot placed, sole uppermost, upon the thigh of the other leg (in full lotus).
2. The spine is upright, not arching backward or slumping forward.
3. The hands are held in the lap, two or three inches below the navel. The palms both face upwards, one over the other so that the thumb-tips touch lightly.
4. The shoulders are relaxed and drawn somewhat back so as to keep the chest open.
5. The head is balanced evenly on the spine.
6. The eyes are directed downwards, either lightly closed or half-open.
7. The mouth is relaxed, the teeth unclenched, the lips held lightly together. The tongue just touches the palate behind the teeth.

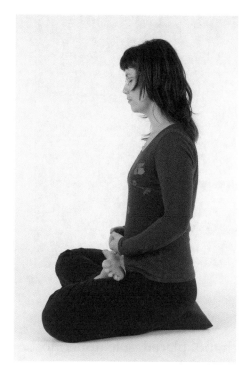

Fig. 4: *Full lotus, side view*

Fig. 5: *Half lotus*

Fig. 6: *One foot on calf*

Fig. 7: *One leg in front*

Fig. 8: *Kneeling with cushions*

Fig. 9: *Kneeling on a stool*

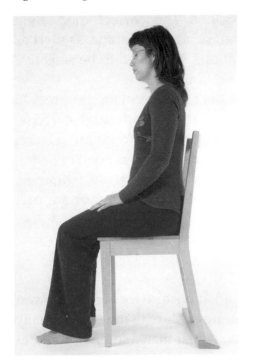

Fig. 10: *Sitting on a chair*

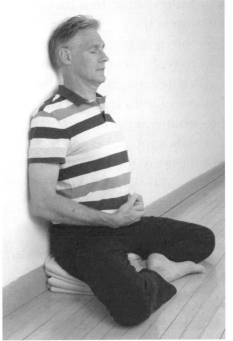

Fig. 11: *Sitting with back against a wall*

In terms of the principles outlined above, some sitting positions are better than others for concentration. The full lotus gives the best skeletal balance and allows easier access to subtle physical energy. It is also the most comfortable for long periods of sitting – once you are used to it.

Next best are other cross-legged postures such as the half lotus. They can be done in a variety of ways, depending on the flexibility of the meditator's hips and knees, using the appropriate cushion height and support under the knees. If sitting cross-legged is simply not possible, a good alternative is kneeling on a low bench or a pile of cushions or sitting on a chair. One can meditate effectively in all these positions. In time, with exercise and more practice, you will perhaps be able to sit in full lotus or half lotus. But if they are new to you, you must be careful when sitting for longer periods until, through appropriate exercise, the hips have loosened and the posture has become fairly easy. Otherwise, the knee joints may be under too much tension and damage could result. Meditators need to take special care of their knees, and there is no point in trying to force them into an ideal position that cannot be sustained. The 'correct' meditation posture is the one that enables you to be as relaxed and as alert as possible within your physical limitations. You need to be sensitive and to work as best you can with what you have.

Whatever your age, it is possible over time to make progress in loosening the joints and strengthening the muscles through exercise. I recommend trainings such as T'ai Chi and Hatha Yoga for keeping the body supple and healthy. Other methods may be as good or better, but these are the ones that I know from experience create awareness of the subtle physical energies that soon become an important part of working in meditation.

A routine for setting up posture

Here is a routine for setting up meditation posture for every time you sit. It offers a systematic way of assessing posture that will eventually become second nature. It might take no longer than a second or two; at other times you may need to spend much more time on it. Remember, however, that the effects of good or bad posture won't usually be clear at first. It may take twenty, thirty or more minutes before you realize that something is wrong or that there has been an improvement. Sometimes a position is comfortable at first but becomes excruciating after ten minutes; conversely, a posture may feel awkward initially, even slightly painful, but become comfortable and stable as the session goes on.

1. Choose a cushion or stool that seems to be the right height and arrange the legs in one of the ways shown. If you are sitting cross-legged, don't be concerned for now if both knees don't reach the ground. Eventually the legs will need to be lower than the hips or the back will slump, but the right seat height will enable that. Most people slump, and need a higher seat than they think. It's worth experimenting with small modifications, as even an inch can make the crucial difference. Eventually, you'll feel the balance to be correct at a certain height, and the awareness arising from that will help you to adjust the legs and back.

   Incorrect cushion height usually causes the main sitting errors: arching backward and slumping forward.

Fig. 12: Overarching backwards   *Fig. 13: Slumping forwards*

Arching or, more exactly, overarching (as the spine naturally arches inwards to some extent) often occurs when the seat is too high. The excessive height causes the upper pelvis to move forward, the tailbone to move backward and the buttocks to protrude behind. This creates a tendency for the body's weight to fall forward, and the upper back arches up and backward to compensate. This strains the lower back, so you begin to feel pain there. The remedy for overarching, if slight, is to relax in the lower back, letting the spine return to a natural position. If that's not enough, you need a lower seat.

Slumping happens when the seat is too low. The upper pelvis tends backward and the tailbone tucks under, causing the lower back to collapse and the body weight to be thrown backwards. Then, in order to avoid falling back, you tend to slump forward and to close up in the chest. This awkward position causes painful tension in the neck and shoulders. The remedy for slumping, if it is slight, is simply to sit up straight – not rigidly straight like a broom handle but with a natural curve. It that is not enough, you need a higher seat. Experiment by adding more layers of cushions or blankets.

2. Become aware of the body's weight as it presses the two sitting bones in the buttocks down on to the seat. Maintaining this awareness as a base and keeping the weight evenly distributed between left and right, allow the spinal column to lift lightly and to straighten without rigidity.

3. Taking a deep breath or two, allow the chest and rib cage to open. Experience the shoulders and arms lifting slightly on the inward breath; and on the outward breath, allow them to roll back and relax down so that the chest stays open.

4. You can then adjust the hands in the lap so that their position maintains the relaxed-down position of the shoulders and arms. It can be helpful to place some padding in the lap so as to support the hands, which can then relax easily. One hand can be placed over the other. This too will help the shoulders to relax.

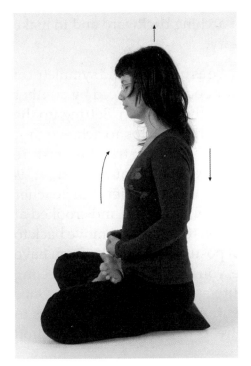

Fig. 14: Direction of spine, chest, shoulders and arms

Fig. 15: Position of head

5. You can now adjust the position of the head. It is important to allow the head to be supported by the spine rather than by the neck muscles. There should be no sense of rigidity, a point worth checking from time to time during meditation. The neck muscles should be completely relaxed, so that the head can move freely. Adjust the head by becoming aware of the neck as an extension of the spine. If it helps, roll the head gently backward and forward until it feels balanced. Experience the point where the skull balances upon the spinal column and let it tilt forward very slightly, so that the gaze rests a few feet ahead on the floor. Lastly, relax the face, jaw, tongue and throat.

6. You can now check the posture as a whole, especially noting the alignment of the trunk from side to side and back to front. It can help to rock gently each way from your pelvis until you feel yourself to be in equilibrium. Now you are in a position to check more thoroughly for the basic sitting

faults of slumping forward or arching backward and to make further adjustments as necessary.

The entire sitting position needs to be as balanced and symmetrical as possible. Ideally, each part of your body is balanced by another part, so that there is minimal strain on the skeleton. Setting up the posture in the systematic way just outlined helps to achieve this. However, you can't always trust your feelings: that the posture feels right doesn't mean it actually is! Often, what feels 'right' is merely what you are accustomed to. When a friend or teacher places us in better alignment, it may feel awkward and crooked at first, and the tendency will probably be to gradually move back to the familiar, incorrect and unhelpful posture. Especially if you have practised meditation for a long time, you should not take the feeling of rightness or wrongness in posture as the only guideline. Once in a while, seek objective assessment. Ask friends and teachers to take a look, and attend classes or retreats where posture instruction is available.

One obvious indication of incorrect posture is pain. Some aches and pains are best ignored – minor discomforts that soon pass, feelings of awkwardness, itches and other irritations. There can be no end to these, and you'll never be able to settle down unless you consciously decide to put up with them. These discomforts are often linked with restlessness, an unsettled mind fastening on to and becoming obsessed by a relatively minor irritation. Indulging this will prevent you from connecting with meditation, and people practising alongside you will be disturbed. If this is really all that's happening, you should recognize the fact and put your attention elsewhere. But it's important to be sensitive in assessing this because some pains may be danger signals. Pins and needles or numbness, for example, should not be ignored. It is certainly not good for limbs to become completely numb. And sharp pains invariably suggest that something is wrong.

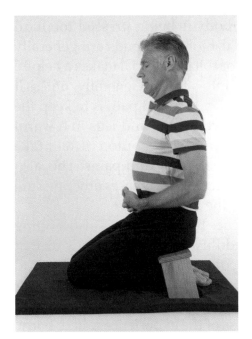

Fig. 16: *Soft floor covering to protect knees and ankles*

Fig. 17: *Padding supporting raised knee*

Fig. 18: *Padding supporting hands and knee*

Fig. 19: *Blanket for warmth*

It may be that one part of your body is being pressed too hard against the floor or another limb. Cushions and pads are generally good for alleviating this; a small pad or roll of material makes a helpful cushion for an ankle that is pressing into a thigh. Generally, unless it is quite hot, a surprisingly effective way to avoid pain is to keep the legs and hips insulated. If you wrap your hips and legs in a warm blanket and sit upon a doubled blanket or a zabuton, it will take the edge off temporary, inconsequential aches and pains. This also protects the knees; and when you are kneeling, it eases any pressure on the ankles and the upper parts of the feet.

The body is where Buddhist practice begins, and it is also a fitting point at which to end this book. Buddhist tradition reminds us that the human body is something exceedingly precious and difficult to obtain. You should therefore treat it with kindness and respect, for it serves as the basis from which everyone can meditate, gain insight and attain Enlightenment. Awareness of the experience called 'body' enables awareness of feeling and the great ethical transformations that become possible when you simply notice your actual emotional responses. Then, taking the Buddha's instruction and looking very deeply into your experience of self and world based on your mysterious embodiment allows the possibility of seeing all things, everywhere, as they actually are.

Endnotes

Preface

1   Ryōkan, *One Robe, One Bowl: The Zen Poetry of Ryōkan*, Weatherhill, New York, 1984, p. 65.

Introduction

2   *Dhyāna for Beginners*, trans. Wai-tao (amended), in Dwight Goddard (ed.), *A Buddhist Bible*, Beacon Press, 1970, p. 437.

3   From Wikipedia, http://en.wikipedia.org/wiki/Zhiyi:

Zhiyi (Chinese: 智顗; pinyin: *zhì yǐ* Wade–Giles: Zhiyi; Japanese: Chigi) (538–597 CE) is traditionally listed as the fourth patriarch, but is generally considered the founder of the Tiantai tradition of Buddhism in China. His standard title was Śramaṇa Zhiyi, linking him to the broad tradition of Indian asceticism. Zhiyi is famous for being the first in the history of Chinese Buddhism to elaborate a complete, critical and systematic classification of the Buddhist teachings, in order to explain the seemingly contradictory doctrines of Buddhism. He is also regarded as the first major figure to make a significant break from the Indian tradition, to form an indigenous Chinese system …

In 575 he went to Tiantai mountain for intensive study and practice with a group of disciples. Here he worked on adapting the Indian meditation principles of śamatha and vipaśyanā (translated as 'zhi' and 'guan') into a complex system of self-cultivation practice that also incorporated devotional rituals and confession/repentance rites.

4   *Dhammapada, The Way of Truth*, trans. Sangharakshita, Windhorse, Birmingham, 2001.

5   Suzuki Rōshi, *Zen Mind, Beginner's Mind*, Weatherhill, New York, 1983, p. 34.

6   Thich Nhat Hanh, *The Sun My Heart*, Parallax Press, Berkeley, 1988, p. 630.

7   Founded by Sangharakshita in 1968; formerly the Western Buddhist Order.

8   The Sanskrit terms *śamatha* and *vipaśyanā* are used throughout this book rather than the Pali *samatha* and *vipassanā*. This is to distinguish its approach from that of the contemporary Vipassanā and Insight Meditation movements, which have popularized what they call Vipassanā Meditation. This in itself is a perfectly respectable and traditional method, but it is only one particular form of insight inquiry. Yet it dominates the popular view of Buddhism in the US especially, so that practitioners are often unaware that there are thousands of other approaches

to vipassanā (or vipaśyanā) in Buddhist traditions. See Bodhipaksa, *Living As A River*, Sounds True, Boulder, 2010, p. 52.

Chapter one

9   T. S. Eliot, 'Burnt Norton', III, from *Four Quartets*.
10 *The Path of Purification*, trans. Ñāṇamoli (some changes), Buddhist Publication Society, Sri Lanka 1975, p. 300.
11 My tradition is known as Triratna. Though the practices in this book will be found in various forms within many other traditional approaches to Buddhism, experienced teachers from the Triratna Buddhist Order will know these methods intimately and will teach them more or less in the way explained here. There are public centres associated with the Triratna Buddhist Community in many cities and towns worldwide. See note 24 for a link to addresses.

Chapter two

12 Ayya Khema's translation from *Being Nobody, Going Nowhere*, Wisdom Publications, Somerville USA, 1987, p. 96.
13 Gampopa, *The Jewel Ornament of Liberation*, trans. H. V. Guenther, Rider, London, 1970, p. 18.
14 *Dhyāna For Beginners*, p. 479.
15 From the *Mettānisaṃsa Sutta*, Anguttara Nikāya V, 342: Mettā bestows the benefits of good sleep (you fall asleep and wake up happily, and don't have nightmares), love and appreciation from other beings (who will feel your mettā for them), protection from violence (others tend to find you less irritating), swift concentration of mind (mettā keeps you connected to the subtle mind), good looks (obviously, harbouring positive attitudes affects your appearance), freedom from confusion at death (due to confidence during life, and practice facing difficult emotions), and rebirth in a happy state of existence.

Chapter three

16 See *Middle Length Discourses of the Buddha*, trans. Bodhi and Ñāṇamoli, Wisdom Publications, Somerville USA, 2001, p. 145.
17 *Thought, I love thought.*
     But not the jiggling and twisting of already existing ideas
     I despise that self-important game.
     Thought is the welling up of unknown life into consciousness,
     Thought is the testing of statements on the touchstone of the conscience,
     Thought is gazing on the face of life, and reading what can be read,
     Thought is pondering over experience, and coming to a conclusion.
     Thought is not a trick, or an exercise, or a set of dodges,
     Thought is man in his wholeness wholly attending.

                                                                    D. H. Lawrence

18 Analayo, *Satipaṭṭhāna, The Direct Path to Realization*, Windhorse Publications, Birmingham, 2003, p. 173.

19 Robert E. Thayer, *The biopsychology of mood and arousal*, New York, NY, Oxford University Press, 1989.

20 *Middle Length Discourses of the Buddha*, p. 146.

21 The others are the five skandhas, the six internal and external sense-spheres, the seven factors of Awakening and the four noble truths.

Chapter four

22 Adapted from W. Y. Evans-Wentz, *The Tibetan Book of the Dead*, Oxford University Press, Oxford, 1984, p. 202.

23 *Dhyāna For Beginners*, p. 482.

24 At the time of writing, there is a list of Triratna Dharma centres at http://www.fwbo-news.org/links.html

25 Abridged from the ceremony of the same title in *FWBO Pūjā Book*, Windhorse, Birmingham, 1999, p. 36.

26 Francesca Fremantle, *Luminous Emptiness: Understanding the Tibetan Book of the Dead*, Shambhala Publications, Boston, 2001, p. 55.

27 See *Vitakkasaṇṭhāna Sutta*, Majjhima Nikāya 20, in *Middle Length Discourses of the Buddha*, p. 211.

28 These three key aspects are known as the Three Jewels, or most precious things.

29 Sanskrit: *dhyāna*; Pali: *jhāna*.

30 From the *Maṅgala Sutta*, trans. Sangharakshita, in *The Enchanted Heart*, Ola Leaves, Norwich UK, 1978, p. 155.

31 Also see note 46.

32 Suzuki Rōshi, *Zen Mind, Beginner's Mind*, p. 21.

Chapter five

33 *Dhyāna for Beginners*, p. 456.

34 See the kamma niyama (ethical nature), presented at the end of Chapter 6.

35 H. D. Thoreau, *Walden*, Harper & Row, London, 1961.

36 *Dhyāna for Beginners*, p. 444.

Chapter six

37 Evans-Wentz, *The Tibetan Book of the Dead*, p. 202.

38 *Dhyāna for Beginners*, p. 454.

39 Pali: *upacāra samādhi*.

40 Venerable Sujivo, Access and Fixed Concentration. Vipassana Tribune, Vol 4 No 2, July 1996, Buddhist Wisdom Centre, Malaysia http://www.buddhanet.net/budsas/ebud/ebmed020.htm

41 *Mahāsaccaka Sutta*, Majjhima Nikāya 36, in *Middle Length Discourses of the Buddha*, p. 332.

42 Sāmaññaphala *Sutta*, trans. T. W. Rhys Davids, Dīgha Nikāya I, 74, Pali Text Society, London, 1977.

43 Buddhaghosa, *Vissuddhimagga* IV, 94, trans. Ñāṇamoli, Buddhist Publication Society, Kandy, 1975, p. 149.

44 I would not recommend taking up one of these practices on a regular basis until a good foundation of mindfulness of breathing and Mettā Bhāvanā are established. Without a qualified teacher, it may be more difficult to sustain this kind of exercise over the long term. But if you are curious, there is no harm in trying it out.

45 Also known as *appanā-samādhi*.

46 There is a considerable difference in quality between the reflex image and the *samāpatti* phenomena referred to in Chapter 3. The *samāpattis* are somewhat coarse and often feel a little odd, though not unpleasantly so. The reflex image is 'friendlier', and indeed can be extremely inspiring.

47 Ayya Khema, *Who Is My Self?*, Wisdom Publications, Boston, 1997, p. 84. A recommended practical guide to the dhyānas, one clearly based on experience.

48 *The Enchanted Heart*, p. 5.

Chapter seven

49 Evans-Wentz, *The Tibetan Book of the Dead*, p. 202.

50 *Dhammapada, The Way of Truth*, trans. Sangharakshita, Windhorse, Birmingham, 2001.

51 Just as one example: Thomas Cleary, *The Flower Ornament Scripture*, Shambhala Publications, Boston, 1993, p. 192. Several other sets of verses (for example at p. 242) also embroider this theme extensively and in detail that is beyond mind-boggling.

52 See, for example, the *Mahāsamaya Sutta* and the *Sakkhapañha Sutta*, Dīgha Nikāya 20 and 21.

53 Buddhaghosa, *Atthasālinī* (expositor, Pali Text Society, p. 360), as explained by Sangharakshita (see note 54).

54 Sangharakshita, *The Three Jewels: An Introduction to Buddhism*, Rider, London, 1968, p. 69ff. For a detailed presentation, see Dharmachari Subhuti, *Revering and Relying on the Dharma*, at www.sangharakshita.org/_notes/revering_relying_dharma.pdf. For a wider discussion of the meaning and origin of the five niyāmas doctrine, see Dhivan Thomas Jones, 'Sangharakshita, the Five Niyāmas and the Problem of Karma', at https://sites.google.com/a/dhivan.net/www2/niyamasessay.pdf.

Chapter eight

55 Evans-Wentz, *The Tibetan of the Dead*, p. 202.

56 *Jñeya and kleśa: āvaraṇa*, the cognitive and emotional veils.

57 *Dhyāna for Beginners*, p. 439.

58 Buddhaghosa's *Visuddhimagga* (see note 43) contains the series of insight stages well known in Theravada tradition as the *vipassanā ñāṇas*, the existence and relevance of which I have only recently become aware. They include references to difficult adjustments that may occur at certain points once insight has arisen. In

addition to Buddhaghosa's classic, I recommend Henepola Gunapala, *The Path of Serenity and Insight*, Motilal Banasidass, Delhi, 1996, p. 159 and Daniel M. Ingram, *Mastering the Core Teachings of the Buddha*, Aeon Books, London, 2008 (or free PDF download), p.195. Both these books are also recommended for material about the dhyānas.

59 Gampopa, *The Jewel Ornament of Liberation*, p. 39. The terms have been adapted slightly.

60 http://www.accesstoinsight.org/lib/authors/thanissaro/affirming.html

61 Gampopa, *The Jewel Ornament of Liberation*, p. 39.

62 From Tom O'Roughly, W. B. Yeats, *Collected Poems*, London, 1994, p. 116.

63 Ratnaguna, *The Art of Reflection*, Windhorse, Cambridge, 2010 is well worth studying in this connection.

64 Gampopa, *The Jewel Ornament of Liberation*, p. 1.

65 Sangharakshita, 'Advice to a Young Poet', in *The Religion of Art*, Windhorse Publications, Cambridge, 2010, p. 159.

66 Udana V, v from *Minor Anthologies of the Pali Canon* Part II, trans. F. L. Woodward, Pali Text Society, Oxford, 1996, p. 67.

67 According to Wikipedia, 'A ḍākinī is a (Buddhist) tantric deity described as a female embodiment of enlightened energy. In the Tibetan language, ḍākinī is rendered *khandroma* which means 'she who traverses the sky' or 'she who moves in space'. Sometimes the term is translated poetically as 'sky dancer' or 'sky walker'. http://en.wikipedia.org/wiki/ḍākinī

68 *Mahāparinibbāna Sutta*, Dīgha Nikāya 16.

Chapter nine

69 See, for example, C. M. Chen, Buddhist Meditation Systematic and Practical, private publication, 1980, p. 131; available online at http://www.yogichen.org/cw/cw35/bm08.html. Yogi Chen was an important influence on my own teacher, Sangharakshita.

70 *Ānāpānasati Sutta*, Majjhima Nikāya 118, in *Middle Length Discourses of the Buddha*, p. 941.

71 Here I follow the approach of Buddhadasa Bhikkhu's ānāpānasati commentary *Mindfulness with Breathing*, Wisdom Publications, Boston, 1996, p. 72.

72 *Dilgo Khyentse Rimpoche*, Editions Padmakara, Dordogne, France 1990, p. 12.

73 Idem.

74 See Sangharakshita, *The Bodhisattva Ideal*, Windhorse Publications, Cambridge UK, 2010 and Śāntideva, *The Bodhicaryāvatāra: A Guide to the Buddhist Path to Awakening*, trans. Kate Crosby and Andrew Skilton, Windhorse Publications, Birmingham 2004.

75 Extracted from the *Tharpe Delam* or 'Smooth Path to Emancipation', rendered into English by Venerable Sthavira Sangharakshita according to the oral explanation of Venerable Dhardo Rinpoche.

76 Evans-Wentz, *The Tibetan Book of the Dead*, adapted, p. 202.

77 *Trikāya* (Skt.): three levels of perceiving the enlightened consciousness. 'Kāya' literally means 'body' or form. The *nirmāṇakāya* is the human historical Buddha as perceived by ordinary sense-based consciousness; the *Sambhogakāya* are his deeper

qualities as perceived by visionary, dhyanic consciousness (in terms of archetypal, ideal form) and the *Dharmakāya* (Pali: *Dhammakāya*) is the essential nature of Reality perceived with transcendental insight.

78 Extracted from the Song of Transience with Eight Similes, *The Hundred Thousand Songs of Milarepa*, trans. G. C. C. Chang, Shambhala Publications, Boulder, 1989, p. 204ff.

79 Buddhaghosa, *Path of Purification* (Visuddhimagga*)*, trans. Ñāṇamoli Bhikkhu, Buddhist Publication Society, Kandy, 1975, pp. 622–623.

80 *Some Sayings of the Buddha,* trans. F. L. Woodward, Oxford University Press, London, 1960, p. 213.

81 The cyclic nidānas are explained in detail in Sangharakshita, *A Survey of Buddhism,* Windhorse, Birmingham UK, p. 128ff. The spiral nidānas are explained in Sangharakshita, *The Three Jewels,* p. 110ff. See also Alex Kennedy, *The Buddhist Vision*, Rider, London,1985. Also recommended is Dhivan Jones, *This Being, That Becomes*, Windhorse, Cambridge, UK, 2011. One source in the Pali canon for these is the *Nidāna-vagga* of the *Saṃyutta Nikāya.*

82 Christof Koch, 'When Does Consciousness Arise in Human Babies?', *Scientific American*, 2 September 2009. http://www.scientificamerican.com/article.cfm?id=when-does-consciousness-arise

83 See the *Saṃyutta Nikāya* 47.7.

Chapter ten

84 *Puja: the book of Buddhist devotional texts*, trans. Sangharakshita, Windhorse, Birmingham, 1999, p. 39.

85 Listed in Buddhaghosa, *Path of Purification* (Visuddhimagga*)*, trans. Ñāṇamoli Bhikkhu, Buddhist Publication Society, Kandy, 1975, p. 112. There are numerous other such lists in the Pali tradition, for example the 101 methods listed in the *Jhānavagga* of the Anguttara Nikāya, Ekaka Nipāta and the sixty-eight found in the *Mahāsakuludāyi Sutta*, Majjhima Nikāya 77.

86 The ten *asubhas* from the Dhammasaṅgaṇī are generally used for the list of kammaṭhānas. They are formulated as specific antidotes to various lustful dispositions. There is a different set, of nine, in the *Satipaṭṭhāna Sutta.* They illustrate the dissolution process of the body.

87 See Paul Williams, *Mahāyāna Buddhism*, Taylor & Francis, London, 2009, p. 209.

88 Dīgha Nikāya 16.

89 *Sutta Nipāta* V, 17 and 18, trans. H. Saddhatissa, Curzon Press, Richmond, 1994, p. 132.

90 Sangharakshita was ordained in the Theravada school but was sent by his teacher Bhikkhu Kashyap to work in Kalimpong, West Bengal, close to the Tibetan border. There he met numerous Tibetan teachers after the Chinese invasion in the 1950s. Sangharakshita studied primarily with the Gelug Lama, Dhardo Rinpoche, who gave him Mahāyāna ordination. His other main teachers were Jamyang Khyentse Rinpoche, Dudjom Rinpoche and Dilgo Khyentse Rinpoche. Later, Sangharakshita also studied with a Ch'an teacher, Yogi Chen (Chen Chien-Ming).

91 See Richard Gombrich, *What the Buddha Thought*, Equinox, Oakville, 2009, p. 183.

92 John Blofeld, *The Zen Teachings of Huang Po*, Rider, London,1958, p. 29.

93 A well-known traditional verse of invocation introducing 'Praise to the 21 Tārās', e.g. http://www.drolkarbuddhistcentre.org.au/?page_id=32.
94 I recommend Vishvapani, *Gautama Buddha,* Quercus, London, 2011 and Bhikkhu Ñāṇamoli, *The Life of the Buddha,* Buddhist Publication Society, Kandy, 1992.
95 *Purābheda Sutta*, Sutta Nipāta IV 10. An edited rendering drawing from several translations.

Appendix one

96 *Dhyāna for Beginners* p. 458
97 Buddhagosa, *Path of Purification,* p. 161, with slight changes.

Resources

The following are some useful web-based resources for meditators.

Access to Insight
www.accesstoinsight.org   A useful source for Pali Canon text material and the Theravada tradition.

Dharma Door
www.dharmadoor.org   Kamalashila's teaching material, news and personal contact.

Free Buddhist Audio
www.freebuddhistaudio.com   A large resource of audio and text Dharma material from the Triratna tradition.

Going on Retreat
www.goingonretreat.com   Retreat information for various UK Buddhist Retreat Centres.

Sangharakshita
www.sangharakshita.org   Sangharakshita is the founder of the Triratna Buddhist Community.

Triratna Community
www.thebuddhistcentre.com   The Triratna Buddhist Community space.

Vajraloka
www.vajraloka.org   The meditation centre where Kamalashila trained and teaches.

Video Sangha
www.videosangha.net   Video talks from the Triratna tradition.

Wild Mind
www.wildmind.com   Learn and discuss meditation online.

Index

absorption, 13, 16, 17, 53, 61, 79, 85, 87, 93, 215
   see also dhyāna, formless absorption
absorption factors, see dhyāna factors
abstract understanding, 96, 111, 115, 123
access concentration, 86–8, 97, 98–100, 107, 112–3, 214–5, 218, 223
ache, 226–7, 238, 240
acknowledgement, 5, 23, 30, 35, 56, 58, 70–1, 216,
acquired image, 97, 99
actions, 28, 67, 69, 71–2, 104, 109–10, 122
   see also *karma*
activity, 34, 48, 49, 68, 74, 78, 81–2
addiction, 80, 122, 175
adhiṣṭhāna (blessing), 194, 198–200
adjustment, 40, 64, 76, 213, 215, 218, 245
Āgamas, 190
ahiṃsā (nonviolence), 69
ākāsa-dhātu (space element), 100, 160, 163–8, 170–2, 191
alienation, 30–1, 38
Ānanda, 26, 174
ānāpānasati, 135–9
   see also mindfulness of breathing
Ānāpānasati Sutta, 135
anattā (non-self), 125–132, 141, 165
animals, 5, 105, 107
anussatis (recollections), 191–2
anxiety, see restlessness
āpo-dhātu (water element), 89–91, 160–172, 167
applied thought, 86, 92–6, 224
archetypal image, 86, 208
archetype, 108, 158, 208, 246
arching, 229, 231, 235–6, 238
art, viii, 4, 73, 124, 202

arūpadhyāna (formless absorption), 100, 107, 131, 191
arūpaloka, 107
associative thinking, 118–9
asubhas (unbeautiful meditations), 192, 246
atmosphere, 50, 76, 123, 152
attachment, 129, 131, 140, 147, 164, 176, 184–8, 203, 209, 224
attention, 11–16, 21–4, 33–4, 38–9, 40–2, 52, 54–6, 61–2, 78, 92, 95, 98–101, 112, 119–20, 125–8, 136, 154–5, 177, 211, 221, 226, 229, 238
attitude, 40, 53, 59, 72, 82, 103, 106, 122, 148, 151, 192, 211–12
authority, 71
Avalokiteśvara, 123
Avataṃsaka Sūtra, 104
avidyā (spiritual ignorance), 173, 176, 181
awakening, viii, 2, 28, 60, 88, 102–4, 110, 120, 133–8, 148–51, 156–8, 184, 189–90, 202–4
awareness (of body), 5–6, 16, 22, 33–4, 38–43, 64, 135–9, 168, 211, 215–8, 227–8, 235–40
   see also reflexive consciousness

back, 17–18, 227–38
balance, 227–38
Bardo Thodol (*Tibetan Book of the Dead*), 54, 102, 154–8, 202
beauty, 53–5, 61–4, 83, 93,
becoming, 105, 176, 184–9, 209
behaviour, 29, 71–4, 82–4, 105, 149, 219
   see also actions
bhava (becoming), 176, 185
bhāvanā (cultivation), 139
big mind, 4

bīja niyāma (biological nature), 109
birth, 104, 175–6, 185–6
blanket, 15–18, 236–40
blessing, 194, 198–200, 207
bliss, 86, 92–6, 137, 176–9, 216, 224
blue sky, 59, 171–2, 196–200, 206, 208
Bodhi, 104, 148
Bodhi Tree, 197
bodhicitta, 9, 122, 132, 148–51, 198, 123
Bodhisattva, 123, 198, 204–8
body, see awareness, physical body
Brahma, 139, 165
brahma vihāra, 9–10, 132–9, 145–8, 191, 208
breadth (of meditation), 211–2
breathing, 7, 9–18, 32, 39, 41, 52, 63–4, 98–9, 111,
    127, 133–8, 191, 198, 205, 222–3, 244
Buddha, viii, 1–4, 7–10, 20, 121–3, 174–5, 190–212,
Buddha Vandanā, 190, 192
Buddhaghosa, 12–13, 109, 164–5, 224
Buddhānussati (Recollection of the Buddha), 9,
    192, 193– 205, 210
Buddhist centre, 47, 76

calm, 17, 61, 83, 176–9, 208
cessation, 139, 176, 186–8
change, 26–7, 34–6, 62, 80, 97–9, 104–10, 128–9, 225
chanting, 7, 50, 87, 198
    see also mantra
citta (heart-mind, mind-state), 1, 137–8, 148
classes in meditation, 18, 238
cognitive dhyāna factors, 91–2, 95
colour, 181, 199, 98, 199, 208, 223
comfort, 14–17, 22, 36, 51, 228–38
commitment, 40, 61, 93, 171, 193–6, 204–5
compassion, 8, 28, 123–4, 132, 139–44, 150–1,
    197–8, 205–7, 211
competitive aspect, 88
complacency, 116
conceit, 133–4, 160
concentration, 7–8, 10–19, 43, 53–6, 58–64, 76–7,
    83–100, 107–8, 111–13, 127, 135–40, 161,
    176–80, 211–25, 226–9
conditionality, see conditioning, wheel of life,
    saṃsāra, nidānas
conditioning, 103–5, 107–10, 133–5, 145–6, 173–89,
    194, 202–5
    see also *niyāma*
confidence, 177–8, 189, 193, 224

consciousness, 3–6, 83–101, 102–10, 154–60, 163–
    171–6, 180–2, 185–9, 202–4
contact, 176–84, 187, 203, 212
contemplation of conditionality, 10, 133–4, 173
contemplation of impermanence, 133–4, 152
conversation, 78, 117
corpse, 152–3, 180, 191
counting, 12–16, 134–6
craving, 35–6, 130– 4, 152–5, 155, 175–6, 180–8,
    191, 209
    see also desire
creativity, 118
cross-legged posture, 230, 234
cushion, 15, 17–18, 50, 233–6, 240
cyclic existence, 177–9
    see also *nidānas*, wheel of life

ḍākinī, 126
dāna (generosity), 69
death, 102, 126, 152–9, 163, 165, 186
    see also impermanence, spiritual death
decoration, 50
dedication ritual, 50–1
desire, 39, 108, 140, 150–1, 184–5, 122–3
desire for sense experience, 54–5, 86, 93, 94–5, 20
deva (divine being), 106
development of loving kindness, see Mettā
    Bhāvanā
dhammaniyāma, see *dharma niyāma*
Dhammapada, 2, 103
Dharma, 53, 114, 116, 123, 124–5, 160, 199
dharma niyāma (ultimate true nature), 109, 110,
    135, 192, 193
dhyāna, 8–9, 17, 61, 81, 83–5, 86–96, 97–101, 106–?
    112–3, 131, 157, 179, 203, 218–9, 222, 223–5
    first dhyāna, 86, 88, 89–90, 95, 108, 112, 161,
        177, 214, 223–4
    fourth dhyāna, 89, 90–1, 95–6, 100, 101
    second dhyāna, 89, 90, 95–6, 223–4
    third dhyāna, 89–90, 95–6, 107, 224
    see also formless absorptions, *arūpadhyāna*
dhyāna factors (*dhyānāṅga*), 91–6, 145–6, 179,
    215–6, 224
diary, 213–4
direct experience, 111, 115
direct seeing, 112, 115, 117, 125–132, 178
    see also vipaśyanā meditation
directed thought, 117, 118–9

Buddhist Meditation: Tranquillity, Imagination and Insight

Mañjuśrī, 198
mano niyāma (perceptual nature), 109
  see also perception
mantra, 50–1, 123–4, 197, 199, 200–1, 207, 208
  see also chanting
meditation, vii, 1, 19, 24, 28–9, 45–6, 52–3, 60, 61–5,
    74, 210, 211
  object, see *nimitta*
  outdoors, 41–4
  system, viii, 7–10, 110
  notebook, see journal
  see also *bodhicitta* meditation, Buddhānussati,
    classes in meditation, concentration,
    contemplation of conditionality,
    contemplation of impermanence, dhyāna,
    Just Sitting, Karuṇā Bhāvanā, Mettā
    Bhāvanā, mindfulness of breathing, Śamatha
    meditation, stūpa visualization, Muditā
    Bhāvanā, Six Element Practice, Upekkhā
    Bhāvanā, Vipaśyanā meditation, walking
    meditation
memory, 98–9, 212, 221–2
mental health, 90–1
mettā, 9, 20–1, 26–29, 31, 131, 139–42, 145–6, 147,
    153, 208, 242 (note 15)
Mettā Bhāvanā, 7–10, 20, 21–31, 39, 43, 64, 131,
    133–4, 139–41, 153, 159, 191, 203, 222, 223,
Milarepa, vii, 160
mind, 1–6, 8, 27, 37–8, 50, 52–3, 59, 65, 66–7, 74,
    84, 85, 87–8, 103, 113, 158, 164, 181–3, 206,
    218–20
  see also dullness, excitement, dhyāna
mindfulness, 6–8, 10, 22, 32–9, 40–4, 82, 85, 124,
    153, 203, 205, 213
  of the body, 226
  sati, 70
  while asleep, 157, 158
mindfulness of breathing, 7, 9, 10, 11–17, 39, 52,
    111, 127–8, 133, 135–9, 191, 205, 222, 223
mind-state (*citta*), 1, 137–8, 148
monkey, 180, 184
mood, 29–30, 33, 37–8, 48, 71–2, 106–7, 148
motivation, 46, 124
muditā (sympathetic joy), 140, 144–5, 147
Muditā Bhāvanā, 139, 144–5, 147, 191
muse, 90

nāmarūpa (psychophysical organism), 176, 181–2
nature of reality, 101, 113, 115, 125, 130
near enemy, 140, 145, 146–7
negative emotion, 35, 71–2, 114, 131, 149, 151, 228
nidānas (links), 175–89
nimitta (sign), 97–100, 107
nibbidā, see *nirveda*
nirveda (disenchantment), 176, 188
niyāma (natural realm), 108–10
nonviolence, 69
no-thingness, see sphere of

object, see *nimitta*
old age and death, 176, 186
one-pointedness, 86, 92, 93, 94–5, 96, 119
opposite quality, 59
outside meditation, see meditation outdoors

padding, 236, 239
pain, 23, 30–1, 34–6, 55–6, 104, 141, 143, 147–8, 187
  physical, 212, 226, 227–8, 235, 236, 238, 240
  see also suffering
parikamma samādhi (preparatory concentration),
    97, 98–9
parikamma-nimitta (preparatory image), 97, 98
passaddhi (rapture into bliss), 96
paṭhavī-dhātu (earth element), 167
paṭibhāga-nimitta (reflex image), 97, 99
Paṭicca Samuppāda (dependent arising), 122,
    173–189
patience, 18, 23, 43, 68, 71, 94, 146, 229,
peace, 50, 56, 61, 93, 96
pema (emotional attachment), 140
perception, 3, 98–9, 109, 138–9, 163
Perfect Wisdom, 40, 130
personal development, see spiritual development
phone, 18
physical body, 5–6, 33, 92, 159, 172, 181–3, 186,
    187, 215–6, 234
  see also posture, awareness of the body, sloth
physical exercise, 48, 64, 80, 217
Piṅgiya, 192–3
pins and needles, 238
pity, 143, 149
pleasure, 20–1, 23, 30–1, 34–6, 53, 55, 88, 92, 93,
    122, 145, 147–8, 177, 180, 183–4
poetry, 4, 74, 90, 99–100, 124–5

WINDHORSE PUBLICATIONS

Windhorse Publications is a Buddhist charitable company based in the UK. We place great emphasis on producing books of high quality that are accessible and relevant to those interested in Buddhism at whatever level. We are the main publisher of the works of Sangharakshita, the founder of the Triratna Buddhist Order and Community. Our books draw on the whole range of the Buddhist tradition, including translations of traditional texts, commentaries, books that make links with contemporary culture and ways of life, biographies of Buddhists, and works on meditation.

As a not-for-profit enterprise, we ensure that all surplus income is invested in new books and improved production methods, to better communicate Buddhism in the 21st Century. We welcome donations to help us continue our work - to find out more, go to www.windhorsepublications.com.

The Windhorse is a mythical animal that flies over the earth carrying on its back three precious jewels, bringing these invaluable gifts to all humanity: the Buddha (the 'awakened one') his teaching, and the community of all his followers.

Windhorse Publications
169 Mill Road
Cambridge CB1 3AN
UK
info@windhorsepublications.com

Perseus Distribution
1094 Flex Drive
Jackson TN 38301
USA

Windhorse Books
PO Box 574
Newtown NSW 2042
Australia

THE TRIRATNA BUDDHIST COMMUNITY

Windhorse Publications is a part of the Triratna Buddhist Community, which has more than sixty centres on five continents. Through these centres, members of the Triratna Buddhist Order offer classes in meditation and Buddhism, from an introductory to deeper levels of commitment. Bodywork classes such as yoga, Tai chi, and massage are also taught at many Triratna centres. Members of the Triratna community run retreat centres around the world, and the Karuna Trust, a UK fundraising charity that supports social welfare projects in the slums and villages of South Asia.

Many Triratna centres have residential spiritual communities and ethical Right Livelihood businesses associated with them. Arts activities are encouraged too, as is the development of strong bonds of friendship between people who share the same ideals. In this way Triratna is developing a unique approach to Buddhism, not simply as a set of techniques, but as a creatively directed way of life for people living in the modern world.

If you would like more information about Triratna please visit www.thebuddhistcentre.com or write to:

London Buddhist Centre
51 Roman Road
London E2 0HU
UK

Aryaloka
14 Heartwood Circle
Newmarket NH 03857
USA

Sydney Buddhist Centre
24 Enmore Road
Sydney NSW 2042
Australia

Buddhist Wisdom in Practice **series**

The Art of Reflection
by Ratnaguna

It is all too easy either to think obsessively, or to not think enough. But how do we think usefully? How do we reflect? Like any art, reflection can be learnt and developed, leading to a deeper understanding of life and to the fullness of wisdom. *The Art of Reflection* is a practical guide to reflection as a spiritual practice, about 'what we think and how we think about it'. It is a book about contemplation and insight, and reflection as a way to discover the truth.

No-one who takes seriously the study and practice of the Dharma should fail to read this ground-breaking book. – Sangharakshita, founder of the Triratna Buddhist Community

ISBN 9781 899579 89 1
£9.99 / $16.95 / €11.95
160 pages

This Being, That Becomes
by Dhivan Thomas Jones

Dhivan Thomas Jones takes us into the heart of the Buddha's insight that everything arises in dependence on conditions. With the aid of lucid reflections and exercises he prompts us to explore how conditionality works in our own lives, and provides a sure guide to the most essential teaching of Buddhism.

Clearly and intelligently written, this book carries a lot of good advice. Prof Richard Gombrich, author of *What the Buddha Thought.*

ISBN 9781 899579 90 7
£12.99 / $20.95 / €15.95
216 pages